RELIGION AND THE
LEGITIMATION OF POWER IN SOUTH ASIA

INTERNATIONAL STUDIES IN SOCIOLOGY AND SOCIAL ANTHROPOLOGY

General Editor

K. ISHWARAN

VOLUME XXV

RELIGION AND THE LEGITIMATION OF POWER IN SOUTH ASIA

LEIDEN
E. J. BRILL
1978

RELIGION AND THE LEGITIMATION OF POWER IN SOUTH ASIA

EDITED BY

BARDWELL L. SMITH

LEIDEN
E. J. BRILL
1978

ISBN 90 04 05674 2

PRINTED IN THE NETHERLANDS

CONTENTS

CONTENTS

Foreword

BARDWELL L. SMITH

THIS VOLUME is one of three collections of essays on the theme of religion and the legitimation of power in South and Southeast Asia.* As a whole, they examine various aspects of Islam, the Hindu tradition and Theravada Buddhism in relationship to the social and political order in several cultural and historical contexts. The present volume deals principally with India, though it contains an essay on Pakistan and another on Sri Lanka. Originally, it was to have included ones on Bangladesh and on Nepal, but these essays were not completed as planned. A second volume is entitled *Religion and the Legitimation of Power in Sri Lanka.* Because of its more limited scope, it is perhaps the most cohesive of the three collections, though it does include consideration of Ceylon's long-term relationship with South India. The third volume, entitled *Religion and the Legitimation of Power in Burma, Laos and Thailand* deals mainly with Burma and Thailand, especially the latter, though two of its essays devote attention to the Laotian context.

In 1973, when the idea for a set of essays on this topic was first considered, the plan called for a single volume, with essentially one chapter on most countries in South Asia and mainland Southeast Asia. At the 1975 annual meetings of the Canadian Association for South Asian Studies and the American Academy of Religion two symposia were held at which the larger share of the essays appearing in these three collections were first read. Both because it did not prove possible to obtain essays on certain countries and because several excellent ones were submitted on the same country (covering different historical periods and diverse aspects of the basic theme), the original plan was modified and the material fell into three groupings rather than one. Subsequent to the 1975 meetings of those two professional associations other papers were solicited from persons known to be working on comparable material and it was also decided to reprint a few previously published articles, in most cases from journals not well-known in North America.

In any collection of essays by several contributors it almost goes without saying, though no reviewer worth his or her salt fails to point this out, that certain chapters are of more enduring value than others and that the volume

* The other two volumes are being published in 1977 by Anima Books, Chambersburg, Pennsylvania 17201.

as a whole does not possess the same cohesiveness a single first-rate scholar could bring to the subject. Certainly, in these collections, there are not only important lacunae, but there is no systematic attempt to relate ideas in one chapter to those in another, let alone to relate one volume to either or both of the others. The attempt here is more modest. It is simply to present together several reflections on a common theme, with breadth of scope and diversity of analysis compensating in part for lack of cohesiveness. Such is the editor's *apologia pro libro suo* in each of these three cases. It is necessary, however, to say something about the theme itself and to indicate how the concept was presented to those who wrote expressly for one or another of these volumes.

On a very general level the theme served to help the contributors focus their attention on how political leaders or a politicized group within a specific religious tradition and its membership (*or* an ideological tradition, for example, Marxism, civil religion in its modern guises, secularism, etc.) made use of "religious" beliefs, practices and institutions to provide cohesiveness to the realm and legitimacy to the holding of power. Examples of this, of course, abound in history. Some of the more famous ones include Constantine in the fourth century A.D., Aśoka in the third century B.C., and Han Wu-ti in the early Han dynasty of the second century B.C.

In the examination of any particular context one needs to consider a number of factors. Obviously, in any short essay only a few considerations can be explored in depth, though one can allude to others which could be examined in a longer treatment. The following factors were suggested to each contributor, though they were not intended to be exhaustive. In fact, part of each symposium's intent was to go beyond the merely descriptive approach to the subject and to help sharpen theoretical tools, i.e., to perceive new ways of analyzing the ongoing relationship between various kinds of ideology and political, social and economic power.

First, some attention must be given to the context itself in an essentially chronological manner. What factors, events, circumstances give rise to a situation in which it becomes possible and/or important for political power to align itself with and make use of a specific ideology or tradition in order to gain credibility and empower its sanctions? One need not begin with this descriptive analysis, but some attention is obviously in order.

Second, beyond the particulars which evolve over time to create a new social context, analysis includes examination of factors of social change, social contact and conflict, forms of cultural and political pluralism, and other aspects of an essentially dynamic picture which prompt different approaches to the organizing and enhancing of power.

Third, other pertinent considerations are the process and forms of legitimation which take place as power seeks to authenticate itself in the minds of potential supporters. Except in circumstances where "naked" or autocratic power is used, one finds a whole spectrum of subtle manifestations of legitimation, e.g., patronage of the arts, the granting of political patronage, direct or indirect support to certain religious groups, etc. Part of the picture here includes exploring how legitimation is nurtured, both within the body politic and within religious communities themselves.

Fourth, in the process of this evolution what happens to the religious tradition (or the ideology) when used in these ways? What happens to the political process, its structures and its goals? One needs to consider the dangers of communalism and the effect upon social, ethnic and religious minorities within the society. Does one find an inevitable corruption of religious tradition and ideology, or may reform and the seeds of a genuine renaissance emerge from these sorts of circumstances? What forms of syncretism emerge and how are these continuous or discontinuous with past forms?

Fifth, part of any such analysis may reveal challenges to the very process of legitimation itself from other forces within the society when threatened by such a development and by members of the political or religious hierarchy who perceive this process as inimical to a healthy social order and/or a given religious tradition. Examining these kinds of factors highlight the complexities of any situation and question univocal interpretations of what may otherwise appear as clearcut and self-evident forces at work.

As implied above, the intent of this endeavor was not to discover one set of criteria by which to examine the relationship between social power and ideological legitimacy, but to open up the investigation in fresh ways. This entails examining critically and with intensity an immense variety of common factors which, while present in most situations of these kinds, assume different forms and possess their own unique dynamics. To identify as many common factors as possible was thus one purpose, but to perceive their idiosyncratic combinations was no less important.

The present collection examines primarily the modern period, though two essays treat earlier developments. The volume deals both with North India and Pakistan and with South India and Sri Lanka, but no attempt is made to cover these regions or countries systematically. As said earlier, these essays are simply examples of reflections upon the central theme.

Since most items listed and annotated in the Goonetileke bibliography have nothing to do with religion in the usual sense, an explanation is called for. Because of the historic connection between political power and the Sangha in Ceylon and because of its reappearance in different forms in the past couple of decades, it is not irrelevant to inquire after the ideological roots of the recent Insurrection in Sri Lanka. The issue is complex and dynamic; this bibliography indicates part of what is central to an understanding of the legitimation of power in that country today.

With regard to diacritical marks, consistency has been sought within each essay and not in the volume as a whole. For various reasons, overall consistency seemed unnecessary in a collection of this sort. In general, diacritics are used here more sparingly in essays dealing mainly with the modern era, which actually is the focus of all but the first two chapters.

Finally, the editor wishes to acknowledge with gratitude the critical reading given to some of these essays by Professors A. L. Basham, A. K.

Ramanujan, and Holly Reynolds. Their seasoned eyes helped to spot some of the more egregious errors in those essays which they read. Needless to say, they are in no way responsible for the content of any essay, nor for the collection as a whole.

Theogony and Power in South India: Some Clues from the Aiyappa<u>n</u> Cult

FRED W. CLOTHEY

I

THE BASIC QUESTION underlying the present inquiry is why gods arise and persist in the history of mankind. More precisely, what are the factors influencing the ways by which man perceives ultimate reality? To what extent does a god's character reflect the socio-cultural-political milieux in which it is worshipped? What can a theogonic myth tell us about the perceptions of a person or a community? And, about the centralization and use of power within a society?

The answers to these questions are complex and many-faceted. This brief statement will explore certain components of the problem as they are illustrated in the mythology and development of one deity: the god known in South India variously as Aiyaṉār or Aiyappaṉ, Hariharaputra, and Śāstā or Dharma Śāstā. The present essay is not an exhaustive historical statement on the development of this god; rather, it reports on some patterns and trends which are illustrated in the history and cultus of Aiyappaṉ. At the outset, let us state several hypotheses about the relationship between theogony and social-political context which have been posited from research into the history and cultus of various deities. These hypotheses, in varying degrees, are applicable in the Aiyappaṉ cult.

First, the manner in which a divine being is perceived reflects particular historical circumstances and geographic contexts (e.g., the phenomena of rivers, mountains, steppelands or farms) which are incorporated into the mythology of certain gods (cf. Pettazzoni, 1965). These historical particulars include economic and cultural factors, as when hunters worship a lord of animals. Early urban civilizations become focal points for regal deities with military attributes and sovereignty; agriculturalists tend to worship the mother goddess, the deity of the liquid principle, or the god of rain and storm (Pettazzoni, 1956; Eliade, 1963). Likewise, sociological factors are reflected in the mythology of gods. For example, a deity can serve as a prototype for the occupational status of a particular social community, as when the god is warrior, king, teacher, smith, servant, etc. (Dumézil). Or, the god's mythology reflects patterns of kinship homologous to those of the social order, particularly in the case of marriage or parentage (Beck, 1975; Spiro, 1967). Or, again, the perception devotees have of their god is often in terms of the social status from which humans are viewing the god. Such is commonly true in the transactional dividual system operative in the Hindu caste system, wherein the degree to which one gives or receives of the god is determined by one's social status (Marriott, 1975). And, certainly, these determinants include the political structure of a particular historical context, as when dynasties of kings and chieftains patronize a particular deity, who in turn is seen as a celestial prototype or patron (Spiro, 1967; Clothey, 1976). All such factors serve as the contexts out of which the images for perceiving the divine are derived. To be sure, in the process, creative idealizations occur and a language of mystery used. Yet seldom is the starting point for conceiving the divine more noble or base than the historical circumstances. Almost always theogony is a commentary on the sociocultural milieux as society's myth-makers perceive them.

Secondly, historical process is a crucial dimension in theogony. Virtually no deity which rises to dominance reflects a contemporary moment alone. Just as social lineage provides identity and place to each person, so divine lineage ascribes continuity, authenticity, identity and power, not only to a god but to his worshippers. In Hindu theogony, especially, each deity reflects not simply a particular cultural moment but an ongoing tradition that by incarnation, generation, homologization, or transference of symbols and meaning derives its authority from a mythic or historical original moment. However "new" the god, he is mythically "from the beginning", an affirmation which affords a devotee a sense of personhood and participation. This is not to claim that deities never become otiose in the Hindu context, only that each "new" or local deity eventually is ascribed some association with the theological mainstream.

Third, this process – and each god developed within it – becomes appropriated personally, not because people are being duped by power-brokers from above, but because a process of personal and/or family interiorization makes a deity existentially real for many devotees. This process has at least two sides. First, there is an enhancement of credibility and intellectual satisfaction (Spiro, 1967). This includes, of course, the ontogenesis of a tradition – the educative process – in which the "wise" tell us it is so and the tradition is handed down from parent to child. There is also the sharing of incidents or stories in which the god has performed miraculous deeds, not only in times past but in one's own time. Contemporary myths are often based on incidents unexplained save in miraculous terms: a friend of a friend of a friend was healed at Paḻaṉi; a pilgrim enroute to Śabarimalai was gored in the jungle by an elephant because he had not observed the rigorous preparatory purifications. The power of the god, in short, is personally credible.

Besides credibility, there are the experiential personal factors of motivation. These include, of course, the perception of the divine in terms that match one's personal needs (Fromm, 1965; Spiro, 1967), as with a god who is completely free, loving, forgiving, dominant or authoritative, etc. This dimension offers insight into the rationale for the existence of putative supernatural figures who personify personal and often unconscious hostilities as in the case of demons and witches, or with the hostile dimensions of parent, society, sociopolitical order, and of cosmos, as with the *nats* in Burma (Spiro, 1967) or the malevolent goddess in many Indian villages. In short, what one needs, one finds in the god; perceptions of the divine reflect the human situation.

If this summary of various factors involved in theogony is not exhaustive, it at least suggests that the relationship between theogony and man is complex. No one hypothesis tells the whole story. It is too simplistic, for example, to argue that theogony is *ipso facto* merely the legitimation of power. The present paper examines briefly some aspects of the rise of the god Aiyappaṉ (or Hariharaputra) to a prominent place in the devotion of South Indians. While the story of this god does not illustrate all the aforementioned factors, the process of his emergence does reveal something of the dynamics between power or, more broadly put, the socio-cultural-political context and theogony. I will concentrate particularly on aspects of the recent surge of popularity of this god in Tamil Nadu, with only passing reference to his earlier history.

II

Aiyappaṉ is the name devotees ascribe to the god whose prototypical pilgrimage center is at Śabarimalai, near the banks of the Pambar river in Quilon District, Kerala. In Tamil Nadu, the cultus is most evident in the westernmost districts during the two months preceding the *uttarayāṇa*, or start of the sun's "northern journey". This is a period climaxed by the beginning of the Tamil month *Tai* (on or about January 15th), when a ritual known as *Makara Viḷakku* is performed. Priests at the temple at Śabarimalai prepare the icon ritually during the preceding two-month period with the *koṭiārcana* (a thousand thousand recitations of praise). This series of ritual acts consists largely of the recitation of the thousand names of Aiyappaṉ (*Śāstā Sahasranāmam*), beginning with *Śivaputrāyanamaha* (obeisance to the son of Śiva) and ending with *Hariharaputrāyanamaha* (obeisance to the son of Harihara [Śiva-Viṣṇu]). Some twenty-five leading priests or *tantrīs* of Kerala preside, all the while scattering thousands of flowers brought to the shrine from the Western Ghats. Meanwhile, some half a million pilgrims gather in small groups during the months of *Kārttikai* (November-December) and Mārkaḻi (December-January), some forty days before the pilgrimage starts. These are usually males of all communities, especially non-brāhmaṇs, but girls and elderly women may also participate. Women between the ages of ten and fifty-five may not go to Śabarimalai, as Aiyappaṉ is still considered a bachelor and the menstrual process is believed to defile the sanctuary. Each participating pilgrim for forty days wears black, blue, or ochre; each observes sexual continence and abstains from meat and intoxicating drink. In all the preparing groups each pilgrim calls the other "Aiyappa" as a sign of the fraternity and classlessness of the worshippers. In pilgrimage, devotees wear *tulasī* leaves or *rudrākṣa* beads as symbols of penitence and carry the two-compartment bag or *irumuṭi* on a stick in a way said to have been done by the god himself when he traversed these same forests while incarnate. As they walk, they raise their communal cry of devotion "*Cāmiyē Caraṇam Aiyappa*" (Aiyappa! the swāmi is my sole refuge). Even if they travel part of the way by bus or car, it is still necessary to walk at least ten miles through a thick forest to the shrine. Only those pilgrims who have faithfully observed all the austerities are considered able even to arrive at the temple, let alone eligible to climb the eighteen sacred steps (*patiṉeṭṭuppati*) leading up to the *garbha gṛha*. Each step represents one of the *indriyas* (senses) or *guṇas* (characteristics of one's humanity) which are mastered in the act of devotion. Pilgrims prostrate themselves before the first step, then slowly ascend each step, bearing the *irumuṭi* on the head. On that step which corresponds to the number of the pilgrimage they are making, they break a coconut. Finally, standing on the eighteenth step they may see the form of Dharma Śāstā holding his hand in the *cinmudrā* pose and seated on his haunches with a belt circling his knee (*padabandha*).

Those pilgrims who are present on the day of *Makara Saṅkrānti* (the first day of the first month following the winter solstice when the light half of the year officially begins) are specially blessed, for it was on this day the temple was said to have been first constructed. On this day, the god makes a special appearance to bless his devotees; indeed, at dusk of this day, many devotees insist, an indescribably splendid light glows in the northeastern skies.

The phenomenon of Śabarimalai, now the most important and popular shrine of the cultus of Aiyappaṉ, remarkable as is its growing popularity, is but one facet of an exploding cultic experience, especially in western Tamil Nadu. Though the god of Śabarimalai was virtually unknown in Tamil Nadu prior to 1952, groups of devotees proliferate and new shrines have been built. In 1968, for instance, a small but highly committed band of devotees in Coimbatore constructed that city's first temple to Aiyappaṉ, a temple which employed a family of Nambūdiri priests from Kerala and has come to have an annual budget of 20,000 rupees. At Ootacamund a temple for Aiyappaṉ received Kumbhābhiṣekam in 1971 when a special fire ritual, a feeding of the poor, a Kathakali dance and a Malayalam play were sponsored. While the influence of Malayalis in these events is obvious, Tamilians in increasing numbers are making this god their own. Who is this Aiyappaṉ and why is he becoming so fondly worshipped by so many Tamilians? Answers to these questions provide clues as to how theogony comments on the human situation.

III

Who is this high god Aiyappaṉ of Śabarimalai, Coimbatore and Ooty? We might start with the myth and from there reconstruct what we can of its history. The myth of Aiyappaṉ as popularly perceived has many variations; one such variation goes as follows:

An *asura* named Śūrpaka, by intense *tapas*, attained the power to turn into ashes anyone whom he touched. Enamored of his own power, he turned against Śiva himself. Śiva sought the help of Viṣṇu, who assumed the form of the beautiful damsel Mohinī, and approached Śūrpaka. Śūrpaka sought to woo Mohinī, who told him that before she would respond to the *asura's* advances Śūrpaka must place his hand on his head and promise never to part from her. Śūrpaka did so and was reduced to ashes. Śiva then wished to see the beautiful Mohinī. Viṣṇu appeared before Śiva as Mohinī; love and union ensued. From the union, Hariharaputra or Aiyappaṉ was born. He was given the name Dharma Śāstā, as he was born for the upkeep of Dharma in the *Kaliyuga* (Narayanaswami, 1970, 30).

The myth of the incarnation of Aiyappaṉ in Śabarimalai continues in this vein. Śiva ordained that Aiyappaṉ should live a mortal life for twelve years in order that the demoness Mahiṣa might be overcome. Hence the lord was found as a babe on the banks of the Pambar river by King Rājaśekhara of Paṇṭalam. The child was brought up in the palace under the name Maṇikaṇṭha, as he had a golden bell around his neck.

After a while, the queen had a son named Rajendiraṉ who grew up with Maṇikaṇṭha. However, the latter exceeded the royal prince in all respects and was designated heir apparent by the king. The queen became jealous for her son and plotted to be rid of Maṇikaṇṭha. She pretended to be chronically ill of severe stomach-aches which, according to court physicians, could be cured only by leopard's milk. Maṇikaṇṭha volunteered to go into the forest to fetch the milk. Accordingly, against the king's better judgment, he set out carrying an *irumuṭi*, (two-compartment bag) on his head, bearing some food and a sacralized coconut.

In the forest, Maṇikaṇṭha met Mahiṣa, and killed her in battle. His divine mission accomplished, he returned to Paṇṭalam, riding a tiger and leading a whole host of leopards. The king recognized Maṇikaṇṭha as divine and implored him to live permanently in his kingdom and bless his people. Therewith, a temple was built in the hills northeast of the Pambar river where the sage Śabari was doing penance and seeking eternal salvation. The divine architect Viśvakarma helped erect the temple and Paraśurāma instructed the king as to the appropriate iconographic features. This is alleged to be the temple which attracts pilgrims to Śabarimalai (Vaidyanathan, 1972, 44). What this myth tells us of the history and sociology of the Aiyappaṉ cultus is difficult to piece together, but certain elements of that history in South India, at least, can be reconstructed in some four stages.

The *first* stage of the god's development in the South is evident by at least the eighth or ninth century A.D. when a god known as Aiyaṉ is worshipped in the region on the Western Ghats of Malabar, then governed by chieftains known as Āys. This god Aiyaṉ is mentioned in the late or post Caṅkam classic, the *Kalittokai*, a work variously dated from the fourth to the seventh or eighth century. There are several references to temples to Aiyaṉ during this period. One such temple is found in a complex of temples associated with Viṣṇu, thought to have been erected in 864 A.D. in Parthivapuram by the Āy-chieftain

Karuṇandakka (TAS, I, 3, 56). In the same region at Alagaiyapāṇḍiyapuram a later inscription (1124) mentions an Aiyaṉ Temple (TAS, I, 59). That these Āy-chieftains were *veḷḷāḷas* and overlords of farmers is attested (TAS, I, 3); that they were associated with the community later known as the Nāyars is also probable, for the Nāyars do play a significant role in the development of the Aiyappaṉ cult. In fact, Parker noted early in this century that tribesmen in Śrī Laṅkā, for whom the god Aiyaṉār was equated to Gaṇeśa, believed the god Aiyaṉār to have come from Madura and to have been originally the god of the Nāyars, an "aboriginal forest-hill peoples" (Parker, 1909, 147). It is also likely that Aiyappaṉ who becomes the folk god of many Tamil villages – the protective horseman god – is a descendent of Aiyaṉ, that god of the Āy chieftains. We know, for instance, that the Pāṇṭiyaṉs who governed Western districts of present-day Tamil Nadu did come into contact with the Āys. In fact, the Pāṇṭiyaṉ Raṇadhīra battled and worsted an unnamed Āy chieftain in the early 9th century (Sastri, 1972, 50). This may have marked the start of Aiyappaṉ's adaptation through Tamil village mythology.[1]

A *second* "element" in the history of this god is associated with the god Śāstā, who comes to relative prominence in Kerala by the tenth century and thereafter. The name Śāstā or Teacher is virtually a generic one, inasmuch as the term is associated with a variety of deities and religious figures. For example, Brahma-Śāstā is a name for Subrahmaṇya or Murukaṉ used in Tamil Nadu, and in Northeastern India inscriptions at times refer to Śāstā as the Buddha (EI, XXI, 99).[2] But in Kerala, the shrine to Śāstā is most commonly within a Śiva or Viṣṇu shrine. One of the earliest references to Śāstā is that found on an inscription ascribed to the Āy King Kokkarunandadakkan about 855 A.D. on a Śiva temple at Padmanābhuram (TAS, I, 39). However, by the 11th century, at least, the Śāstā shrines are increasingly independent and the deity has been explicitly combined with Aiyappaṉ.[3] Both ksatriya and brāhmaṇ communities are identified with Śāstā and his motifs as "teacher". On the one hand, the kṣatriya kings of the epic era in Northern India had claimed the role of "teacher of brāhmaṇs" and patron of the arts as well as that of warrior-preservers of the state (Mukhopadhyay, 1931, 310). The assumption is unavoidable that the Aiyappaṉ-Śāstā fusion, whatever else it

1 This raises questions about the meaning of the name Aiyappaṉ. It is commonly assumed Aiyaṉ derives from the term *Ārya* and connotes "brāhmaṇ" or Āryan elements. While the term Aiyar is found in some Caṅkam passages (e.g., Akam 240: 6) and appears to refer to "respected" ones, like "sages", at least one scholar, N. Subrahmaniam (1966, p. 177), believes this term to mean "brāhmaṇ" only derivatively. Nor is it clear what relation this term has to the god Aiyaṉ. On the other hand, the term Āy apparently is related to the term Āyar – cowherd or protector – which was an appropriate appellation both for the Āy chieftains and for the god they patronized.

2 See, for example, a Nolanda inscription of Vipulasrimitra in the first half of the 12th century.

3 An inscription found on the southeast side of a Guhānātha-Svāmi Temple in Kanyakumari, as ascribed to the 31st year of the Cōḷaṉ Rājarāja I, refers to a shrine for Aiyappaṉ-Vediya-Śāstā.

represented, reflected a claim by Kerala chieftains to the power and authority of epic kings. At the same time, Śāstā was a prototypical figure for the brāhmaṇ community, serving in the capacity of teachers in the South from an early date. In fact, Śāstā's iconographic features are largely brāhmaṇic, most often characterized by the *yajñopavīta* (sacred thread), jaṭā (braid of the ascetic), and *yogapatta* (posture of the yogin) forms.

It is also clear that by the 13th century at least the Śāstā cultus had combined aspects of both Śaiva and Vaiṣṇava ritual and myth. That Kerala was relatively early an area generally more conducive to Śaiva-Vaiṣṇava cooperation than was the case in Tamil Nadu is suggested by several factors. There are, for example, hints of Nammāḻvār writing in western Pāṇṭiyaṉ country about the 8th or 9th century to the effect that God manifests himself in all forms without prejudice (*Tiruvāymoḻi* 1:1:5). This syncretism may have been in part a reaction to the presence of *nāstika-s* in Kerala, presumably Muslims and Syrian Christians as well as Buddhists.[4] It is a syncretism which, incidentally, Rāmānuja was unable to convert to a more orthodox Vaiṣṇavism despite efforts in the mid-13th century.[5] Whatever the basis of the eclecticism, the ritual life of the Śāstā cultus as with much ritual life of both Śaivism and Vaiṣṇavism in Kerala came to be based in the *Tantrasamuccaya*, a manual reflecting both Śaiva and Vaiṣṇava traditions. This manual is still the basis for ritual in Śabarimalai and often requires the presence of both Śaiva and Vaiṣṇava priests.[6]

A *third* stage in the history of the god represents the merging of the Śāstā cultus with the Harihara cultus and the eventual emergence of the Hariharaputra mythology. The rise of this mythology is difficult to date as there are virtually no inscriptional references to Hariharaputra in the South, particularly in Tamil Nadu; nor are there allusions to the mythology of Hariharaputra in the epic literature or in most of the major purāṇas.

However, the process of combining the cultus of Aiyappaṉ-Śāstā with that of Harihara seems to have been stimulated in Tamil Nadu by political developments occurring during the thirteenth century. It is clear that Harihara was

4 This is the suggestion of K. K. A. Venkatachariar, referring to observations made by Periyavāccam Piḷḷai in Maṇiprabandham 1228, written late in the 13th century in Cēnkanūr, as a commentary on Tiruneṭuntaṇṭakam or Tirumañkaiyāḻvār.

5 An observation of K. K. A. Venkatachariar, commenting in conversation on references found in the *Kuruyiṉappaṭi Kuruparamparai pirapāvam* by Piṟpaḻakaiya perumāljīyar.

6 A myth is told by the elderly chief *Tantrī* at Śabarimalai about the Śaiva and Vaiṣṇava origins of the priests. It seems years back that Lord Paraśurāma visited the Krishna District of Andhra Pradesh and invited two brothers in a family of brāhmaṇ yogins to serve in temples founded by him in Kerala. The Krishna River was dry at that time, but, as he left, Paraśurāma caused a flood. Each of the brothers crossed the river by using his yogic powers. The younger brother walked across the waters. His progeny came to be known as the "Tharanallūr" family – acknowledged authorities in the ritual techniques of Viṣṇu. The older brother waved his hand and made the waters part, thereby acquiring the title "Thaḻaman", and producing a family of priests skilled in the ritual techniques of Śiva and Śāstā.

a deity patronized by the Hoysaḷas of eastern Karnāṭaka into the thirteenth century.[7] But the reigns of Jaṭāvarman Sundaram Pāṇṭiya I (1251–1268) and of his son Māravarman Kulaśekhara I (1268–1284) apparently mark the point at which these streams come to focus in a single context within Tamil Nadu. Jaṭāvarman waged war successfully against both the Cheras and the Hoysaḷas, but he was reportedly weary of certain acrimonious disputes that occurred between two adjoining temples in Pudukkōṭṭai – one Śaiva, the other Vaiṣṇava. Worship in both temples temporarily ceased and a military officer of the Hoysaḷas, one Vīra Somēśvara, was appointed mediator. Jaṭāvarman himself worshipped at Śrīraṅgam and Chidambaram, Vaiṣṇava and Śaiva temples respectively, giving extensive gifts to both. Similarly, at least one inscription dated during the reign of Māravarman claims that all religions flourished in friendly toleration at the time (Sastri, 1975, 160). In this same period, an interesting incident occurs at the famed Vaiṣṇava temple at Śrīraṅgam. The *jīyar* at Śrīraṅgam (apparently one Śrīraṅga Nārāyaṇam Jīyar), acting in the middle of the thirteenth century to control erosion of the temple grounds and to prevent the interference of śūdra elements by the river, consecrates to the north and to the east a deity known as the Śūdradevatā, and a village goddess known as Tiruvaraṅkaccelvi. At least one editor believes this Śūdradevatā to be the same as Śāstā, or, more accurately, a deity already used in folk religion to avert evil spirits in villages, namely the deity Aiyaṇār, now adapted as a brāhmaṇic deity for the purpose of averting evil in a Vaiṣṇava cult (EI, XXIX, 73–75, citing Kōyiloḷuku XXIV, 289).

Apart from this one incident, however, one finds few references in official documents to Hariharaputra or Śāstā within Tamil contexts up to recent times. To be sure, references to Harihara can be found. For example, at least two Vijayanagar kings assumed the name Harihara – the first, according to inscription, to combine the functions of protecting the good and destroying the evil (EI, XIII, 10). The second, starting a new dynasty, was a native of Tulu Nadu and a patron of both Harihara and the Śrīraṅgam temple (EI, III, 224 and I, 362). And, despite the relative absence of references to Hariharaputra or Śāstā, we know of the persistence of Aiyaṇār as a folk deity in villages of Tamil Nadu. That god was observed by B. Ziegenbalg, the first Protestant missionary to India in the early eighteenth century; by Oppert and Whitehead in the nineteenth century; and by such anthropologists as Dumont

7 Some of the earliest archeological references to Harihara are found in S. Karnāṭaka and Telugu areas. The Hoysaḷa king Narasiṃha II constructed a temple to Harihara in 1224 A.D. in Devanagere. A Kadamba inscription of 1171 A.D. begins with an invocation to Harihara. Another inscription, dated about 1104, unearthed in Nagpur, Andhra Pradesh, refers to the combined forms of Śiva and Viṣṇu. Further, Peyāḷvār had earlier sung of the combined form of Viṣṇu and Śiva in the Tirupati hills, while Poykaiyāḷvār speaks of the combined form of Hara and Nārāyaṇa.

Abundant references to Harihara in purāṇic sources suggest the cult was widespread in the North considerably earlier than in the South (e.g., *Bhāgavata Purāṇa* VIII. 6–7; *Liṅga Purāṇa*, Pūrvādha, Adh. 96; *Skanda Purāṇa* VII. 2, 17, 187ff.; *Matsya Purāṇa*, Adh. 260; *Nāradīya Purāṇa*, Adh. 83, 23ff.). (P. Jash, 1974, p. 134ff.).

in more recent years. This Aiyaṉār remains the relatively un-brāhmaṇized averter of evil spirits whose cultus is often combined with that of the goddess, especially during a festival in the month of *Puraṭṭāci* (September-October), and with that of the so-called servant god, Karuppaṇṇasvāmi.

This brings us to a *fourth* stage in the god's history – the stage in which Hariharaputra, the fully orthodox god, becomes incarnate as the child of a South Indian king, and this cultus is brought into Tamil Nadu. Tradition has it that this king was named Rājaśekhara, that he lived in a kingdom called Paṇṭalam, and that the name of his divine son was Maṇikaṇṭha. It is virtually impossible to place this myth into any historical context. But the most plausible historical figure on whom the myth may be based is the seventeenth century Pāṇṭiyaṉ, Varaguṇa Śrīvallabha, alias Kulaśekhara, who performed a Vedic sacrifice to demonstrate his wealth and status (Sastri, 1975, 230). A Sanskrit treatise refers to a great king of the legendary Mūṣika Kingdom (said to have existed in the general area where the Āys once governed) whose name was Vallabha. Vallabha is said to have set up the god Śāstā or Āryaṉ in a shrine together with a fort and towers erected at Vallabhapaṭṭinan (TAS, II, 113, citing the Mūṣika-Vamsār Sarga XIV). A later prince – one Bālarāmavarma Kulaśekharapperumāḷ (1758–1798) – is believed to have built roads to a Śāstā shrine at Āryaṉ Kāva in the jungles halfway between Quilon and Shencottah (TAS, V, 12). Āryaṉ Kāva is another name associated with Śabarimalai.

IV

Whatever the historical origin of the myth of Aiyappaṉ's incarnation, certain elements in the cultus' recent spread afford clues into some political, social, and psychological factors in the god's popularity. In the early 1920's, oral tradition claims, a group of Nambūdiri brāhmaṇs and non-brāhmaṇ Nāyars determined together to renovate the shrine of Śabarimalai and to make its god a popular alternative to Murukaṉ, the god of Paḷaṉi in Tamil Nadu who attracted many pilgrims from the area now known as Kerala. Part of the motivation involved was financial – to re-direct funds being funnelled into the Paḷaṉi devasthānaṉ.[8] By 1951, the icon of Śāstā was reinstalled at Śabarimalai. In 1952, P. T. Rajan of Madurai, a non-brāhmaṇ who, in fact, had been actively involved in non-brāhmaṇ movements of Tamil Nadu, was asked to parade the icon of Aiyappaṉ throughout Tamil Nadu. For some nine months, P. T. Rajan organized such an effort, believing Aiyappaṉ to be a god who was not brāhmaṇ in background and who could be worshipped by

8 This is the account of Mr. A. S. Gnanasambandan, formerly professor of Tamil at Madurai University. I have been unable to confirm this report with historical records. However, this "pragmatic" consideration is not uncommon in South India today. Mr. Nedunchelian, former minister of tourism of Tamil Nadu, was quoted in 1975 as pleading that Tamil pilgrims, before travelling to Tirupati (in Andhra Pradesh) should visit Tiruttaṇi (in Tamil Nadu) and leave their offerings there.

one and all in a manner transcending caste boundaries.[9] A number of Tamilians still remember Aiyappaṉ's appearing in their town in Tamil Nadu. This event marked the beginning of the surge of interest one now finds proliferating, especially in western Tamil Nadu.

What then are the cultural factors represented in Aiyappaṉ's current growth in popularity? It is too early to offer definitive conclusions as to the relationship between this theogony and the socio-political matrices involved, but perhaps a few tentative conclusions can be suggested.

First, many Tamilians see in Aiyappaṉ a syncretizing agency who transcends sectarian, communal, and linguistic boundaries. We have already observed that the Śāstā cultus incorporated aspects of both Śaiva and Vaiṣṇava ritual and mythic heritages. Its ritual texts, the *Tantrasamuccaya*, combine elements of both traditions; its priests claim inheritance from both; and its basic myth combines the power and authority of Śiva and Viṣṇu alike.[10] The iconographic arrangements in the newly constructed Aiyappaṉ temples reflect this syncretism even more completely. At Coimbatore, for example, enshrined to Aiyappaṉ's left is Guruvāyūrappaṉ, a manifestation of Viṣṇu common to Coimbatore District; on the right is Murukaṉ, Śiva's second son; in the rear is Durgā said to be both the consort of Śiva and the embodiment of all indigenous goddesses; beside Durgā is Vināyakar, Śiva's other son. Oral tradition carries the syncretism further: Aiyappaṉ is said to be the third son of Śiva; Māriammāḷ (or the embodiment of all other local goddesses) is his elder sister (thereby retaining the relationship found on the folk level between Aiyaṉār and the village goddesses); Karuppaṇṇasvāmi, the folk "servant god", is enshrined at Śabarimalai and at Ooty. Tradition also persists that a great Muslim leader worshipped at Śabarimalai, who has been memorialized with an icon; in popular parlance, this Muslim leader is considered the elder brother of Aiyappaṉ. Pilgrims also insist that even Christians travel to Śabarimalai to witness the power of the god. In short, it is a cult seen to transcend sectarian provincialisms and boundaries. He is the god above gods, superseding all other manifestations.

Secondly, there is a creative ambivalence about Aiyappaṉ's cultural identity. While many brāhmaṇs claim Aiyappaṉ as part of the Sanskritic theological mainstream, non-brāhmaṇs, especially those from castes once called "backward", claim him as their own and believe him to be free of the alleged brāhmaṇ imperialism associated with other deities. A number of these "backward" castes have in recent years developed mythologies which enable them to believe in the nobility and honor of their origins. Hindu Nādars, for example, until recently disenfranchised from orthodox temple ritual as śūdras, have developed an elaborate mythology within the last century that purports to

9 P. T. Rajan, in an interview in July, 1972.

10 Despite the official syncretism of the Śāstā cultus, the impression persists from several interviews that Aiyappaṉ's most enthusiastic worshippers are Vaiṣṇava in background, many of whom see Śāstā as the syncretizing alternative to the more Śaiva Murukaṉ. (See Clothey, 1972.)

show they were originally Pāṇṭiyaṉs or "Dravidian *kṣatriyas*" (Hardgrave, 1969, 80 ff). Such groups find in a god like Aiyappaṉ a prototype of these "noble origins", affirmation of this authenticating mythological history. In such communities Aiyappaṉ is accepted not only as the god of "our forefathers", but also as he who represents that which "we were intended to be". At the same time, the god is increasingly identified as the new hope for Tamil Nadu, more powerful than all other gods, a supra-Tamil, universal deity above the regional, linguistic, and caste barriers that are sometimes divisive. Thus the community created in pilgrimage is one based on uniformity of practice and devotion, not on status or name. Every pilgrim is theoretically equal to every other. Many of the perquisites and transactional inter-caste reciprocities that have become a part of much worship in Tamil Nadu have been abrogated and suspended. There is a certain freedom from all societal norms. In that sense, though in that alone, there is a Bacchanalian character to the Aiyappaṉ experience.

Thirdly, this experience of freedom is basic to the cultic experience. Not only are caste and societal patterns suspended, but the pressures of modern life and the tedium of the world of work are circumvented in pilgrimage – especially in the Śabarimalai pilgrimage. There is acted out a certain nostalgia for wilderness, an abrogation of the demands of urbanization, a suspension of the newer economic hierarchies of industrialized society, an escape from depersonalization, a return to rootedness and community.

Fourth, there is genuine awe at the power of the god. His very remoteness enhances this aura, as does the rigorous preparation demanded of pilgrims who visit him. Stories circulate of pilgrims who were killed en route because they had not taken the trip into the god's presence seriously enough, for even wild beasts act in accordance with the purposes of the god. Shop owners and medical students speak earnestly of the lights which glow in the heavens on the day of Aiyappaṉ's appearing; tales of the god's miraculous feats abound.

And, *fifth*, as always in the Indian religious experience, history, both actual and mythic, is important. Despite the vicissitudes of history, and the probable use and misuse of power even in the Aiyappaṉ tradition, history still authenticates, gives identity, provides a sense of hope that the emerging new religious consciousness characterized by radical democratization and freedom is, after all, forged from the long-standing vision of the Ancients. The future and the change it implies, the dawning of new community, are neither traumatic nor frightening. They are consistent with all that has gone before.

This fourth stage of Aiyappaṉ's history is not complete. It seems probable that the village shrines to Aiyaṉār will in the near future either be revived into or replaced by shrines that incorporate more fully the cultic and mythic life of the Śabarimalai Aiyappaṉ – the new "high god" of Tamil Nadu. That is, the village shrines may be increasingly brāhmaṇized, though selectively, without sacrificing their identity with the aspirations of non-brāhmaṇs. Members of so-called "backward classes" especially may find in reviving Aiyaṉār shrines an opportunity to express and symbolize their newly emerging social power. The ritual and mythic gulf between the village Aiyaṉār and the Śabarimalai Aiyappaṉ may be bridged within the next generation. The process should be interesting to observe and may provide further insight into the complex patterns which exist in Tamil India.

BIBLIOGRAPHY

BECK, Brenda E. F.
1975 *A Study of the Structure and Basic Themes of the Skanda Purāṇa* (unpublished paper).
CLOTHEY, Fred W.
1972 "Pilgrimage Centers in the Tamil Cultus of Murukaṉ", *Journal of the American Academy of Religion*, XL, 1 (March, 1972): 79–95.
1977 *The Many Faces of Murukaṉ: The History and Meaning of a South Indian God.* Hague: Mouton & Co.
DUMÉZIL, Georges
1952 *Les Dieux des Indo-Européens.* Paris: Presses Universitaires de France.
DUMONT, Louis
"A Structural Definition of a Folk Deity of Tamil Nad: Aiyanar, the Lord", in Lessa and Vogt (eds.), *Reader in Comparative Religion: An Anthropological Approach.* Third Edition. (New York: Harper and Row), 189–195.
ELIADE, Mircea
1963 *Patterns in Comparative Religion.* New York: The World Publishing Company.
E.I.
Epigraphica India and Record of the Archeological Survey of India. E. Hultzsch, ed., I: 362 f; III: 224 ff; XII: 274 ff; XIII: 10 ff; XVI; 268 f; XVIII: 182 ff; XXI: 99 ff; XXIX: 13 f, 73–75.
FROMM, Erich
1965 *Escape from Freedom.* New York: Avon Books.
HARDGRAVE, Robert
1969 *The Nadars of Tamiland.* Berkeley: University of California Press.
Hindu, The
"Ayyappa Temple in Coimbatore" (November 18, 1971).
"Ayyappa Temple for Ooty" (May 28, 1972).
"Harihara Temple off Devanagere" (December 8, 1971).
"Record Crowd at Sabarimalai for Samkranam" (January 15, 1972).
"Significance of Sabarimalai 'Kodi, Archana'" (November 19, 1971).
JASH, Pranabaranda
1974 *History of Śaivism.* Calcutta: Roy and Chandhurg.
KRAMRISCH, Stella
1969 "Indian Varieties of Art Ritual", in Joseph M. Kitagawa and Charles H. Long, eds., *Myths and Symbols: Studies in Honor of Mircea Eliade.* Chicago: University of Chicago Press.
MARRIOTT, McKim
1975 "Hindu Transactions: Diversity without Dualism", in Bruce Kapferer, ed., *Transactional Analysis.* London: Tavistock Publication.
MUKHOPADHYAY, M.
1931 "Some Notes on Skanda-Kārttikeya", in *Indian Historical Journal*, VIII (1931): 309–318.
NARAYANASWAMI, V. R.
1970 "Sabaramalai", in *Vivekananda College Magazine* (1970): 30–31.
PARKER, H.
1909 *Ancient Ceylon.* London: Luzac and Co.

PETTAZZONI, Raphael
1956 *The All-Knowing God.* Trans. by H. J. Rose. London: Methuen & Co., Ltd.
SASTRI, K. A. Nilakanta
1975 *The Pandyan Kingdom.* Madras: Swathi Publications.
SPIRO, Melford
1967 *Burmese Supernaturalism.* Englewood Cliffs, N. J.: Prentice-Hall, Inc.
SUBRAHMANIAM, N.
1966 *Pre-Pallavan Tamil Index.* Madras: University of Madras.
TAS
Travancore Archeological Series. K. V. Subramanya Aiyar (ed.) Trivandrum Government Press, 1910–31. I: 3–59; II: 120–140; III: 28–59; IV: 43 ff; I: 12 ff; 140 ff.
VAIDYANATHAN, K. R.
"Pilgrimage to Sabarimalai", in *The Illustrated Weekly of India* (January 16, 1972), 44–45.

Crisis of Authority in a Hindu Temple under the Impact of Islam

Śrīraṅgam in the Fourteenth Century

GEORGE W. SPENCER

As ONE OF the most illustrious Vaiṣṇava temples in South India, the Śrī Raṅganāthaswamy temple at Śrīraṅgam is rich in legend and history.[1] Celebrated in the devotional hymns of the Āḻvārs and famous for its role in the early history of Śrīvaiṣṇavism, the Śrīraṅgam temple has been the object of both devotion and conflict. Its location, on an island in the Kāverī river, has rendered it vulnerable to natural disasters, as well as to the rampages of invading armies – Hindu, Muslim, and European – which repeatedly commandeered the site for military encampments. The political dimension of its history is colorful, for it is a mixture of patronage and plunder, of royal endowments and political interference in its internal affairs, even from its ostensible protectors. Nor were the temple's political problems all external ones; like other complex institutions, large temples like the one at Śrīraṅgam were prone to internal conflicts, reflecting not only the ambitions of individuals, but also jealousies and rivalries among groups of temple servants over the control of specific duties and perquisites. Such internal tensions were readily aggravated by external pressures and wider societal crises. The problem of temple "authority" was a dual problem, with both internal and external dimensions, and these dimensions interacted. Thus, major Hindu temples were never isolated from larger political developments, and the problem of maintaining a temple's institutional integrity and internal order was naturally more difficult in periods of general crisis.

One such period of crisis was the Tamil country's transition from the classical era of the Pallava, Pāṇḍya, and Cōḻa kingdoms to the era of Islamic confrontation, a transition which was marked initially by the Muslim incursions of the early fourteenth century and followed thereafter by the consolidation of the great Hindu empire of Vijayanagar. This period of crisis had a drastic impact upon the Śrīraṅgam temple. It is clearly reflected in the temple chronicle, known as the *Kōil Oḻugu*, or Temple Record. In the following

1 An earlier version of this article was presented as a lecture to students and faculty in South and Southeast Asian studies at the University of Michigan, Ann Arbor, in October of 1973.

pages I shall examine the evidence of the *Oḻugu* in order to indicate how that transition and its attendant problems affected the temple servants and how the memory of that time of trial was preserved in temple tradition.

What sort of document is the *Oḻugu*? In spite of considerable confusion in its chronology (erroneous Śaka dates, events discussed in scrambled sequence, etc.) as well as an infusion of apocryphal lore, the Śrīraṅgam chronicle is one of the most reliable of the surviving temple records. It is an invaluable repository of detailed information regarding ritual activities, the organization of temple servants, personal and factional disputes within the temple, and related matters. Therefore, the *Oḻugu* can be utilized by scholars who have many different questions to ask of it. Recently, Professor V. N. Hari Rao of Venkatesvara University in Tirupati undertook to edit, translate from Tamil into English, and as far as possible to reconcile the surviving printed and manuscript versions of the chronicle in order to bring it to the attention of a wider scholarly audience.[2] The *Oḻugu* purports to be a record compiled periodically by successive generations of Vaiṣṇava Ācāryas, a claim which, if true, may help to explain the gaps and occasional contradictions in the narrative.[3] As the text testifies, the chronicle's present form dates from 1803 A.D., when British Collector John Wallace submitted a request to the temple authorities to amalgamate the surviving, fragmentary *Oḻugu* manuscripts into a single, coherent account. Although the resulting amalgamation contains many patent interpolations, anachronisms, and myths, the high degree of reliability of most of the *Oḻugu* has been confirmed by reference to contemporary inscriptions, which also serve to correct the chronicle with regard to dates and other specific details. But we should remember that the chronicle as a whole constitutes the "institutional memory" of the Śrīraṅgam temple; hence, the editorial biases and mythological elements are no less pertinent to the temple's story than are "historical events" which can be verified by scholars.

But what is most important for our present inquiry is that a careful study of the chronicle's information can reveal which periods of rapid change had the greatest impact upon the temple, as reflected in the reactions of its record keepers. Specifically, the testimony of the *Oḻugu* reveals that the two Muslim raids which struck the temple in 1311 and 1323 A.D. had a highly disruptive effect upon its administration and services, and that the southward expansion of the Islamic frontier into peninsular India, of which these raids constituted only one rather dramatic manifestation, set in motion certain wider changes in the political structure of southern India, transformations which drastically altered the temple's relationships with the outside world. These changes

2 V. N. Hari Rao, *Kōil Oḻugu; The Chronicle of the Srirangam Temple With Historical Notes* (Madras: Rochouse and Sons, n.d.). Footnote citations to the chronicle refer to this annotated edition. For further information, see K. V. Subrahmanya Aiyar, "Koyilologu," *Indian Antiquary*, XL (1911), pp. 131–44.

3 Professor Hari Rao suggests that it may have been compiled by temple accountants, but many of the opinions expressed in the chronicle make that suggestion difficult to accept. Some combination of these, and perhaps other, attributions should not be ruled out.

prompted the temple's chroniclers to look back to the age of the philosopher-saint Rāmānuja, in the late eleventh and early twelfth centuries, with admiration and nostalgia, and to perceive the disruptions and intrusions which began in the early fourteenth century as sad departures from the divine plan which Rāmānuja had ordained for the temple. So before we can discuss the events of the fourteenth century, we must first consider the system of temple governance which was established in the twelfth century by Rāmānuja, since it was this system which was disrupted by the Muslim raids and their aftermath – a fact which is repeatedly emphasized, and lamented, in the *Oḻugu.*

Rāmānuja's System and the Orissan Challenge

The chronicle contains a lengthy discussion of Rāmānuja's career at Śrīraṅgam, particularly in connection with his reform of the temple's administration. According to the *Oḻugu,* Rāmānuja, already renowned for his piety before he came to Śrīraṅgam, was sought out by Āḷavandār ("the Victor", also known as Yāmunācārya), grandson of the great Vaiṣṇava Ācārya Nāthamuni, to be groomed as Āḷavandār's successor as Ācārya and Śrīkāryam,[4] the Chief of Servants at the Śrīraṅgam temple. After Āḷavandār's death, Rāmānuja assumed control at Śrīraṅgam and undertook a meticulous examination of temple finances, in spite of being strenuously opposed – even to the extent of an attempted poisoning[5] – by the temple accountant (Viḻupparaiyan)and other servants who felt threatened by such an inquiry. Rāmānuja then proceeded to deliberately weaken the office of accountant by splitting it into two parts. The Viḻupparaiyan was now exclusively assigned the tasks of writing documents for the Śrīkāryam and of carving inscriptions, while the newly-created office of Vaṇsaṭakōpadāsan was charged with the tasks of writing leases for temple lands and making copies of the documents and inscriptions executed by the Viḻupparaiyan. In addition, Rāmānuja delegated to the two accountants joint responsibility for maintaining accounts relating to the storehouse and temple lands.[6] He apparently designed this tandem arrangement to make concealment of any transactions from the Śrīkāryam (i.e., himself) more difficult. However, this system was no doubt rather cumbersome as well, for many years later, after Rāmānuja's time, a failure of heirs brought the office of Viḻupparaiyan to an end and the Vaṇsaṭakōpadāsan took over all treasury duties.[7] This appears to be the only major feature of Rāmānuja's system which was allowed to lapse without the pressure of outside political interests effecting the change.

4 To avoid confusion, only the term Śrīkāryam will be used in this article, but Sēnāpati Durantara and other synonyms appear in the *Oḻugu.*

5 *Oḻugu,* p. 44.

6 *Ibid.,* pp. 90–91.

7 *Ibid.,* p. 91.

Apparently Rāmānuja had originally intended to remove all of these accounting duties from long-standing Veḷḷāḷa (non-Brahman) control and assign them to fellow Brahmans, but the temple servants prevailed upon Rāmānuja to respect the established customs and privileges of the temple's non-Brahman functionaries.[8] This information is very interesting in light of the conventionally-accepted picture of Rāmānuja as a friend of the lower classes. On the other hand, he did succeed in organizing the temple according to principles laid down in the Pañcarātra Āgamas, the ritual precepts of Bhāgavatism, by curbing the authority of the Vaikhānasa priests, who followed more conservative principles, based upon rigorous mastery of Sanskritic lore, which restricted worship to specially-trained Brahman priests and did not sanction the worship of the popular saints known as the Āḻvārs. He also increased each of the two divisions of temple servants, i.e., Brahman and non-Brahman, from five groups to ten. The names, duties, and privileges of these twenty groups are specified in detail in the chronicle. It is evident that these duties and privileges came to be jealously defended, particularly among the ten groups of Brahmans, and that threats of encroachment by one group upon the province of another constituted a major source of inter-group tension and conflict within the temple. Yet there seems to have been curiously little conflict between Brahmans and non-Brahmans on this score, perhaps because the detailed specification of non-Brahman functions – as artisans, garland-makers, musicians, holders of torches and other items during processions, and so on – already implied substantial involvement in temple affairs.

Preeminent among the ten groups of Brahmans was that of the Tiruppatiyār, or Kovaṇavar, who consisted initially of Rāmānuja's closest followers. The Śrīkāryam also served as leader of this group. The Śrīkāryam's authority over temple administration was greatly strengthened by Rāmānuja before he retired from that office, handing over the "mace of authority" to his trusted disciple Āṇḍān, in whose line the position became hereditary. As might be expected, the Kovaṇavar proved to be the strongest defenders of Rāmānuja's system of temple governance, particularly of the enhanced powers of the Śrīkāryam, and hence were the first to oppose the weakening of that office which took place following the Muslim incursions.

One passage in the *Oḻugu* asserts that a contemporary Cōḷa king, as a gesture of repentance for a recent period of Śaivite-inspired persecution by the royal court which had forced Rāmānuja into temporary exile from Śrīraṅgam, had relinquished royal authority over the temple and had vested control wholly in Rāmānuja.[9] Since this claim to total institutional autonomy is self-serving, that passage is naturally suspect, but it does emphasize the contrast, which is repeatedly stressed in the *Oḻugu*, between the relative independence

8 He also intended to replace a man of weaver caste, who performed a number of minor temple duties, with a Brahman, but changed his mind when convinced of the man's piety. *Oḻugu*, pp. 94–95.

9 *Oḻugu*, p. 107 and note beginning p. 108.

enjoyed by the temple during the Pallava-Cōḷa period and the constant interference which characterized relations between court and temple in the subsequent Vijayanagar era.

In spite of this alleged autonomy, one serious disruption of Rāmānuja's system which took place even *before* the Muslim invasions is recorded in the chronicle. About a century after Rāmānuja's time, the temple was occupied for roughly two years by the "Oḍḍas", i.e., the army of an Eastern Ganga king of Orissa, until 1225 A.D., when the Orissans were driven out by the forces of Sundara Pāṇḍya.[10] During the Orissan occupation, worship was carried on by priests "well-versed in the Vaikhānasa Āgama" (as opposed to the Pañcārātra), a serious departure from Rāmānuja's system. In addition, non-Vaiṣṇavas established themselves near the temple and may have taken over some temple duties, although no details are given. Furthermore, "some servants remained in the temple and appropriated to themselves the income from the temple lands and thus proved false to God."[11] A Pāṇḍyan inscription[12] confirms and elaborates this episode, charging that the heads of the ten groups of Brahman servants had entered into traitorous collusion with the Orissans and collected an extortionate duty (*Oḍḍukāsu*, "Orissan money"). This record observes that the Pāṇḍyan restoration was followed by a purge of the ten servants and the introduction of a system of elections to those offices.[13]

But the Orissan episode is given scant attention in the *Oḻugu*, and appears to have been only a temporary disruption of Rāmānuja's system. As such it did not have the more serious repercussions of the later Muslim raids.[14] Nevertheless, it illustrates the sensitivity of temple governance to outside political and military developments, as well as the dependence of temple authorities upon the benevolence and protection of kings. When disruptive forces intruded into temple affairs, internal control could also break down and ritual functions could be interrupted. The Orissan incident also illustrates how easily sectarian religious rivalries could affect court-temple relationships, since royal preferences for Śaivism over Vaiṣṇavism, or vice versa, could have adverse effects upon institutions controlled by the less favored sect.[15]

---

10 Sundara Pāṇḍya's name is not mentioned in the *Oḻugu*'s account of this episode, however. In fact, the chronicle erroneously attributes this incident to the tenth century. More accurate details are provided by inscriptional evidence, as noted below.

11 *Oḻugu*, p. 91. The Viḻupparaiyan is said to have joined them in this treachery.

12 No. 53 of 1892.

13 See pp. 100–01 note.

14 The significance of this fact is somewhat obscured by the scrambled sequence in which the chronicle discusses these events. The first Muslim raid, which actually took place in 1311 A.D., is discussed *before* the Orissan occupation of 1223-25 A.D. and the Orissan episode is mentioned *before* the career of Rāmānuja (early 12th century) is discussed.

15 Similar difficulties, in centuries subsequent to the period which we are considering here, were caused by rivalries between the Vaḍagalai and Teṅgalai (roughly speaking, pro-Sanskrit vs. pro-Tamil) sects of Śrī-Vaiṣṇavism. The temple fell into the hands of the Teṅgalais, as noted below, and remained there, in spite of periodic challenges from the rival branch. The *Oḻugu* itself has a pronounced Teṅgalai bias, particularly in its discussion of the succession of Ācāryas.

The Delhi Sultans and the Pursuit of Plunder

For the Delhi Sultans, the thirteenth century had constituted an initial period of consolidation of power in northern India. The so-called Slave Kings who controlled the throne prior to 1290 A.D. were largely preoccupied with subduing the recalcitrant rājas of the upper Gangetic valley and Rajasthan, as well as contending with the repeated incursions into the northwest of Mongol forces from Central Asia. Until these initial difficulties were resolved, it was difficult for the sultans to consider ordering military expeditions to venture into the south.

But this period of consolidation was followed by the dramatic expansion of Delhi's power during the three decades when the Khalji sultans occupied the throne (1290–1320 A.D.). They pursued a bold, new policy of launching long-distance raids into the peninsula, intended to secure the short-term economic benefits of plunder – gold, jewels, elephants, and other forms of portable wealth – but aiming as well to secure annual tribute payments from the nearby centers of Hindu power in Maharashtra and Telengana. From the very beginning, these raids were intimately connected with court politics in Delhi, for as Baranī's critical account in the *Ta'rikh-i-Fīrūz Shāhī* suggests, Alāuddīn Khalji, while still serving as provincial governor during the reign of his uncle and father-in-law Jalāluddīn Fīrūz, secretly and without authorization launched the first invasion of the Deccan early in 1296 A.D. for the express purpose of securing treasure with which to buy his way to the throne in defiance of the claims of the sultan's two surviving sons. The enormous treasure which Alāuddīn extracted from the Yādava king of Devagiri, on the pretext of smiting the infidel, soon enabled him to have the sultan murdered and to ascend the throne himself in June of 1296. Baranī sarcastically observes that "he scattered so much gold about that the faithless people easily forgot the murder of the late sultan and rejoiced over his accession."[16]

The desire of Alāuddīn and subsequent Khalji sultans to secure a steady flow of treasure with a minimal investment of administrative manpower quickly institutionalized this "southern" strategy, which brought both rewards and dangers to the throne. The principal danger was that the practice of assigning command of expeditionary forces to court favorites created continual threats to the throne by giving those generals an opportunity to demonstrate their leadership capacities and by whetting their appetites for the further exercise of power. In short, this practice produced its own crisis of authority, for it created power without legitimacy. It is no mere coincidence that the three notable examples of usurpation of the throne in the Khalji period – namely that of Alāuddīn in 1296 A.D.; of his famous eunuch general Malik Kāfūr,

16 John Dowson, ed. *The History of India as Told By Its Own Historians; The Muhammadan Period. The Posthumous Papers of the late Sir H. M. Elliott.* In the reprint edition of Susil Gupta Ltd., it appears under the title of *Later Kings of Delhi or Tarikh-i Firoz Shahi of Zianud din Barni* (Calcutta, 1953), p. 71.

who placed a minor on the throne and named himself as an all-powerful regent in 1316, following Alāuddīn's death; and of the slave general Khusru Khān in 1320 A.D., after he had murdered Sultan Mubārak Shāh – all were instigated by individuals who were not in the direct line of succession to the throne, but who were precisely the men who had led the major Khalji raids into southern India. Both Kāfūr and Khusru Khān were slaves of Indian ancestry; after their usurpations both were murdered by cabals of hereditary Muslim nobles who resented the rapid rise of such ambitious but base-born individuals. In fact, Khusru Khān, a convert to Islam, was actually accused by Turkish nobles of harboring crypto-Hindu tendencies, a false charge but one which reflected genuine factional divisions and prejudices within the Muslim ruling class.[17]

Although the implications of this period of predatory activity for court politics in Delhi clearly have a fascination all their own, we are primarily concerned with the momentous implications of these raids for the history of the south. Their impact upon the southern courts and temples was highly disruptive. It was Malik Kāfūr's spectacular southern raid of 1310–11 A.D. which resulted in the initial plundering of the Śrīraṅgam, Chidambaram, and other famous temples of the Tamil country. This disaster was repeated at Śrīraṅgam a decade later, in the early Tughluq period, in the year 1323 A.D., by Ulugh Khān. His subsequent ascent to the throne of Delhi in 1325 A.D. as Sultan Muḥammad bin Tughluq, possibly after the murder of his father, suggests some interesting parallels with the Khalji career pattern noted above. The major difference, of course, is that Muḥammad was in fact in the line of succession.[18]

At the time of these raids, the Hindu empire of Vijayanagar had not yet been founded. Indeed, historians have long recognized that the raids contributed to the rise of Vijayanagar by crippling the regional Hindu kingdoms which preceded it. On the eve of Malik Kāfūr's raid, the Pāṇḍyan kingdom, the only important political system in the Tamil country at that time, was already weakened by internal conflicts between rival claimants to the throne. When Kāfūr's army arrived in 1311, the Pāṇḍyas were virtually helpless and unable to prevent the Muslims from plundering court and temples as they pleased. Nor was any effective resistance organized anywhere in the south until after the founding of Vijayanagar in 1336 A.D. But, for reasons which we shall refer to later, the eventual rise of Vijayanagar would not mean for Śrīraṅgam a simple return to the relative tranquility of the pre-Islamic era,

17 See the remarks by S. Roy and M. W. Mirza in *The Delhi Sultans*, ed. by R. C. Majumdar et al., *History and Culture of the Indian People*, Vol. VI (Bombay: Bharatiya Vidya Bhavan, 1960), pp. 44–46 and 608.

18 There is some doubt about the exact date of the second attack upon Śrīraṅgam, since it could have occurred later, in connection with Muḥammad's southern raid of 1327–28, launched after he had ascended the throne. See S. Krishnaswami Aiyangar, *South India and Her Muhammadan Invaders* (London, etc.: Oxford University Press, 1921), p. 158. The Śrīraṅgam evidence points to the earlier date; the Muslim chronicles, to the later date.

for the temple could not remain immune to the more intensive militarization of the medieval period.

Physical Damage and Healing Myths

What were the initial effects of the Muslim raids upon Śrīraṅgam? Although the physical damage which resulted from the two raids and the military occupation of the temple grounds was extensive, it stopped well short of total destruction. Moreover, most of the chronicle's references to structural damage are embedded in discussions of subsequent repairs and benefactions, and hence are scattered and probably incomplete. And the *Oḷugu* tends to confuse details of the two raids, so it is seldom possible for us to distinguish their effects, even when the chronicle attempts to do so. Whenever the chronicle mentions a specific cause of damage – and it usually does not – that cause is always fire. Many of the flammable structures in the temple, particularly the large *gopurams*, were partially or totally destroyed. Some other wooden structures – the "beams of the third, fourth and fifth granaries of the storehouse" are specifically mentioned[19] – were simply allowed by the Muslims to deteriorate, presumably during the lengthy second occupation.

While the chronicle claims that the procession-images were miraculously spared destruction on both occasions, it admits that many of the remaining images of gods and saints, as well as the guardian figures at the gates, were damaged or destroyed.[20] Even the copper Garuḍa-vehicle in the great *maṇḍapam* was destroyed, although its procession-image was safely hidden in a garden.[21] During the second raid, the entrance to the sanctum had been blocked with large stones prior to the Muslims' arrival, and thus the image of the reclining Raṅganātha was saved from destruction, at the cost of an interruption of services.[22] Several of the pillared halls, which were located in various temple enclosures, were wrecked.[23] The embankments around the island were also damaged, although it is not clear from the chronicle whether this was deliberate.[24] The gold staff of Viṣṇu was destroyed. The central sanctum and the various satellite shrines were less vulnerable to serious damage than were the flammable structures such as gates, but the text does mention damage to the northern face of the Nammāḻvar shrine[25] and observes that the Dhanvantrī shrine, dedicated to the patron-deity of healing (Dhanvantrī-Emberumān), had to be rebuilt.[26] In its discussion of the first raid, the chronicle admits

19 *Oḷugu*, p. 169.
20 *Ibid.*, pp. 148, 157, 163.
21 *Ibid.*, pp. 148–49, 157.
22 The *Oḷugu* suggests that the temple servants somehow managed to surreptitiously enter the sanctum and attend to the needs of the Perumāḷ.
23 *Oḷugu*, pp. 142, 156.
24 *Ibid.*, p. 152.
25 *Ibid.*
26 *Ibid.*, p. 156.

that the Muslims made off with all of the temple treasures,[27] but no details are provided, since the chronicler was evidently more interested in discussing the fate of the sacred images.

A mere recital of acts of destruction would have constituted a rather bleak narrative, so the chronicle was embellished with pious apocrypha. The longest and most colorful of these tales concerns the fate of the procession image of Viṣṇu – known as Aḷagiyamaṇavāḷa Perumāḷ, the handsome bridegroom – which was carried away by the Muslims in 1311.[28] According to this story, a local woman of great piety, referred to as Pinchenravalli ("She who followed"), was so devoted to the divine image that she followed the Muslim army back to Delhi and there entered the sultan's palace by disguising herself as one of the palace women. She discovered that the sultani, the ruler's daughter, was so enchanted by the idol that she had removed it from the palace store-room to use as a plaything. Pinchenravalli then returned to Śrīraṅgam to inform the temple servants of the image's disposition. Suspending all services at the temple, sixty of them followed her back to Delhi, where they so delighted the sultan with song that he agreed to return the image to them. The sultani, who had been placed in a deep sleep by the god, awoke the next day, horrified to find the beloved image gone, and threatened to end her life. The alarmed sultan assembled his troops and the girl herself led them in pursuit of the idol. Aware of pursuit, the temple servants halted at Chandragiri and dispersed, three of them ascending the Tirupati hills and concealing the idol in a remote place. Unable to locate the idol even at Śrīraṅgam, the sultani sickened and died, and the army returned to Delhi empty-handed.

Meanwhile, the story continues, the other temple servants drifted back to Śrīraṅgam, having lost track of the idol and its three guardians. Nearly sixty years later, a group of tribal hunters discovered the last of the three servants, living alone in a hut of leaves and worshipping the image, so they brought word of his existence to the Rāja of Chandragiri. With the rāja's assistance, the image was returned to Śrīraṅgam, but it was installed in the sanctum only after its authenticity had been established by some miraculous proofs, since the older generation of temple servants had all passed away.

The function of this miraculous tale was, of course, to embellish the harsh facts of disaster in a manner which would sustain a pious world-view. The raid was thus made the occasion for a triumphant demonstration of piety, righteousness, and the god's divine powers. Potentially embarrassing questions about the god's failure to prevent the raid in the first place were simply ignored, and His powers were demonstrated in other ways. The historical reality was no doubt more prosaic: The Muslims simply made off with the image, which was never heard of again.[29]

---

27 *Ibid.*, p. 25.

28 *Ibid.*, pp. 24–31.

29 This fate is suggested by the *Oḻugu's* observation that after the temple servants had waited in vain for the reappearance of the divine image, a fresh image was cast and used in its place. See p. 28.

The raid of 1323 A.D. is given similar treatment, but in a later part of the chronicle, separated from the account of the first incursion by a lengthy discussion of the connections of successive Vaiṣṇava Ācāryas, beginning with Nāthamuni, with the temple. The second account, although shorter than the first, is less fanciful, and is discussed in a sequence more closely approximating its actual occurrence, i.e., *after* the age of the great Ācāryas rather than before. This suggests that the account of the restoration which followed the first raid, the Pin̲chen̲ravalli story, was simply a fanciful projection into the earlier years of the authentic restoration which followed the second raid. According to the *Oḻugu*, as the Muslim army approached the temple the (new) procession image was placed in a palanquin and sent with attendants away from the temple, toward the south, while the sanctum was sealed to protect the sanctum image. The Muslims, who not only captured the temple but also occupied the grounds for many months, slaughtered many priests and ascetics and caused extensive physical damage to the temple, but were prevented from destroying it utterly, the chronicle informs us, when their leader succumbed to the charms of one of the dēvadāsis. Meanwhile, after travelling across the far south from one sanctuary to another, the Perumāḷ finally stopped at Tirumalai, where it remained in the Tirupati temple until the liberating Vijayanagar forces restored it to Śrīraṅgam.[30]

Restoration, Innovation, and Vijayanagar Authority

In 1371 A.D., Vijayanagar generals restored the sacred images to Śrīraṅgam, but the temple administration was a shambles, and the temple had lost its lands and other endowments during the intervening half-century. Piḷḷai Lokācārya, head of the Uḍayavar Maṭh, had died in exile, and the living descendants of Āṇḍān, whose family had hitherto monopolized the post of Śrīkāryam, remained in exile – in Vijayanagar itself, according to one passage – even after the restoration. Some groups of temple servants had begun to encroach upon spheres of activity originally reserved for others.[31] Because of these and other disruptions, Vijayanagar chiefs and court-appointed officials were able to introduce major innovations while ostensibly restoring order.

The court proceeded to impose upon the temple a new office, that of warden. He reported directly to the court, and thus served as a kind of proconsul while at the same time acting as a conduit for gold and other gifts from the court to the temple. Appointed to this post in 1371 A.D. was a Brahman named Periya Kṛṣṇarāyar Uttamanambi, founder of a line of Uttamanambis who were destined to exercise authority at Śrīraṅgam. Far from being a total

30 *Ibid.*, p. 131.

31 For example, the Viṇṇapan-saivār, a group of temple singers (number five in Rāmānuja's system), "created for themselves" the right of entering the sanctum to assist in worshipping the Perumāḷ during the *nivēdanam* (rice-offering). *Oḻugu*, p. 80.

stranger to the temple, Periya Kṛṣṇarāyar was descended from generations of temple servants who – from the time of Rāmānuja himself, according to the chronicle – had performed the ritual duties connected with medicinal offerings to the Perumāḷ, examined the kitchen, and performed related tasks. Now elevated to a position of extraordinary authority, with a strong political mandate, he proceeded to institute some drastic changes.

Whereas Rāmānuja's system of governance had aimed at strengthening the office of Śrīkāryam and weakening the treasury, Uttamanambi's policy was the reverse. The functions of the Śrīkāryam were now divided among several different offices. At the same time, authority over the ten groups of Brahman servants was consolidated in the treasury, which also became a politically appointive office under the control of the warden.[32] The chroniclers clearly perceived this kind of blatant political interference as a disturbing departure from the cordial but distant relationship between court and temple which had prevailed prior to the fourteenth century. The complaint is explicit:

> At the time when the Chera, Chōḷa, and Pāṇḍya kingdoms were ruled over by a single king, and later on, when three different kings ruled over the three kingdoms... kings refrained from ruling over the lands that had been granted to temples and Brahmans. These donations were left under the control of the Brahmans themselves. The kings interfered only to investigate into misdeeds and punish wrongdoers. ... After [1371 A.D.] all the [southern] kingdoms passed under the control of the Rāya-Narpati. The Rāya and the various Durgadipatis gave many pieces of land to the temple as gifts. They appointed their own men as accountants and superintendents of the temple, *as if it were an item of royal administration from the palace.*[33]

And again:

> The order of things established by [Rāmānuja], according to the sāstric injunctions enunciated by the Perumāḷ Himself in the Pañcarātra, fell into ruins.[34]

Many of these innovations were introduced gradually, however. Thus, the first step in bringing the treasury under political control was the introduction of a new accountant, who was given various titles by successive wardens.[35] This new accountant steadily encroached upon the duties of the Vaṇsaṭakōpadāsan, despite resistance from the latter, until he had finally acquired complete control over all accounts.[36] At the same time, the treasury was allowed to encroach upon the duties of other groups, on the theory that these duties had "lapsed" to the treasury due to the lengthy disruption of the traditional system of administration. In this manner, the wardens exercised effective control over

32 *Ibid.*, p. 173.
33 *Ibid.*, pp. 171–72; emphasis added.
34 *Ibid.*, p. 173.
35 He is said to have been brought from an unspecified settlement on the northern bank of the Kāverī. *Oḻugu*, p. 92.
36 This, at any rate, is my interpretation of the *Oḻugu's* discussion, which is unfortunately rather disconnected. See pp. 92–93.

the temple's administration and greatly enhanced the powers of their appointed accountants.

Yet the regime of the Uttamanambis was scarcely one of unrelieved oppression. In fact, the generosity of the Vijayanagar kings and the vigorous activities of the wardens in securing endowments and in directing repairs and construction projects are acknowledged, and described in some detail, in the *Oḷugu*. One of the wardens acted as the temple's spokesman at the Vijayanagar court in order to resolve a lengthy and violent boundary dispute, which is also discussed at length in the chronicle, between the Śrīraṅgam temple and the neighboring and rival Śaivite temple at Jambukēśvaram.[37] Other examples of the Uttamanambis' valuable services to the temple and their wholehearted participation in its activities are noted in the *Oḷugu*.

These administrative arrangements of the Vijayanagar period have some interesting political implications. The earlier relationship of the Delhi Sultans to the temple, though crude, is easy to understand; they were after plunder. But what were the aims of the Vijayanagar kings, who provided generous donations to the temple, bestowing resources rather than removing them? They must have sought some other kind of benefit than mere material profit. Yet what, apart from the presumed satisfaction of pious inclinations, could they have received in return for their generous gifts and their solicitude for the temple's internal affairs? To understand what they were after, we must bear in mind that temples confer honor and legitimacy upon the hero-kings who patronize them.[38] Gifts of land and other valuables, obtained by military means, were donated to the temple in exchange for ceremonial honors. This kind of ritual legitimation by the temple was of crucial importance to Telugu warriors who were seeking to consolidate their control over the distant Tamil country, which had its own cultural traditions and established institutions. Only an extensive network of these symbiotic relationships between the court and major temples could provide strong ideological links for such a far-flung empire, which would otherwise be of a purely military character. This network of relationships was carefully constructed by the Vijayanagar kings. Their success in this endeavor not only helped to consolidate their conquest regime, but also had some important effects upon the direction of religious change in the south. Above all, it gave strong impetus to the growing strength of the Teṅgalai or Southern school of Śrīvaiṣṇavism, at the expense of the Vaḍagalai or Northern school. This is clearly seen at Śrīraṅgam, where the Uttamanambis soon established close ties with the Ācāryas of the Southern school, particularly with the illustrious Maṇavāḷa Māmuṇi. The Southern school gradually became

37 *Ibid.*, pp. 139–41.

38 For this portion of my argument I am indebted to my colleague Arjun Appadurai, who has explored this theme in an illuminating paper entitled "State and Sect in South India: The Vijayanagara Period." It was presented at the Association for Asian Studies meetings in Toronto in March, 1976 on a panel ("Kingship and the Social Order in South India") for which I was the moderator. Dr. Appadurai's thesis is too complex to summarize here, but I have adapted portions of his argument to my own interpretation.

predominant at Śrīraṅgam, thanks in part to its connections with this vitally important source of patronage.

Later Developments

Rāmānuja's system of temple administration was partially restored, in the third quarter of the seventeenth century, by the Ācārya Śrīnivāsa Dēsikar. The chronicle notes that this sage became famous in the vicinity of Śrīraṅgam because of his learning, and that he converted many of his listeners from Śaivism to Vaiṣṇavism through his skill at public disputation. He carried out extensive repairs to the Śrīraṅgam temple with the assistance of the Nāyak of Madurai, and he set out to restore Rāmānuja's system of temple governance.[39] He even forbade non-Vaiṣṇavas to enter the temple. Since he was also a descendant of Āṇḍān, his reforms represent a resurgence of the authority of that line, lost when the Uttamanambis curbed the powers of the Śrīkāryam. Thus, Vijayanagar imperial decline was marked at Śrīraṅgam by at least a partial renascence of the system which the Vijayanagar regime had undermined, although the *Oḷugu's* rather sketchy account of this period makes it difficult to assess the exact degree of restoration. The Uttamanambis did continue to exercise some power at the temple, but were now forced to survive in the rougher game of multi-polar power politics, in which success depended upon allying one's self with the right provincial court at the right time. In fact, the role of warden appears to have become increasingly "internalized", i.e., transformed from proconsul into temple functionary, taking on the role of protecting established customs and properties, especially against expropriation by unruly Nāyaks, the former provincial governors of the Vijayanagar empire who now acted with both independence and pugnacity. Various temple authorities, including the wardens, were periodically forced to pay extortionate levies to them, sometimes selling offices and lands in order to do so.[40] Factional disputes within the temple were convenient for the Nāyaks, since rival functionaries could be played off against one another, with politically-confirmed temple offices as the reward.

During the eighteenth century, which was notoriously turbulent in the south, Hindu, Muslim and European armies invaded the temple precincts on several occasions. Troops of the Nizām of Hyderabad, the Nawāb of Arcot, Haidar Ali and Tīpū Sulṭān of Mysore, various Marāṭhā chiefs, and the French all intruded at one time or another, frequently imposing arbitrary levies of gold, paddy, etc. upon the temple as tribute. The French are accused by the chroniclers of outright plunder of the temple.[41] Yet it is significant that, as the *Oḷugu* repeatedly states, the Perumāḷ (i.e., the image of God) did not

39 *Oḷugu*, p. 188.
40 *Ibid.*, p. 181.
41 *Ibid.*, p. 197.

find it necessary to "quit" the temple on any of these occasions. This observation, plus the rather cursory treatment given to each of the eighteenth century intrusions, suggests that these disturbances, although frequent, produced less trauma, were less disruptive of ritual activities, and created less need for apologetic mythologizing than had the Muslim incursions of the early fourteenth century. By the beginning of the nineteenth century, when the temple came under British authority, the fourteenth century upheavals were still "remembered" in the temple with stronger feelings of shock and revulsion than were the more recent events.

Modernization and Religious Legitimation in India 1835 - 1885

GERALD JAMES LARSON

Introduction

THE PRESENT PAPER is in two parts. In Part I, I briefly address problems of definition; and in Part II, I attempt to set up a typological, analytic perspective regarding a specific research area – namely, the fifty-year period in nineteenth-century India (specifically 1835–1885) during which time an all-India national consciousness emerges in a specific segment of society that appears to be inextricably allied with certain developing religious legitimations. I shall try to argue that nineteenth-century Indian social reality is dialectically related to these developing religious legitimations; that these dialectical relationships are complex, plural and cross-cultural; and that the study of such relationships, though exceedingly difficult, may lead to some useful perspectives with respect to the volume's theme: Religion and the Legitimation of Power. My intention in the paper is not so much to begin to do a history of religion of nineteenth-century India as it is to inquire into the assumptions and perspectives for such a history. Thus, the paper is prolegomenon, or perhaps better, hermeneutic in the sense that I am interested primarily in interpretive perspectives for doing Religious Studies.

Part I: Definitions

For a collection of papers on the theme "Religion and the Legitimation of Power", it is not necessary that all contributors use the same definitions, but it is helpful for each contributor to make clear the definitions that are operating in his or her particular presentation. My own view (and, I would hasten to add, the view of many researchers in the newly emerging field of Religious Studies) is that religious traditions are best studied holistically, comparatively, and historically as part of a social or cultural system. Religious traditions are inextricably involved with the larger social reality in a given place and time, and function on various levels of personal and social awareness within that larger social reality. Oftentimes, religious traditions correlate positively and explicitly with the functioning of the total social order as can be seen, for example, in many ancient Indo-European religious traditions (Larson, 1974: 9–11). On the other hand, in numerous social contexts, the claims made by followers of a religious tradition may radically call into question the ontological or moral validity of a particular social context or institution, but even such a negative claim or critique feeds upon the social reality it attacks and is inconceivable apart from it. One thinks, for example, of Hindu notions of *mokṣa* which call into question and, finally, go beyond *varṇāśramadharma*, but it is clear enough that the very value of *mokṣa* presupposes *varṇāśramadharma* or some comparable social valuation *from* which release is imagined or attained.

Within the larger social reality, a religious tradition or "religion" furnishes meaningful interpretations of the world and the human condition, both theoretically and practically, by means of which individuals and various social groups fashion, maintain, and act out their identity with respect to "ultimate" issues. In terms of definition of the word "religion", perhaps Peter Berger has offered the most useful characterization. Says Berger,

> Religion is the human enterprise by which a sacred cosmos is established. Put differently, religion is cosmization in a sacred mode....... Every human society is an edifice of externalized and objectivated meanings, always intending a meaningful totality. Every society is engaged in the never completed enterprise of building a humanly meaningful world. Cosmization implies the identification of this humanly meaningful world with the world as such, the former now being grounded in the latter, reflecting it or being derived from it in its fundamental structures. Such a cosmos, as the ultimate ground and validation of human nomoi, need not necessarily be sacred. Particularly in modern times there have been thoroughly secular attempts at cosmization, among which modern science is by far the most important. It is safe to say, however, that originally *all* cosmization had a sacred character....
>
> It can thus be said that religion has played a strategic part in the human enterprise of world-building. Religion implies the farthest reach of man's self-externalization, of his infusion of reality with his own meanings. Religion implies that human order is projected into the totality of being. Put differently, religion is the audacious attempt to conceive of the entire universe as being humanly significant. (Berger, 1969: 25, 27–28.)

Equally useful for purposes of this paper is Peter Berger's definition of the term "legitimation". Says Berger,

> By legitimation is meant socially objectivated "knowledge" that serves to explain and justify the social order. Put differently, legitimations are answers to any questions about the "why" of institutional arrangements. (Berger, 1969: 29.)

Legitimations, then, are ways of ordering, of giving meaning and sanction to social reality. Such legitimations may be "cognitive" and/or "normative" and operate to some extent on the level of self-conscious theoretical elaboration, but also and more importantly, on the level of practical, day-by-day life. Referring to Berger again,

> ...it would be a serious mistake to identify legitimation with theoretical ideation. "Ideas," to be sure, can be important for purposes of legitimation. However, what passes for "knowledge" in a society is by no means identical with the body of "ideas" existing in the

> society. There are always some people with an interest in "ideas," but they have never yet constituted more than a rather small minority. If legitimation always had to consist of theoretically coherent propositions, it would support the social order only for that minority of intellectuals that have such theoretical interests – obviously not a very practical program. Most legitimation, consequently, is pretheoretical in character. (Berger, 1969: 30.)

This latter point about "legitimation" holds also for an adequate understanding of religion. That is to say, although religious ideation is important to some people, such ideation is not at all the only or even the dominant mode of the manifestation of religion. Religious conceptions are frequently naive and simplistic – one might say, to be more precise, "pre-theoretical" or "pre-reflective" – but nevertheless they serve as powerful and practical legitimations on the level of everyday life.

By opting for definitions of "religion" and "legitimation" like the ones briefly indicated, I am, of course, indicating a certain methodological perspective. In other words, by stressing the social reality of religion and by stressing the "pre-theoretical" or praxis-dimensions of "religion" and "legitimation", I am obviously favoring an approach to Religious Studies which emphasizes such problems as process, transformation, change, dialectical interaction, and everyday social-psychological behavior in concrete, practical social situations. Such an approach seeks to go beyond an "isms-approach" to religion, an "essentialist-approach", or a purely "structural-functional approach". The methodological perspective is, rather, in the direction of a more open-ended "totalizing" approach which construes religion in dialectical tension with a total social reality, and more than that, construes the study of religion itself and the practitioner of that study as moments in an on-going social-historical praxis. I call this methodological perspective "socio-analytic criticism" or "praxis-analysis", and I have discussed the theoretical basis for the perspective elsewhere.[1] In any case, I propose to employ "socio-analytic criticism" or "praxis-analysis" as I turn now in Part II to an examination of "Modernization and Religious Legitimation in India: 1835–1885".

Part II: Religious Legitimation and Nineteenth-Century India

As is well-known, by 1920 Gandhi had consolidated his leadership of the Indian nationalist movement, and sentiment had already arisen for complete independence from British rule. An all-India political movement was underway which would eventually result in independence in 1947. Apart from Gandhi himself, the nationalist movement was made up of and led by a newly emergent elite, men and women numbering in 1921 about 2.4 millions out of a total population of 305 millions (*Census of India 1921*, vol. I., pt. 2, p. 72, Calcutta), who spoke and read English; who had been exposed to the concepts of Western science, politics, literature, thought and religion; who were aware of and to some extent in contact with one another in various parts of the country because of a vigorous free press and an efficient railway system; and whose occupations included modern trade, manufacturing, government service, commercial agriculture, and the new professions of law, journalism and education. (Mehrotra, 1971: 51–106; Spear, 1961: 277–288.) From a religious point of view, this new class was made up of Hindus, Jains, Muslims, Parsees, Theosophists, a smattering of Christians and various kinds of secularists. In terms of caste heritage, the Hindus in the class came primarily from various *brāhmaṇa*, *bania* and *kāyastha* groups, although here and there lower castes were also represented. Geographically, the new class came overwhelmingly from the urban centers of Calcutta, Bombay and Madras.

To some extent, it can be argued that the growing all-India awareness of this class was brought about by negative or antagonistic social forces vis-à-vis British rule including, for example, the refusal of the British Raj to allow Indians into the higher levels of the Civil Service; the slow pace of the British in allowing political representation for Indians on the various levels of government; the suspicion that the British were employing a "divide-and-rule" tactic which was encouraging religious communalism; a concern that government economic policy was taking too much money and too many resources out of India while at the same time discouraging the development of indigenous industry; and a growing resentment to the racism and attitudes of European superiority which manifested themselves not only in official government policies in education and politics but also on local level among non-official foreign residents like the so-called "interlopers", the Anglo-Indians and various types of over-zealous missionaries. (B. B. Majumdar, 1965: 1–21; B. B. Majumdar, 1967: 1–21; Mehrotra, 1971: 3–9; D. E. Smith, 1963: 65–99; D. E. Smith, 1966: 21–48; D. E. Smith, 1974: 3–28.)

It can also be argued with some plausibility, however, that the growing all-India awareness of the new class was shaped by an equally large number of positive social forces including a recognition of the obvious benefits of improved education, medical care, communication and travel; a realization of the value of uniform government administration, law, and revenue-collection; and a social awareness of increased wealth made available through free trade, extensive investment with reasonably cheap money, and a long period of internal peace that provided a context in which the economy could develop. Perhaps, most important, there was a recovered pride, self-confidence and respect for India's own remarkable cultural heritage in such areas as art, language, philosophy and spirituality. (Kopf, 1969: 1–49; R. C. Majumdar, 1965: 89–96; D. E. Smith, 1974: 3–28.)

As one begins to get a totalized picture of this new class together with the incredibly complex social reality in which the class functioned, one is struck by the paradoxes, contradictions, tensions and polarities which characterized these people and which call into question most of the categories used in historical description and other modes of scholarly analysis. Tradition-modernity, continuity-change, centralization-communalism, alienation-identification, secularization-religious values, westernization-Indianization; all of these and more are operative forces in dialectical interaction with one another. (Palmer,

1961: 2.) Moreover, as one begins to get a totalized picture of this new class and its complex social reality, one begins to realize that it is a picture without a frame, or perhaps better, that the very image of a picture is inadequate. One begins, rather, to think of a series of pictures, or a motion-picture, or some sort of image that allows one to include both a global perspective and a much more sophisticated grasp of the notion of time; for it begins to become apparent that this new class and its social reality, reaching forward in time, has become the India that even now is struggling for political identity and social legitimation. As such, it is inextricably allied with our own understanding of ourselves and of our own way of life. Similarly, this new class and its social reality reaches back in time to the eighteenth and nineteenth-centuries wherein there is still a direct connection with our own social reality, for, to cite just one minor example, the Cornwallis who surrendered his troops to the American revolutionaries at Yorktown in 1781 is the same man who, in 1793, set up the Permanent Settlement with the *zamindars* in Bengal, thereby establishing for the first time in India a kind of private-property system which proved to be an important economic factor in the emergence of the new elite in the nineteenth-century. (Mehrotra, 1971: 6ff.) In one broad but, I suspect, significant sense, then, to inquire into the question of "Religion and the Legitimation of Power" among the the nineteenth-century Indian elite is to inquire into a similar issue with respect to our own social reality.

Apart from this general totalized context, however, the significant evidence suggests that this new class had its roots primarily in nineteenth-century India and especially in the remarkable period of 1835–1885: 1835 marking Macaulay's famous "Minute on Education" and the official decision to introduce English education on an all-India basis as well as to make English rather than Persian the language of all government communication; and 1885 marking the first meeting of the Indian National Congress in Bombay. Prior to the 1830's (and after Robert Clive and Warren Hastings had ended the earliest nabob-period of plunder and fortune-seeking), the East India Company had been basically conservative regarding its cultural and social policies. (Spear, 1961: 203–214; D. E. Smith, 1963: 72–78.) Beyond the actual conquest itself (completed by the early nineteenth-century and consolidated everywhere by mid-century), the only important changes introduced by the British in the early decades of rule were the reorganization of the judicial system, the Permanent Settlement or land reform with systematic revenue-collection in Bengal carried out by Cornwallis in 1793, the introduction of the *ryotwar* system of land reform in the Madras Presidency between 1819 and 1827, and the *talukdar* land reform system in the North-Western provinces. (Mehrotra, 1971: 1–50; Moore 1966 : 5–15.) Nothwithstanding these changes, whenever possible in this early period the Company tried to avoid meddling in internal affairs, and indeed like the princely states had actively supported local temples, important festivals and other traditional institutions both administratively and financially. Moreover, this early period saw the rise of British Orientalism in Calcutta symbolized in the College of Fort William and the pioneering research into India's classical and vernacular languages sponsored by Warren Hastings and Lord Wellesley and carried out by such Orientalists as William Jones, H. T. Colebrooke and William Carey. (Kopf, 1969: 45–94.) The first serious challenge to this early policy was the Charter Act of 1813 – a challenge mounted in Britain by Grant, Wilberforce and other Evangelicals – which allowed missionaries to enter the country for the first time and also established a direct connection between the government of India and the Church of England. (Kopf, 1969: 129–144.) Nevertheless, it should be noted that the decision was also made to continue the strict policy of religious neutrality in terms of government pronouncements and actions. With the publication in England of James Mills' *History of British India* in 1817, together with the rise of radical utilitarian programs and liberal reformist policies in economics and social life, all of which tendencies correlated with the transformation taking place in England as a result of growing industrialization, the older Company policy of cultural neutrality was seriously called into question. (Kopf, 1969: 236–272; Stokes, 1959: 1–47.) Indeed, by 1833, the Company's commercial activities were taken over by the British government and Lord Bentinck was on the scene in India as Governor-General dispensing what he himself called the "pure milk of the Benthamite word", together with what Croce has called the "nineteenth-century religion of liberalism". A peculiar alliance of "merchant, manufacturer and missionary" appears to have emerged, fired on one level by a faith in quantitative political economy, on another level by a vision of free trade and universal education, and on yet another level by an Evangelical conviction that somehow God wanted all these things. (Spear, 1971: 169–186; Stokes, 1959: 27–31.) The alliance led to a policy of active engagement with respect to Indian culture after 1835, the goal of which in the famous words of Macaulay was to create "...a class of persons, Indian in color and blood, but English in tastes, in opinions, in morals and in intellect." (deBary, 1958: 601.)

The more strident forms of the new policy were moderated to a large extent as a result of the Sepoy Mutiny in 1857, and in 1858, when the Company was dissolved and India taken over by the British Crown, Queen Victoria in her proclamation, while explicitly referring to Britain's reliance on the "truth of Christianity", went on to assert, however,

> ...and we do strictly charge and enjoin all those who may be in authority under us that they abstain from all interference with the religious belief or worship of any of our subjects on pain of our highest displeasure. (D. E. Smith, 1963: 72.)

This at least officially eliminated the missionary from the "peculiar alliance" already referred to, and more than that, generally led to a more moderate approach to reform. Thereafter, the government of India moved more and more into a ponderous, albeit efficient, imperalist presence, and in the later decades of the nineteenth-century larger social forces came into play with the establishment of a strong, utilitarian-inspired central government and legal system, massive capital investment with the building of an all-India railway system, and the development of commercial agriculture and general economic development, greatly accelerated by the opening of the Suez Canal after 1869. (R. Iyer, 1971: 163ff; Moore, 1966: 15–62; Stokes, 1959: 81–139.)

The Indian response to these incredible changes taking place was, of course, complex and multi-dimensional. On one level, there was a rapid and favorable response especially in Calcutta, Bombay and Madras to English education, government service, and new economic opportunities. (R. C. Majumdar, 1965: 1–85; B. B. Majumdar, 1967: 7–21; H. Mukherjee, 1957: 21–69.) Moreover, British Orientalism had had an important impact on Bengali intellectuals leading not only to the well-known Bengali renaissance but also eventually to an all-India appreciation of the country's rich cultural heritage. (Kopf, 1969: 284–289.) On another level, there was a widespread revulsion against Evangelical Christian missionizing efforts especially in Calcutta, Madras and Bombay. Indeed, S. R. Mehrotra has clearly documented, mainly from Indian newspapers of the period, the extent to which Evangelical missionizing functioned as a crucial negative force in helping to bring about an all-India social awareness. An article in a Calcutta newspaper of December, 1845, illustrates well this level of response:

> In this crusade against Christianity we find men of all sects and parties meeting on common ground... men who have faith in idols, and those who despise them... the Hindoo Pharisee, and the Hindoo libertine, – the man whose kitchen is limited to the most ritualistic food, and the man who eats beef and drinks champagne, without scruple – brahmuns and soodras – young Bengal and old Bengal, – the well-educated Hindoo youth who has studied Shakespeare and Bacon, and the old Hindoo who believes that the world rests on the back of a tortoise, – all are united in one general opposition to the truths of Christianity and in efforts to oppose its progress. (*Friend of India*, Calcutta, December 1845, in Mehrotra, 1971: 38.)

Or, again, in an article during the same year one reads,

> ...the bigoted and the liberal, orthodox and reformer, the gross idolater, and pure Vedantists, all are united in hatred and opposition to the gospel. (*Calcutta Christian Advocate*, May 31, 1845, in Mehrotra, 1971: 38.)

On yet another level, many traditional Hindus and Muslims had no comprehension of what was happening, and simply despised the British and other foreign "interlopers" as *mlecchas* ("barbarians") and *feringhees* ("infidel foreigners"), who should be violently expelled. (Mehrotra, 1971: 51–106.) It was not until the failure of the Sepoy Mutiny in 1857 that it was realized that this traditional Hindu-Muslim vision of violent expulsion was only a hopeless dream. On still another level, many English-educated Indians opted not only for the new language and the resulting benefits to career and personal wealth, but also for British ideas like liberalism, representative democracy and social reform. It was this level of response that led to the first indigenous political associations as those in Calcutta, Bombay and Madras in the 1840's, the British Indian Association in 1851, the Indian Association of 1876, and the Indian National Congress of 1885. (C. F. Andrews and G. Mookerjee, 1938:

97–140; Karunakaran, 1964: 1–55; Lewis, 1962: 64–81; B. B. Majumdar, 1965: 22–64; R. C. Majumdar, 1962: 321–416; R. C. Majumdar, 1965: 418–463; Mehrotra, 1971: 51–106; Spear, 1961: 298–319.)

In terms of specifically religious legitimation, I have already suggested that this new class for the most part clearly rejected Evangelical missionizing as well as the purist Hindu-Muslim view that the despised *mlecchas* ("barbarians") and *feringhees* ("infidels") should be violently expelled. (Mehrotra, 1971: 51–106.) In rejecting Evangelical Christianity, the new class was not unique. As is well-known, Christianity has been rejected generally in India except among low-caste or outcaste groups. In rejecting the purist Hindu or Muslim views, the new class did so not simply because of the political realities after the defeat of the Mutiny in 1857, but also because the purist model of religious identity represented an obvious negation of the new class' very existence. The new class, in other words, was already deeply involved with the "barbarian" and the "infidel" and thus almost by definition was polluted and outside the framework of that kind of religious legitimation. What appears to have happened, in the fifty-year period under review, is that the new class opted for various kinds of hybrid religious legitimation. Some, for example, identified with systems of ideas and patterns of behavior made available through enlightenment and romanticist classicism, liberal humanism, representative democracy and various other formulations of modern Western thought and practice. Perhaps more became involved with one or another variety of a reformed indigenous spirituality like the Brahmo Samāj (founded in 1828), the Prārthanā Samāj (of 1867), the Ārya Samāj (of 1875), the Theosophical Society (after 1882), the Rāmakrishna Mission (of 1887), or some other form of neo-Hindu tradition. (R. C. Majumdar, 1965: 97–156.) The Parsees formed a hybrid Religious Reform Association in Bombay in 1851, and many of the Muslims in the new class eventually identified with Syed Ahmed Khan's hybrid Aligarh Movement (from 1875 onwards). A few preferred one or another variety of Protestant Christianity, but, as mentioned above, the Evangelical Christian model functioned more as a kind of *via negativa* among members of the new class. (Pathak, 1967: 3–89.) In almost every instance, then, the emerging religious legitimations were mediated by the rapidly changing social reality of the nineteenth-century, and in each instance the religious options in turn doubled back upon the larger social reality and acted upon it. Taken together, it appears that the various religious legitimations that emerged were neither Eastern nor Western, ancient nor modern, national nor communal, but rather, hybrid formulations that correlated with the pluralistic, cross-cultural and composite identity of the new class.

In view of this incredibly complex contextual environment, it may seem impossible to say anything about the problem of "Religion and the Legitimation of Power" other than to point at this problem of hybrid formulation. Recalling, however, the definitions of "religion" and "legitimation" referred to in the beginning, which emphasized the pre-theoretical or pre-reflective aspects of "religion" and "legitimation", it is possible to say something, at least by way of clarification, regarding the issue at hand. To understand the hybrid formulations, it is useful to turn away from the study of religion as ideational-constructs and to attend more to the level of praxis or usage. I would like to argue that it is not very helpful when studying nineteenth-century hybrid religious legitimations to ask what role did Christian ideas play, or Hindu ideas, or Muslim ideas, etc. A more useful approach might be to ask to what extent are religious legitimations idiomatic usages in highly complex social situations? From this perspective hybrid religious legitimations are "idioms" in the sense that they have a meaning which cannot be derived as a whole from their conjoined elements. They are specific to a particular context and lead to immediate comprehension only in that context. Such hybrid religious legitimations as "idioms" are socially objectivated "knowledge" in Peter Berger's sense, operate on a pre-theoretical level, and "bestow" a "valid ontological status" or "aura of factuality" on the social reality that has been created by the praxis of a particular group. Such religious "idioms" are what operated among members of the newly emerging class in nineteenth-century India and functioned as pre-theoretical systems of valuation or ways of giving expression to their composite identity.

The political scientist, W. H. Morris-Jones, was the first to call attention to "idioms" like this, only he did so in the realm of modern Indian politics. (Morris-Jones, 1971: 273ff.) He identified three "idioms" that appear to be operative in modern Indian political life: a "modern" idiom, a "traditional" idiom, and a "saintly" idiom. By the term "idiom", Morris-Jones calls attention not so much to a self-conscious, theoretical system of ideas, but, rather, to a set of operative valuations which function almost unconsciously or pre-theoretically – the kind of "idiom" used, for example, while making a political "deal" during a coffee break, rather than the more formalized and self-conscious ideation evident in an official session of parliament. It is clear that pre-theoretical "idioms" like this are apparent throughout the history of religion in nineteenth-century India among the members of the new elite in terms of their religious legitimations. The "modern-idiom" is composed of the more or less taken-for-granted valuations of liberal humanism, representative democracy, science and technology, and a general orientation to the social reality of the present. The "traditional-idiom" may be seen in the pre-theoretical or pre-reflective valuations of certain sacred texts, festivals, social relationships, etc., clearly in need of reform but also clearly a set of criteria for valuing and thereby allowing an orientation towards the past. And, finally, the "saintly-idiom" is found in the pre-theoretical valuations of immediate or experiential religion which is almost free-floating in that it does not necessarily identify with the traditional or the modern, even with any particular institutional articulation, and which, as it were, breaks through all religious forms.

In addition to these three "idioms" or "usages", however, there is also an obvious polarity manifesting itself again and again throughout nineteenth-century Indian religion and which has to do with behavioral mode, or style, or manner of presentation of the various idioms. One style or mode might be called coercive, or aggressive, or exclusive; the contrasting style or mode could be described as subversive, or passive-aggressive, or inclusive.

Putting the idioms together with the behavioral mode or style of presentation, one could set up an analytic scheme wherein would exist a "modern idiom" of religion with a coercive or a subversive mode; a "traditional idiom" of religion with a coercive or a subsersive mode; and a "saintly idiom" of religion with a coercive or subversive mode. Within the "modern idiom" in its coercive mode one might place what Croce has called the "nineteenth-century religion of liberalism" as well as what Bentinck characterized as "the pure milk of the Benthamite word" – liberalism and utilitarianism not as philosophical positions or modern ideologies but rather as religious idioms in the context of a particular social reality. (Somewhat later than the fifty-year period considered in this paper, Marxist valuations came to play an important role under this type.) Within the "modern idiom" in its subversive mode one might place the enlightenment classicism of British Orientalism with its universalist vision of civilization and its profound appreciation for India's cultural past which, however, was always interpreted in terms of a modern, rational and enlightened vision of what India should be in the present. Indian intellectuals, scholars and political leaders have been especially attracted to both these types of "modern idiom".

Within the "traditional idiom" in its coercive mode, one might place the Ārya Samāj with its strident pride in the ancient Veda as a sole criterion, yet which also was deeply concerned with modernization and reform – but modernization and reform looking back to the Vedic past for its primary orientation. Within the "traditional idiom" in its subversive mode might be placed groups like the Brahmo Samāj, the Prārthanā Samāj, and the Theosophical Society, all of which affirmed the ancient valuations of the Indian tradition but also accepted the valuations of other religious traditions – a passive-aggressive or inclusive spirituality, profoundly aware of the need for a type of modernization which could be achieved through the appropriating of a great variety of religious traditions. Also, within the "traditional idiom" in its subversive mode, one might place both the Church of England in India in the nineteenth-century as well as the Serampore Protestant mission near Calcutta in its early nineteenth-century form. (Kopf, 1969: 284–289; D. E. Smith, 1963: 78–84.) The Church of England, of course, was legally prohibited from being coercive and operated simply as a presence in India, but nevertheless served as an important symbol of the possibility of religious freedom in Indian self-consciousness. The Serampore Mission is a particularly interesting case. As David Kopf has shown, under the guidance of William Carey and Joshua Marshman, the mission disseminated a sort of Protestant Reformation model of spirituality, not by coercively attempting to convert Indians but, rather, by encouraging a reformation from within Indian culture. Thus, it was Christian in its valuations, but its mission strategy was subversive and inclusive, and it is no accident that some of the Serampore missionaries worked closely with the British Orientalists in Calcutta early in the century. The few Indians from the newly emerging class who became Christians often did so with this "idiom".

Within the "saintly idiom" in its coercive mode, one might place the sort of Christian mission valuation that one finds in a man like Alexander Duff in Calcutta. As David Kopf has commented, "Duff aimed at transforming Calcutta Bengalis into Scottish Presbyterians." (Kopf, 1969: 260.) His goal was to convert all of Calcutta, and it never seemed to bother him that the Hindu and Muslim population of Calcutta was greater than the population of his native Scotland. What appears so obviously incongruent is not to a certain kind of evangelical who, as Eric Stokes points out, combines an intense individualism with the conviction that human character can be "suddenly and totally transformed". Such a religious valuation is much more than coercive from within the "traditional idiom" that was mentioned earlier. The intensely evangelical spirit of an Alexander Duff represents a critique of all social reality, whether traditional or modern. Few Indians accepted this "idiom" and, as mentioned earlier, it tended to serve in the nineteenth-century as a negative limiting "idiom" over against which the newly emerging class tried to express itself religiously.

Finally, within the "saintly idiom" in its subversive mode, one might place the nineteenth-century Hindu saint, Rāmakrishna, and his disciple, Swami Vivekānanda, the founder of the Rāmakrishna Mission (in 1887). (R. C. Majumdar, 1965: 116–131.) One might also perceive within this type the religious valuation and behavioral style of some of the later nationalist figures like Gandhi, Vinoba Bhave and Jayaprakas Narayan. This idiom of religious valuation looks for the immediate or experiential dimension in all traditions while refusing to concede that any one social reality, either traditional or modern, is the primary source for religious valuation. In so far as this idiom engages in mission activity, it does so in a passive-aggressive mode, as can be seen in the quiet, low-key strategy of the Rāmakrishna mission, as well as in the later non-violent non-cooperation movement of Gandhi which was designed not simply as a political device but also to "convert" the British by passively encompassing them in a larger vision of non-violent social reality that would be multi-national and multi-religious.

All of these "idioms", then, served as hybrid religious legitimations in nineteenth-century India among the members of the new emerging class. Indeed, they continue to be operative in present-day India as well. It is not unusual to find Indians using several of these idioms in one conversation, for these idioms are not perceived to be mutually exclusive ideational constructs. They are, rather, as I have tried to show, pre-theoretical systems of valuation in dialectical interaction with one another. They have emerged out of the incredible transvaluation of values that took place in nineteenth-century India and have emerged out of the class of people who were caught up in that transvaluation. In terms of final assessment, one is tempted to interpret these hybrid religious legitimations as being unique to the very specific, indeed highly eccentric, social reality of nineteenth-century India. On the other hand, what happened in nineteenth-century India may have been the first, halting step of what Erik Erikson would call the loss of our identity as "pseudo-species" and the "quest" in the social praxis of our time for the "anticipatory development of more inclusive identities". (Erikson, 1969: 431–433.)

Note

I have discussed what I call "socio-analytic criticism" or "praxis-analysis" in two other essays: (a) "The *Bhagavad Gītā* as Cross-Cultural Process: Toward an Analysis of the Social Locations of a Religious Text" (Larson, 1975: 651–669); and (b) "Revolutionary Praxis and Comparative Philosophy" (Larson, 1973: 333–341). Rather than repeat the more detailed treatments set forth in these two articles, let me simply quote one short passage from the former article, which will briefly indicate the direction of my thinking with respect to the issue of methodological perspective. In the article I suggest a

> ...methodological perspective which would allow us to look at common problems and to ask questions that lead us in two seemingly opposite directions: (a) a totalistic or "telescopic" direction that causes us to reflect upon the whole range of our problems, and (b) a specific or "microscopic" direction that leads us to take seriously the empirical data in our cultural studies. One such experimental method might be what I would call "socio-analytic criticism" or "praxis-analysis." The expressions are my own invention, although the perspective is derived primarily from the methodological reflections of Jean-Paul Sartre in his *Critique de la raison dialectique*, in which he sets forth a method which he calls "totalization," "dialectical knowing," or the "progressive-regressive method" – a method which involves simultaneously the study of social structure, historical experience, and individual praxis both of the investigator and that which is being investigated....
> I call the approach "socio-analytic criticism" or "praxis-analysis" in the hope that such phrases indicate a position which transcends either a humanistic/historical or social-scientific preference but which makes use of elements from both. Moreover, I prefer naming the approach "socio-analytic criticism" or "praxis-analysis" in the hope that such a naming will enable one to pursue the methodological perspective without getting completely caught up in Sartre's philosophical position of existentialistic Marxism. In any case, I suggest that what I am calling "socio-analytic criticism" or "praxis-analysis" be tried as a methodological approach which involves the following elements: (a) historical and textual research in the framework of an intention reaching for an understanding of the larger, "totalistic" social reality; (b) a focus on praxis both of the material being studied and of the researcher; (c) an approach which moves forward and backward, so to speak, and attempts to make connections between ancient and modern, "eastern" and "western," and so on; and (d) an approach which focuses more on process, transformation and change in Religious Studies. (Larson, 1975: 657–658.)

I should perhaps also indicate that my attempt to develop the methodological perspective of "socio-analytic criticism" or "praxis-analysis" explains my preference to use Peter Berger's definitions of "religion" and "legitimation" already referred to, for Berger's own work is heavily dependent on Alfred Schutz's phenomenological sociology as well as the praxis-orientation of the early Marx and the social-psychology of George Herbert Mead – all of which motifs or strains are congenial to the methodological perspective that I am trying to develop.

REFERENCES

ANDREWS, C. F. and G. MOOKERJEE
1938 *The Rise and Growth of the Congress in India*. London: George Allen and Unwin Ltd.
BERGER, Peter
1969 *The Sacred Canopy*. New York: Doubleday Anchor.
1973 *The Homeless Mind*. New York: Vintage, Random House.
DE BARY, W. Theodore, *et al.*, eds.
1958 *Sources of Indian Tradition*. New York: Columbia University Press.
ERIKSON, Erik
1969 *Gandhi's Truth*. New York: W. W. Norton.
IYER, Raghavan
1971 "Utilitarianism and Empire in India", in T. R. Metcalf (ed.), *Modern India: An Interpretive Anthology*. London: The Macmillan Co.
KARUNAKARAN, K. P.
1964 *Continuity and Change in Indian Politics*. New Delhi: People's Publishing House.
KOPF, David
1969 *British Orientalism and the Bengal Renaissance*. Berkeley: The University of California Press.
LARSON, Gerald James, ed.
1974 *Myth in Indo-European Antiquity*. Berkeley, Los Angeles, London: The University of California Press.
LARSON, Gerald James.
1973 "Revolutionary Praxis and Comparative Philosophy", *Philosophy East and West*, 23 (July), 333–341.
1975 "The *Bhagavad Gītā* as Cross-Cultural Process: Toward an Analysis of the Social Locations of a Religious Text", *Journal of the American Academy of Religion*, XLIII (December), 651–669.
LEWIS, Martin D., ed.
1962 *The British in India: Imperialism or Trusteeship?* Lexington, Mass.: D. C. Heath and Co.
MAJUMDAR, B. B.
1965 *Indian Political Associations and Reform of Legislature (1818–1917)*. Calcutta: Mukhopadhyay.
1967 *History of Indian Social and Political Ideas (from Rammohan to Dayānanda)*. Calcutta: Bookland Private Ltd.
MAJUMDAR, R. C.
1962 *History of the Freedom Movement in India*, Volume I. Calcutta: Mukhopadhyay.
MAJUMDAR, R. C., ed.
1965 *British Paramountcy and Indian Renaissance*, Part II. Part of the series, *The History and Culture of the Indian People*. Bombay: Bharatiya Vidya Bhavan.
MEHROTRA, S. R.
1971 *The Emergence of the Indian National Congress*. Delhi: Vikas Publications.
METCALF, Thomas B., ed.
1971 *Modern India: An Interpretive Anthology*. London: The Macmillan Co.
MOORE, R. J.
1966 *Liberalism and Indian Politics*. London: Edward Arnold Publications.
MORRIS-JONES, W. H.
1971 "India's Political Idioms", in Thomas B. Metcalf (ed.), *Modern India: An Interpretive Anthology*. London: The Macmillan Co.
MUKHERJEE, H. and U. MUKHERJEE
1957 *The Growth of Nationalism in India* (1857–1905). Calcutta: The Presidency Library.
PALMER, Norman D.
1961 *The Indian Political System*. New York: Houghton Mifflin.

PATHAK, S. M.
1967 *American Missionaries and Hinduism.* Delhi: Munshiram Manoharlal.
SMITH, D. E.
1959 *India as a Secular State.* Princeton: Princeton University Press.
SMITH, D. E., ed.
1966 *South Asian Politics and Religion.* Princeton: Princeton University Press.
1974 *Religion and Political Modernization.* New Haven: Yale University Press.
SPEAR, Percival
1961 *India.* A Modern History. Ann Arbor: The University of Michigan Press.
1971 "Bentinck and Education", in T. B. Metcalf (ed.), *Modern India: An Interpretive Anthology.* London: The Macmillan Co.
STOKES, Eric
1959 *The English Utilitarians and India.* Oxford: Clarendon Press.

The Religious Legitimization of Change among Modernists in Indo-Pakistani Islam

SHEILA McDONOUGH

"C'est un devoir, nous dit Ibn Taymiyya, de considérer l'exercise de pouvoir comme une des formes de la religion, comme l'une des actes par lequel l'homme se rapproche de Dieu." (Gardet, 1961: 107.)

"Question: Will Pakistan be a secular or a Theocratic State?
Mr. Jinnah: You are asking me a question that is absurd. I do not know what a Theocratic State means." (Ahmad, 1960: 422.)

PAKISTAN CAME into existence in August, 1948 because many Muslims had decided against the option of life in Congress-dominated India. The masses who voted for Pakistan were responding to an appeal to the ideal of Muslim solidarity. Those who made the appeal were mainly products of a Western type of educational system. But the need to define their position over against the claims of the secular ideal of the Congress made it necessary for the political leaders of the anti-Congress Muslims to put forward an alternative. The anti-Congress position necessarily took the form of an appeal to Islamic religious ideals.

Yet this problem was not the only reason why the modernist leaders claimed to be in some sense spokesmen for their religion. Within the structure of Islam, the modern period has witnessed a breakdown of traditional modes of authority, and much experimentation with new forms. The traditional pattern had consisted of at least five types of authority. Firstly, the Caliph had taken over from Muhammad the function of symbolic head of the community, and political and religious leader. The Caliphs did not, however, take over the function of interpreting the religion. The *ulama* class gradually came into being as a group of experts who were acknowledged to have the authority to interpret the scripture. A third form of the authority came to be the *Shariah* itself. Although the *ulama* created the *Shariah*, by a long process of discussion and gradual arriving at consensus, once agreement had been reached the actual religious law took on a certain autonomy because the *ulama* had agreed that further discussion was not necessary, and that the questions could not be re-opened. The subsequent function of the *ulama* tended to be limited to commentary only.

A fourth form of authority rested in the later medieval period with the leaders of the Sufi orders. They gradually took on the function of spiritual advisers, often to the political leaders. And, a fifth type was that of the Mahdi, a charismatic leader, not legitimated by the political or religious authorities, but gathering support by his claim to divine inspiration. That such leaders often gained support from the Muslim masses indicates that readiness to respond to such appeals is an aspect of the complex whole of Muslim expectations.

In the context of Indian Islam, the medieval authority patterns were dislocated by the final collapse of Mughal political authority in 1857. The loss of the central form of Muslim political authority meant that the other types of authority also lost their sense of their relationship to the whole. It is hard to be one prop of a system when the other props have fallen down. The *ulama* in particular have been in a sense struggling ever since trying to discover how to perform their traditional role in a changed world. In part, especially in Pakistan, they have been tempted to try to exercise political authority themselves, or at least to control the political authorities more thoroughly than they had done in the medieval period. In other words, the collapse of the Mughal rulers left the *ulama* with a certain feeling that they ought to have greater authority, and that the community needed them more than ever.

One indication of this concern of the *ulama* was the founding of a new training institution for religious scholars, the Dar ul Ulum at Deoband. This happened ten years after the failure of the Mutiny. The founder of Deoband had taken part in the fighting earlier. The establishing of the seminary was a conscious effort to try to accomplish with pen and book what swords had failed to do. (Faruqi, 1963: 23.) The activity of the teachers, students and supporters of the new institution indicates a certain resilience and vitality among the *ulama*. The leaders of the Sufi orders by contrast have not exhibited noteworthy new activity in the face of change, and the orders have gradually declined. Both the modernists and the new *ulama* have tended to disparage Sufism as a source of Muslim backwardness and unhealthy other-worldliness. Further, although some modernists might be said to have manifested charisma, the traditional type of Mahdi, promising millenarian perfection, has not appeared. The Caliphate also, in spite of the efforts of the *Khilafat* movement, has ceased to exist.

The *ulama* and the *Shariah* thus remain the main forms of traditional authority still functioning actively. This has probably meant that the *ulama* have tended to feel an even greater need to keep the *Shariah* unchallenged, since its status is linked with their role as interpreters. The Deoband school has not been willing to encourage new modes of thinking about religion and religious law.

The Western-educated elite responded differently to the problems of the new age. One finds almost all the themes which are characteristic of the modernist position in the writings of Maulana Muhammad Ali, leader of the *Khilafat* movement and founder of the Jamia Millia Islamia (National Muslim University). In his autobiography, he says:

> Like other men of my own class, particularly the 'Old Boys of Aligarh', I was now impelled to make a close study of my religion.... Both my brother and I now turned more and more to the Qur'an. (Afzal Iqbal, 1942: 44.)

Muhammad Ali's own class were those who were conscious of themselves as the probable future leaders and spokesmen for their community. They were more or less aware that they would have to communicate with members of their community from different levels of society, and also to articulate what their own community's position was over against the English and the Hindus. Thus, although Muhammad Ali was thinking of becoming a leader of the Muslim community within the context of an independent India, he still felt strongly the need to be clear in his ideas about his religion. His leadership took the form of journalism, and educational reform, as well as political agitation, and in all these roles he needed to be sure he could use language that would be familiar to Muslims and that would move them to support his causes. After he and his friends, in response to Gandhi's call for the abandoning of the British-supported universities, had left Aligarh and founded the Jamia Millia Islamia, Muhammad Ali wrote a curriculum for the religious education of the new generation of Muslims.

The emphasis of the curriculum was on the Qur'an and on Islamic history. The new generation of leaders were expected to steep themselves in the spirit of the Qur'an. Muhammad Ali has told us how intoxicated he was with the driving force he had appropriated from his personal study of the Holy Book.

> Ever since, this book... has had the invariable effect of intoxicating us, with its simple grandeur, its intense directness and its incessant flow of motive power for the manifold activities of life.
> And long before I had read it through, Eureka! I had found a new meaning in life and in this world and an entirely new significance in Islam. I had been familiar enough with the main tenets of Islam; but they had been little more than a bundle of doctrines and commandments each for a particular department of life or situation.... Now, however, they acquired a new coherence.... They were no longer a bundle of doctrines but a single Divine Purpose running through all creation... man made a voluntary and complete surrender of himself and became the rightless slave of his creator.... This rightless slave of Allah became free forever.... Then as the Vicegerent of God he had the full force of the universe at his beck and call. He could now use it whenever, and wherever His Divine Purpose necessitated its use... (Afzal Iqbal, 1942: 88–90.)

The modernist as typified by Muhammad Ali is thus one who seeks from his religion fuel – energy and drive that will enable him to transcend present obstacles and create better conditions of life. He needs a vision of what ought to be, and assurance that if he acts rightly "the full force of the universe" will flow into him and enable him to fulfill his purposes. The modernist political leader expects all his supporters to share his vision and his causes. Of necessity, therefore, this view of Islam has little room for the idea that only one group of Muslims are qualified to interpret religious meaning. In Muhammad Ali's words:

> Islam had no apostles, no Church, and no Church Councils like Christianity to dictate her creed to the believer. It has not even a clergy and the whole spirit of Islam is consistently and relentlessly opposed to such a thing as "experts" in religion. It wants all alike to know their faith, and religion should be the province of all the faithful. That is why, unlike Christianity, it has had no "Theology by Committee..." (Afzal Iqbal, 1942: 158.)

Such relentless opposition to experts in religion would understandably not sit well with the *ulama*. The same situation after 1857 which had led the *ulama* in the direction of claiming a greater right to leadership was also leading political leaders like Muhammad Ali to disparage the medieval system and to claim their own rights as representative political leaders to speak on religious questions as well. Thus, as the *ulama* were becoming more interested in politics, the politicians were moving into religion.

Another aspect of the modernist position was appeal to what might be called the "Abraham" motif, namely that when believers found themselves in a bad situation, they ought to pack their bags and go off to found a better society elsewhere. The young Maulana Abul Kalam Azad, like Maulana Mohammad Ali a self-appointed religious authority, and an active journalist and politico-religious agitator, had supported agitation in 1920 which had called upon the Muslim masses to leave India.

> The movement involved 18,000 Muslims, most of them of poorer classes, in great suffering as they were turned away from the Afghan border, and thousands died on the road of sickness and hunger. (Ahmad, 1967: 136).

It is not difficult to see this abortive emigration as a forerunner to the movement to Pakistan that was to occur twenty-eight years later. Both are indications of a latent readiness of Muslims to accept the view that difficulties can be remedied by movement elsewhere. A political leader working with Muslims knows that this is one of the appeals that he can make. Any political leader in any actual situation might or might not make such appeal. In the 1920 instance, Maulana Azad supported the call, whereas Jinnah did not. By 1948, the position was reversed. What the religion does is provide a number of options which are likely to move believers if they are stressed; political leaders then select what seems appropriate at a given time.

The Abraham motif in the Qur'an is similar to its Biblical counterpart, but there are certain differences. In the Qur'an, there is not an emphasis on a specific promised land. The stress is rather on Abraham as the one who departs from idolatry: he says a vehement no to false gods. Where he should go, or what he should do is not spelled out: he will follow as God commands.

Neither Abraham nor Moses in the Qur'an is linked with the idea that God is leading the people to a specific place that has been fore-ordained to be theirs.

Muhammad is the basic prototype of Prophet in the Qur'an. The symbols of Abraham and Moses are cast in his image, as are those of all the other Qur'anic prophets. They all suffered from persecution by idolaters, as he did, and they all warn that destruction will fall on the heads of those who fail to heed the prophetic warning. But Mohammad left his home only because the unbelievers refused to hear. The emigration might have been to any place where God's commands could have been put in action. Thus Muslims are not told that there is one promised land, but rather that if any situation becomes intolerable they will have to start again somewhere else.

Much of the imagery used in the case of the movement that led many Indian Muslims to decide to opt for Pakistan came from the pen of the poet Iqbal. He often appealed to images of Abraham and Moses. For example:

> You, shut in by walls, have never known that moment when the shrill
> Bugle-call that sound the march goes echoing over wood and hill....
> Nor the going-down of sun in stillnesses of desert ways,
> Twilight splendour such as brightened Abraham's world-beholding gaze,...
> Wildernesses ever new love's fever seeks and thirsts to roam –
> You the furrowed field and palm-grove fetter tight to one poor home; (Kiernan, 1955: 19.)

The appeal in such verses is for courage and imagination: believers are promised that if they can be brave enough to leave all known security, including the security of knowing what their religion is, they can expect the fresh air of the desert. That image suggests both the first Muslims, and also the state of abandoning all settled places. Abraham's gaze is world-beholding because he has freed himself from all that is particular. With absolute freedom comes omniscience.

An example of Iqbal's use of the Moses' theme is as follows:

> If a man deems himself earthly
> The light divine dies in his heart.
> When a Moses loses hold of his own self,
> His hand becomes dark and staff merely a rope.
> Life is nothing without the capacity for new creations.
>
> (Dar, 1964: 70.)

The hand and the staff of Moses recur frequently in these verses as reminders that Moses triumphed over the black arts of the Pharaoh's magicians. Because of his faithfulness in a time when he was alone in the face of vast and threatening power, Moses' hand turned white and his staff became a snake. Thus the faithful can ever expect, as Muhammad Ali had said, that the full force of the universe will come to their aid.

The impact of Iqbal's poetry has tended to liberate those who have responded to it to be ready to deal in new ways with whatever might happen. It would be an improper over-simplification to suggest that Iqbal's use of

Abraham is intended to urge Muslims literally to emigrate from their homes. The intention is rather to urge believers to liberate themselves from whatever impedes their individual and social creativeness.

The example of the energizing force which Muhammad Ali said was released in him by his appropriation of the spirit of the Qur'an is typical of what the modernists claim as the fruits of their new understanding of their religion. The psychological forces involved seem to be complex. Probably release comes partly from acceptance of the new imperative to change. If, for other reasons, change is perceived as necessary, the modernist legitimization of continual change as a way of life can liberate believers from a split in their consciousnesses.

Further, acceptance of an ideal of change requires that individuals appropriate the symbols for themselves, since the need for on-going decision-making necessitates self-conscious individuals who can debate among themselves and work out what should be done. Iqbal urged that believers should be integrated persons if they were to be creative. This meant not only that they could not allow any external authority to interpret their religion for them, but also that their own lives should not be compartmentalized. From his perspective the phrase "Islam is a code for the whole of life" meant that the believer should bring to bear in all his decisions the awareness that he had of ultimate values.

This phrase has been used a great deal in the speeches and writings of Pakistani leaders of all schools of thought. For modernist political leaders such as Jinnah and Ayub Khan it has tended to mean a personal code of ethics. For the conservatives and fundamentalists it has rather meant the medieval system of religious law. For doctrinaire socialists, such as Parwez, it has meant a socialist system.

The phrase itself has been one of the expressions the modernist leaders have used to justify their leadership by arguing that they would create a better society than that associated with Western countries and secularism. One finds this idea also in Muhammad Ali. He quotes the classical Qur'anic version of what the Islamic community ought to be:

> But the Prophet, knowing the divine purpose, insisted... that what was read could be easily assimilated. It was this kind of teaching which produced the first evangelists of Islam, men of whom the Qur'an only too truly says:
> 'Ye are the best community that hath been raised up to mankind. Ye enjoin the right and ye forbid the wrong and ye believe in Allah.' (3: 109) (Afzal Iqbal, 1942: 84.)

The phrases "enjoin the right and forbid the wrong" are the classical descriptions of the *raison d'être* of the Islamic community. They provide the basic justification for any Islamic state, although they are also used to describe the function of other types of Muslim groups; for example, an a-political group of pietistic Muslim religious reformers in contemporary India also uses these phrases. (Haq, 1972: 168, 169.)

It is noteworthy that Muhammad Ali was expressing himself in this vein in 1920 long before the Indian Muslims had seriously thought of attempting to set up a new Muslim state. He was preparing himself to be a political leader of the Muslims within the context of an independent India. Nevertheless, almost all the expressions characteristic of the later modernist Muslim leadership of Pakistan are present in his writings.

Muhammad Ali said that the essence of Muslim responsibility for the world was summed up in two phrases "the Kingdom of God" and "Vicegerency of man". Kingdom of God is not an Islamic term, and subsequent Muslim modernists have not used it. The idea, however, remains central to modernist concerns. For example, in his speech moving the Objectives Resolution for the Constituent Assembly in 1949, Liaquat Ali Khan said:

> It is God-consciousness alone which can save humanity, which means that all power that humanity possesses must be used in accordance with ethical standards which have been laid down by inspired teachers known to the Prophets of different religions. (Smith, 1971: 32.)

Muhammad Ali also used the term theocracy.

> This was nothing else but the Divine Purpose for which Theocracy existed in the Universe and once man identified his Life Purpose with God's Purpose running through all His creation, he set to work to demolish all the intervening obstructions. (Afzal Iqbal, 1942: 118, 119.)

In this case, the later modernists have been careful to disavow such terminology. In his speech, Liaquat Ali explained why theocracy would be an inappropriate term for the new Islamic nation.

> It is true that in its literal sense, theocracy means the Government of God; in this sense, however, it is patent that the entire universe is a theocracy.... But in the technical sense, theocracy has come to mean a government by ordained priests... I cannot overemphasize the fact that such an idea is absolutely foreign to Islam.... If there are any who still use the word theocracy in the same breath as the polity of Pakistan, they are either laboring under a grave misapprehension, or indulging in mischievous propaganda. (Smith, 1971: 33.)

By 1949, the modernist leaders were well aware that the term theocracy was being used by advocates of secular India to disparage Pakistan. Since Muhammad Ali had been well known to the Congress leaders, it might even be that their disparagement of theocracy was related to what they had heard from him.

Some scholars have suggested that the terms "nomocracy" or "lay theocracy" might be adequate for the Islamic political ideal. In the case of the modernists of the sub-continent, however, these terms are not adequate, because the modernists are concerned with the notion that individuals by appropriating what Liaquat called "God-consciousness", or what Muhammad Ali called "the force of the universe", might become creative. This position leaves little room for restrictions on the creativeness of individuals. The modernists tend to make their case in part by a description of what they are not. Both Muhammad Ali and Liaquat Ali characterize the lack of "God-consciousness" as corrupt and Machiavellian. The evils of the twentieth century are attributed to those who possess technique but have little sense of brotherhood and justice. Thus, whether the modernist Muslims were to be part of independent India, as Mohammad Ali expected, or citizens of a new Islamic state, as in the time of Liaquat Ali's leadership, they would expect to be powerful since they maintained that their adherence to the task of implementing brotherhood and justice would fill them with energy.

Although generally the *ulama* had not supported the movement for Pakistan, in part because they distrusted the modernist leadership, many of them did move to Pakistan. Once there, they tended to assume that they ought to have a function in society roughly comparable to their status in medieval times. The modernist leaders, on the other hand, needed to legitimize their claims. The result has been a long process of experimentation in trying to devise structures whereby the *ulama* could be consulted and could be used to legitimize the activities of the politicians without impeding the actual processes of government.

Largely because of the difficulty of devising a formula that would be satisfactory to the diverse political units that constituted Pakistan, an acceptable constitution was many years in the making. In the successive phases of the nation's brief history, the long years without a constitution, the period of martial law, the period of basic democracies, and the latest democracy, the lack of definition of the nation's constitution has meant an absence of precision as to the role of the *ulama*. This has been one of the many unsettling factors in the nation's life.

In the years before the first constitution of 1956, the *ulama* had taken part in advising the constituent assembly. Most of them agreed that

> the Head of the State should be the actual executive, that he should preside over the parliament, that his cabinet should be responsible only to him, that he must be a male Muslim and a pious one, and that all acts of government must be guided and limited by the *Shariah*. (Binder, 1963: 213.)

The latter issue has been the most serious point of difference. In the brief history of Pakistan there has already been diversity in the amount of power exercised by the Head of State. But the Heads of State have all had similar views on the *Shariah*, namely, they have not been willing to limit their capacity to legislate.

President Ayub Khan in his autobiography gave vent to his objections to the attitudes of many of the *ulama*, and in particular to the fundamentalist leader Maulana Mawdudi. Ayub wrote:

> The *ulama* knew that the leadership of the Muslims... was gradually passing to the modern educated classes.... It was this new leadership that the *ulama* dreaded and against which they aligned themselves with the Indian National Congress.... Pakistan was the

> greatest defeat of the nationalist *ulama*. But they are a tenacious tribe and power is an irresistable drug.... Among the migrants was Maulana... Maudoodi... who had been bitterly opposed to Pakistan. He sought refuge there and forthwith launched a campaign for the 'Muslimization' of the hapless people of Pakistan. This venerable gentleman was appalled by what he saw in Pakistan: an un-Islamic country, un-Islamic government, and an un-Islamic people! ...So he set about the task of convincing the people of their inadequacies, their failings, and their general unworthiness.
> All this was really a facade. The true intention was to re-establish the supremacy of the *ulama* and to reassert their right to lead the community.... They succeeded in converting an optimistic and enthusiastic people into a cynical and frustrated community. (1967: 202, 203.)

Ayub was unusually frank for a political leader in stating explicitly that the issue was a contest for leadership. His exasperation with the tenacity of the *ulama* is probably fairly typical of what many modernist leaders have felt. He also points to another noteworthy aspect of the conflict between the two groups, namely, that the modernists think that the *ulama* induce feelings of guilt and unworthiness among the people, whereas the modernists see themselves as encouraging life-affirming activism.

It was during Ayub Khan's regime that the Muslim Family Laws Ordinance was promulgated. This law, by changing the regulations concerning polygamy and divorce, did away with the absolute authority of the *Shariah* in these areas of personal law.

The commission which originally studied the problem and put forward the recommendations which later became law was composed mainly of modernists. In arguing their case, they stated many of the themes we have noted. They argued that Islam is well capable of meeting the challenge of evolutionary forces. They said of Islam:

> Its basic principles of justice and equity, its urge for universal knowledge, its acceptance of life in all its aspects, its world-view, its view of human relations and human destiny, and its demand for an all-round and harmonious development, stand firmly like a rock in the tempestuous sea of life. (Smith, 1971: 73.)

These sentiments might have come straight from the pen of Muhammad Ali, although more than forty years had passed since he wrote of his "Eureka" discovery of modernist faith.

The one representative of the *ulama* on the commission was outspoken in his disagreement with the modernist position. He stated his view that the authority of the *ulama* was being usurped. He noted that the faithful ordinary people remained loyal to the *ulama* in spite of modernist propaganda against the religious authorities.

> But in spite of the destructive propaganda Muslims had enough religious consciousness and feeling for faith to turn for religious guidance to the pious *ulama* who possess the knowledge of the Shariah and act upon it.... This prerogative of the specialist is not based on any racial or tribal group but is rooted in reason. When people did not take any notice of the nontechnical *Ijtihad* and opinions of these anglicized West-ridden Sahibs, they started propaganda against the *ulama* that they have created priesthood in Islam, so that

> their own opinion may have the right to encroach upon their domain.... *Ulama* is not the name of any race or tribe but everyone who devoted the greater part of his life to the acquisition of knowledge of religious subjects is an *alim*. This right of theirs is based on their erudition and experience in exactly the same way in which the right of explaining and interpreting the provisions of the Pakistan Penal Code vests in lawyers and barristers only. (Smith, 1971: 77.)

This representative of the *ulama* seems to think that "priests" are a racial or tribal group. Perhaps he is thinking of Hinduism. When Muhammad Ali or Iqbal condemned priestcraft, they were thinking explicitly of Christianity. That confusion may be some indication of the way in which the modernists and the *ulama* have been arguing at cross-purposes. The modernist claim has been that every believer has a right to interpret his own religion, and that within the nation the elected leaders should have final authority for any legislation that affects religion. The *ulama* have claimed that only persons with their educational experience have the right to interpret religion.

Another instance of conflict between the two attitudes has been the matter of the Ahmadiyah. The question has been whether this group of followers of the late nineteenth leader Mirza Ghulam Ahmad ought to be considered Muslims. The problem is whether the Ahmadiyah are giving more religious stature to their leader than is permissible for Muslims.

When the issue first came to the forefront in 1952, the *ulama* were severely criticized for having incited civil disturbances over a theological question. Some of them were imprisoned. At that time the modernists' position, as expressed in the judgement of the court known as the Munir Commission Report, was that such issues ought to be excluded from political life. Twenty years later, however, the modernists adopted a different tactic. This time the parliament has taken action directly. The parliament has said that the members of the Ahmadiyah groups are not to be considered Muslims. By taking such action, the members of parliament have affirmed that the right to decide such questions rests finally with the elected representatives of the people.

Many modernists have thought that the *ulama* might eventually be reconciled to modernist attitudes if the methods of religious education in the training institutions could be changed. Iqbal emphasized this point. During Ayub Khan's regime, a religious trusts department was set up for West Pakistan. It reorganised the *Madrasah* (seminary) system at all levels to include general subjects, and also set up a post-graduate institution at Bahawalpur to provide advanced training in religious subjects. (Sayeed, 1967: 168.)

In addition, a Central Institute of Islamic Research was set up to undertake Islamic Research for the purpose of "assisting in the reconstruction of Muslim society on a truly Islamic basis". (Sayeed, 1967: 166.) The Institute has continued to publish journals regularly.

In one of his books, Fazlur Rahman, the first director of the Central Institute, argued for a position that would transcend both simplistic modernism and rigid conservatism. He wanted the scholars to re-open the problems relating to religious law that had ceased to be debated by the *ulama* from the tenth century. If this were to happen, the function of the *ulama* would become that of participants in an on-going discussion as to how religious values could best be implemented. The authority of the *ulama* as experts would remain, but the *Shariah* would not retain its unchangeable status. Fazlur Rahman maintained that the process of continuing discussion was the original Muslim way of dealing with such problems, and that the ossification of religious law had been a later development, brought about in part by the principles of jurisprudence developed by al-Shafi. (1965: 1–24.)

REFERENCES

AHMAD, Aziz
1967 *Islamic Modernism in India and Pakistan, 1857–1964.* London: Oxford University Press.

AHMAD, Jamil-ud-Din, (ed.)
1960 *Speeches and Writings of Mr. Jinnah.* Lahore: Ashraf.

AYUB KHAN, Mohammad
1967 *Friends Not Masters. A Political Autobiography.* Lahore: Oxford University Press.

BINDER, Leonard
1963 *Religion and Politics in Pakistan.* Berkeley and Los Angeles: University of California Press.

DAR, Bashir Ahmad, (trans.)
1964 *Iqbal's Gulshan-i Raz-i Jadid and Bandagi Namah.* Lahore: Institute of Islamic Culture.

FARUQI, Ziya-ul-Hasan
1963 *The Deoband School and the Demand for Pakistan.* New York: Asia Publishing House.

GARDET, Louis
1961 *La Cité Musulmane Vie Sociale et Politique.* Paris: J. Vrin.

HAQ, M. Anwarul
1972 *The Faith Movement of Mawlana Muhammad Ilyas.* London: Allen and Unwin.

IQBAL, Afzal, (ed.)
1966 *My Life a Fragment. An Autobiographical Sketch of Maulana Mohamed Ali.* Lahore: Ashraf.

KIERNAN, V. G., (trans.)
1955 *Poems from Iqbal.* London: John Murray.

SAYEED, Khalid, B.
1967 *The Political System of Pakistan.* Boston: Houghton Mifflin.

SMITH, Donald Eugene
1971 *Religion, Politics and Social Change in the Third World. A Sourcebook.* New York: The Free Press.

RAHMAN, Fazlur
1965 *Islamic Methodology in History.* Karachi: Central Institute of Islamic Research.

Rajaji, the Brahmin

A Style of Power

JOANNE PUNZO WAGHORNE

> ...Do not think of me as Governor-General. You should look upon me as a teacher for whom you should care.[1]

WHEN CHAKRAVARTI RAJAGOPALACHARI assumed the office of Governor-General of India in 1948, he became both the symbol of traditional British India and the first representative of the coming republic. As Governor-General he was the last representative of the British King and of a system which had attempted to blend its governmental structure with much of traditional Indian royal polity. The new republic in theory put an end to royalty and substituted free elections for all forms of traditional birthrights to power. With India's government so balanced between a royal colony and a new republic, Rajagopalachari's style of leadership during this transitional period is crucial for a study of the traditional forms of legitimation of power in modern India. For Rajagopalachari (also called C.R. or Rajaji), the office of Governor-General represented not primarily an honorary position but rather an opportunity to reinterpret much of the old religiously-based polity through the language of a democracy. The particular style of leadership which C.R. chose to adopt to bring a sanctity to the new state beyond the ballot box is the subject of this essay. The thesis that follows is based upon the theory that as Governor-General he retained various ingredients of a very particular style of Brahmin religious leadership – a style long connected to the kings and royal courts of India.

The line connecting his leadership with the style of the royal Brahmins proves to be a matter of inheritance in many respects. C.R. was born into a Brahmin family of teachers and government servants – a family in which many aspects of the royal Brahmins appear to have been maintained.

In spite of his removal of the sacred thread,[2] his stand on untouchability,[3] and his neglect of all Brahmin rituals,[4] C.R. was nevertheless accorded the full rites of a Brahmin at his funeral. He had remained a Brahmin in worldly

1 C. Rajagopalachari, *Rajaji's Speeches* (New Delhi: Ministry of Information and Broadcasting, Government of India, 1948), p. 36.

duties, if not in his ritual status. Unlike Gandhi, the son of a merchant turned saint and political leader, Rajaji did not have to deny his inherited status to establish his right to deal in political issues. C.R. could state with impunity that a true Hindu must perform "fully and conscientiously... all duties devolving upon him as a result of birth, or of events and circumstances or arising out of his place in society."[5] For C.R., birth as well as circumstance played an important part in the development of his self-image as a leader.

The Iyengar from Hosur: The Silent Tradition

> Kshatriyas prosper not without Brahmanas, Brahmanas prosper not without Kshatriyas; Brahmanas and Kshatriyas, being closely united prosper in this world and in the next. – Laws of Manu (IX. 323)[6]

Chakravarti Rajagopalachari was born in Thorapalli village, Hosur Taluk, in the Salem District of the Madras Presidency in 1879. This Brahmin family owned land in the small village which had once been granted solely to this community as an *agrahāram* but was by now sold off in part to other communities.[7] Rajaji's family moved when he was five to the nearby town of Hosur where his father took up the hereditary position of village *munsif*. His father was considered a very orthodox scholar who followed the tradition of learning and expounding the Sanskrit scriptures.[8] Although small land owners,

2 It is not clear when C.R. removed his thread. He never was photographed with it while he held public office. The thread was replaced at the time of C.R.'s funeral rites. Close members of his family continued to undergo the *upanayana* ceremony. C. R. Vasudev, personal interviews in Madras, February and May, 1974.

3 C.R. later became well known in the state for refusing to transfer *harijan* water workers from duty in a Brahmin neighborhood. This particular story is often cited by Rajaji's supporters to illustrate his early stand against caste. Actually, when C.R. retold the incident, his position was that caste had no place in the public government, but he had not consciously assigned the *harijans* to the *agrahāram* as a "caste breaking measure." He told the Brahmins, "You may have your religion or whatever it may be in your private capacity. The Municipality cannot make distinctions of caste". Cf. C. Rajagopalachari, *Chats Behind Bars: Essays on Various Subjects* (Madras: S. Ganesan, 1931), pp. 71–72.

4 C.R. did pray and considered himself "a devout though very imperfect Hindu Vedantin". See C. Rajagopalachari, *Rajaji's Speeches*, Vol. I (Bombay: Bharatiya Vidya Bhavan, 1958), pp. 19–20. But C.R. dropped the personal ritual cycle of daily and monthly prayers which mark the life of an orthodox Brahmin.

5 C. Rajagopalachari, *Vedanta: the Basic Culture of India* (New Delhi: The Hindustan Times, 1946), pp. 37–38. This work was later revised and published under the title *Hinduism: Doctrine and Way of Life* (Bombay: Bharatiya Vidya Bhavan, 1964).

6 As translated by G. Bühler in Vol. XXV of the *Sacred Books of the East*, p. 399.

7 Raj Mohan Gandhi, personal interview held at the Kalki Buildings, Madras, December 18, 1973. (Mr. Gandhi is the grandson of both C.R. and Mahātma Gandhi. C.R.'s daughter Lakshmi married Devadas Gandhi.)

8 Nilkan Perumal, *Rajaji: A Biographical Study* (Calcutta: Maya Publications, 1948), pp. 11–13. Perumal's biography is very unreliable on these early years. The description of Rajaji's family in these pages borders on myth. However, interviews with members of C.R.'s family confirm that C.R.'s father was a landowner, something of a scholar, and a village officer.

the family has been described as "poor";[9] Rajaji himself considered his father "uneducated" in that he knew no English and probably had no formal schooling.[10] The family maintained a traditional occupation and a hereditary claim to a small piece of land.

Although traditional, Rajaji's father was apparently committed to his son's career in law.[11] He never put his son under a *guru*, nor did he teach him Sanskrit. In 1930, C.R. in his *Chats Behind Bars* claimed that he had no formal religious education: "My religion I have learned only from my mother".[12] But C.R.'s father did insist that his son receive a formal English education. C.R. was sent to the English medium school at Hosur, and, at the age of fourteen, to college in Bangalore. At seventeen he entered Madras Law College and by twenty-one he had defended his first murder case.[13] C.R. never returned to live in Hosur, beginning his law practice in Salem; much later, he went to Madras.

Throughout these changes, C.R. never left his father behind. While at Salem and even at Madras when C.R. interrupted his law career to join Gandhi's movement, his father continued to live with him. C.R. never directly mentioned his father during this period. Again, Rajaji in his old age wrote nothing about his family, but he was never separated from his sons, grandchildren, and widowed daughter by more than a few miles. No matter what mental distance he travelled, Rajaji remained physically close to a line of blood relations which linked him to Thorapalli village in Hosur. In his life, there were none of the radical breaks with immediate family ties that are usually associated with a man "coming up in the world".[14]

Rajaji's immediate environment during most of his life was within a Brahmin household. Though dropping all Brahmanical rituals from his own

---

9 K. Santhanam, personal interview at the Kalki Buildings, Madras, November 28, 1973; and C. R. Narasimhan, personal interview at 60, Bazullah Road, Madras, December 12, 1973.

10 In an interview with Rajaji, Monica Felton asked specifically about the Perumal biography. Rajaji dismissed Perumal's image of his father as a famous scholar. C.R. said of his father, "He was an uneducated man... He was a scholar in Sanskrit but he did not know English. He was the *village munsif* in Hosur. English was not a necessary accomplishment in a place like that." Monica Felton, *I Meet Rajaji* (2nd. ed., Bombay: Jaico Publishing House, 1964), p. 23. First published in London by MacMillan, 1962.

11 *Ibid.*, p. 23 (Jaico Edition).

12 C. Rajagopalachari, *Chats Behind Bars*, p. 84. C.R. adds, "I did not learn it from any book or under any Guru..."

13 From an interview with C.R., in Felton (Jaico Ed.), p. 24.

14 C.R.'s family still lives in Madras city. With the exception of his daughter Lakshmi, the family has married within the Brahmin Iyengar community. Contacts are still maintained with relatives in Thorapalli for marriages and other important family functions. C.R. Vasudev, personal interviews, in Madras, February 21, 1974; February 22, 1974; and May 23, 1974.

regimen, he did not demand an end to such rites for the rest of his family.[15] These facts seldom appear in C.R.'s public writings; the father, children and grandchildren who surrounded him continued to live much like other households in the neighborhood. This family environment was not a direct psychological factor in C.R.'s political development, but it clearly provided a background which did not conflict with his growing career in law and politics. This silent Iyengar heritage provided in some sense a natural setting for his public life.

Careful investigation shows that C.R.'s family had for generations been part of a vital network of governmental power in South India. C.R.'s father was a *munsif* from an *agrahāram* village; the titles *munsif* and *agrahāram* Brahmin have rich connotations in a small place like Hosur and Thorapalli, going beyond C.R.'s unassuming self-description as the son of a poor Brahmin village officer. The *agrahāram* Brahmins, especially those with hereditary judicial offices such as *munsif*, held real power. This stemmed from a combination of ascribed religious sanctity and the knowledge important for administration of the state. Brahmins were part of that cycle of royal power made legitimate by Brahmin participation in the state.

"Thorapalli *Agrahāram*"[16] in the 1880's was officially recognized as an enfranchised *inām* village.[17] An *inām* is an old form of land tenure recognized by the British in which land was held at a reduced rate of tax, or tax-free, in return for services rendered to the state or the public.[18] In the case of the *agrahārams*, whole villages had long been gifted to groups of Brahmins[19] by

---

15 C.R.'s family continues to observe Brahmanical family rites. The investiture of the sacred thread, *upanayana*, was performed for C.R.'s sons and grandsons at the time for their marriage, which is the normal custom for more modern Brahmin households. C.R. himself took part in the family rite of marriage, *upanayana*, et cetera. No members of the family to whom I informally spoke could remember C.R. personally performing either *pūjā*, or any household sacrifice. In an interesting article, Mrs. Lakshmi Devadas, Gandhi's daughter-in-law, does remember that as a child in Salem she saw her father dressed for court in a turban "*tirunāmam*" – the *vaishnava* mark of a red streak inside a white U – "was always there on his forehead", in "A Daughter's Reminisences", in the *Rajaji: 93 Souvenir*, (Madras: by the 93 Souvenir Committee, 1971) p. 69. I have the impression that C.R. may have personally followed more of the ritual customs at Salem than after his conversion to the Gandhi movement.

16 Thorapalli is called "Thorapalli *agrahāram*" in a local myth which is narrated in Henry Lefenu, *A Manual of the Salem District of the Presidency of Madras* (2 Vols; Madras: The Government Press, 1883), Vol. I, p. 171. Hereafter cited as *Salem Manual 1883*.

17 Cf. the list of *ināms* in Vol. I of the *Salem Manual 1883*, p. 504.

18 See under "inām" in the Glossary, Vol. III of [MacClean] *Manual of Administration of the Madras Presidency in Illustration at the Records of the Government and the Yearly Administration Reports* (3 vols; Madras: The Government Press, 1885), p. 352.

19 Brahmin *agrahārams* were also called *brāhmadeya* villages but apparently were not inhabited only by Brahmins. The Brahmins were the dominant caste and controlled the administration of the village. Cf. T. V. Mahalingam, *South Indian Polity* (Madras: University of Madras, 1967), p. 349.

the reigning king, but the nature of the service expected is a complicated matter. The gift of land to Brahmins by a ruler had long been an act of religious merit in India, but land was never granted to just any Brahmins. The recipients were expected to be "learned" and "venerable".[20] *Agrahārams*, in fact, have been described by some South Indian historians as centers of learning where education was dispensed free to worthy students.[21] But these land grants to support learning had an importance for the royal authority which went beyond collecting religious merit or providing public education. When the grants themselves are read, it becomes clear that the donor-king expected his establishment of *agrahārams* to directly confirm the legitimacy of his own authority and that of his dynasty.

An appendix to the *Manual of the Salem District 1883* contains a valuable collection of *agrahāram* grants found in various inscriptions in the district.[22] In these inscriptions the donor kings are careful to establish themselves as true royalty through their special relationship with the Brahmins. One king expected his establishment of *agrahārams* to prolong his lifetime, increase his power,[23] and send his ancestors to the heaven reserved for true royal warriors.[24] Another king had himself described as a great patron of the Brahmins, one who confirmed their divine rules of conduct through the might of his own arm.[25] Such descriptions reflect the ancient Vedic image of kingship: rule by a true line of warriors (*kshatriya varna*) whose might confirms and protects the sacred law of the Brahmins. The protection and patronage of that Brahmanical law had been publicly demonstrated through land grants to learned Brahmins

---

20 This epithet is usually added to the descriptions of the Brahmin recipients of *agrahāram* grants. An excellent example of this is in an inscription establishing an *agrahāram* by a king of the reigning dynasty of Mysore. The inscription is translated in an appendix to *Salem Manual 1883*: The Brahmin grantees are described as "thoroughly versed in the Vedas and Vedāngas, well acquainted with the traditions of religion and law, learned in all the different branches of knowledge, ceremonially pure, of good families, householder, full of the true Brahmanical spirit, and of gentle disposition" (p. 421).

21 For example, see Anant Sadashiv Altekar, *Education in India: A Comprehensive Work on the History, Aims and Ideals of Ancient Indian Education* (Benares: The Indian Book Shop, 1934), p. 60.

22 *Salem Manual 1883*, Vol. II, pp. 349–435. These inscriptions were edited and translated by T. Foulkes. Each inscription has an explanatory introduction and is especially useful here because the grants are confined to Salem District alone. The Brahmins and Brahmanical institutions and power varied throughout South India. Here my remarks are confined to the Brahmin villages of Salem, although the relationship between the Brahmins and the court may be similar throughout the South. Brahmins and donations to Brahmins may have been particularly important in South India where dynasties could not claim pure kingly caste status, since the caste hierarchy in the South breaks sharply between the 'twice born' Brahmins and the next lower castes – the land owners who have been classified as '*shudras*' – a caste below the Āryan *kshatriyas* and *vaishyas*.

23 *Ibid.*, p. 351.

24 *Ibid.*, p. 367.

25 *Ibid.*, p. 351.

from Vedic times. Support from this source made a ruler more than a tax collector – it made him a king.[26]

The *agrahārams*, then, were symbols of kingly rule; they attested to the local lord's willingness to at least pay homage to, if not heed, the sacred laws. These laws, however, had a complicated structure. Sometimes the law was described as "the Veda", which in other Sanskrit usage referred to ritual as well as social regulations. By modern times in South India, state Vedic rituals were no longer performed for the king. Only those sacred regulations for the right order of society remained part of the Sanskrit tradition connected to the court. These regulations were traditionally understood to be embodied in the *dharmashāstras*, codes of religious-civil law, and in the epics and *purānas* which were said to be the practical examples of that righteous order.[27] The recitation of the *Rāmāyana* and *Mahābhārata* was provided for by the king in the temples, other public places, and a court.[28] One king of Mysore, in fact, was pictured in a Salem inscription as rising every morning to listen to the reading of the heroic poems and historic tales.[29] This most certainly refers to the epics and *purānas* and presumedly implies that the king took these as models for his rule. Here again, the ancient examples of ordered conduct, the epic tale, was connected to kingly rule. And, at this time, Brahmins were the keepers of those stories of righteousness now considered sacred scripture and law.

The *agrahārams* were linked to kingly rule in yet another way: their founding coincided with the establishment or re-establishment of new royal sovereignty over an area. The establishment of these *agrahārams* was especially important in Salem District, which passed constantly from dynasties centered in such diverse places as Vijayanagar, Madurai, Tanjore, Kancheepuram and Mysore.[30] As the collection of inscriptions in the *Salem Manual* shows, *agra-*

---

26 Descriptions of great kings who donated the traditional gift of land and cattle fill the epics and purānas. The *Laws of Manu*, in fact, ordain the three means of livelihood for the Brahmin as "sacrificing for others, teaching, and accepting gifts from pure men." (X.77). The very acceptance of a gift, then, attested to the purity and honor of the donor. Cf. *The Laws of Manu*, Vol. XXV, *The Sacred Books of the East*, p. 419.

27 V. Raghavan, "Methods of Popular Religious Instruction in South India", in Vol. IV of the *Cultural Heritage of India* (4 Vols; 2nd. ed.; Calcutta: The Ramakrishna Mission Institute of Culture, 1962), p. 503.

28 There was a special *inām* grant made for these recitations. See "inām" in the Glossary, Vol. III of [MacClean] *Manual of Administration*, p. 352 ff.

29 This inscription presents the reigning king in words which nearly quote *The Laws of Manu*, which says: "Let the King, after rising early in the morning, worship Brahmanas who are well versed in the threefold sacred science and learned [in polity] and follow their advice." (VII. 37) *Sacred Books of the East*, Vol. XXV., p. 221. King Krishna Raji of Mysore is described: "He awakes at day break and... after he has made many gifts of cows and money to the Brahmins, he listens to the readings of the heroic poems and historical tales." *Salem Manual 1883*, p. 420.

30 The rapid succession of dynasties in this area, traditionally called the *Kongu*, is well narrated by M. Arokiaswami, *The Kongu Country: Being a History of the Modern Districts at Coimbatore and Salem from the Earliest Times to the Coming of the British* (Madras: University of Madras, 1956).

hārams were established over this area by each successive dynasty from the 7th or 8th century A.D. One grant coincided with victory in a battle in the area, another with a special propitiation of ancestors, and a third with a royal marriage. All these events were closely related to the continuance of dynastic rule. In this sense, the founding of an *agrahāram* functioned like a ritual to mark and confirm kingly rule.

The *inām* grants to Brahmins creating *agrahārams* were important state religious charities, but they were not co-terminous with religion itself. Temples also secured public funds and support through land grants.[31] Nor did the *agrahāram* Brahmins have a monopoly in religious learning; non-Brahmins conducted numerous village festivals and ceremonies, even taking an important part in temple rites.[32] Yet the religious learning and power of *agrahāram* Brahmins did have a special place in the religious life of the area; they were closely connected with the sacred laws and sanctification of the state itself.

If Rajagopalachari's family history is correct, the Brahmins of Thorapalli secured their *agrahāram* under the last Hindu dynasty before Mughal and British conquest.[33] Though Thorapalli is not a temple town and C.R.'s family strongly maintains they had never been priests, C.R.'s father was learned in the Sanskrit tradition. The religious power of this family was not set in the village ritual cycle, nor in temple worship, but rather in the special Sanskrit learning related to the power of court and king.

C. Rajagopalachari's father also entered directly into the practical roots of government service in Salem District: he was *munsif* at Hosur. While the formal connection between the king and the *agrahāram* took place on a level of ritual and religious ideology, the Brahmins held real political power at the royal court. The office of *munsif* is a reflection of this power. The *munsif's* office was a hereditary position under the Hindu and later Muslim rulers of Salem, combining the powers of judge and revenue officer. While many other types of local tribunals existed, the *munsif's* office was a link between the central royal authority and the village.[34] He was a minor state official. Judging by

---

31 Temple villages were also called *agrahārams*, but the system of religion on which these centered was not so much the Brahmins themselves but the whole temple complex. I am using the term *agrahāram* to apply specifically to land grants to "learned" Brahmins which, at least in the Salem District, are clearly separate from temple land grants.

32 The non-Brahmin priests are called *Pantārams*. There is a manuscript in the MacKenzie collection which records a change in temple management whereby Brahmins were appointed in place of these non-Brahmin priests. Cf. T. V. Mahalingam, ed., *MacKenzie Manuscripts: Summaries of the Historical Manuscripts in the MacKenzie Collection* (1 of 2 planned volumes; Madras: The University of Madras Press, 1972), p. xxxix.

33 Raj Mohan Gandhi, Personal interview at Kalki Buildings, Madras, December 18, 1973. The grant was confirmed by the Mughal conqueror Tippu Sultān and then reconfirmed by the British.

34 The Brahmin dominance and place in such state offices are described in Frederick John Richards, *Salem District Gazeteer* (2 parts; Madras: The Government Press, 1918), Part I, p. 137. Richards says, "The Brahman's position in Salem District is, as elsewhere, pri-

early European accounts of Salem District, the Brahmins dominated such minor state appointments as well as the administrative machinery of the royal court itself.[35] When the East India Company took over the administration of the area, they eliminated the revenue powers of many such minor officials, including the *munsif*, but they absorbed this officer into their Anglo-Indian Court System.[36] The office of *munsif* remained even under the British as the lowest judicial organ of the central authority.[37] But while the laws of the district court were anglicised, the court of the village *munsif* conducted cases outside English law.[38] The village *munsif* at the turn of the century was thus part of the new central authority as well as a "left-over" from the traditional Hindu royal judicial system in which Brahmins had held major offices.

The power of Brahmins in the judicial system reflects that same power to legitimize which had connected them to the royal court. As J. Duncan Derrett has pointed out, Brahmins exercised the power not to make statutory laws but to formulate a "reasoned and complete system" which would assure the king that his legal system functioned in accord with orthodox Hinduism.[39] Within the Brahmin community lay the power to formalize local customs along more universal standards. Brahmins provided sanctification for the law; just as their presence in the kingdom and the court legitimized the king himself. While

---

marily political in origin... Many of the village officers are still practically, though not theoretically, hereditary in Brahman families and the origin is proudly traced to the grant of some Raja whose name is long since forgotten. Brahman officers are, from time immemorial the links that connect the village administration with the centre of political power..." There were non-Brahmin village headsmen and institutions like caste tribunals which still held judiciary power over their members. But, C.R.'s father's office appeared to operate closely with the central authority rather than on the purely local level. He was not strictly a village *munsif*, for he inherited his position not in Thorapalli, but in Hosur, the district capital. This means that his jurisdiction was more likely over a group of villages. *The Salem District Gazeteer, 1918*, mentions that there were intermediary judicial authorities over some groups of villages (part I, p. 127).

35 The Brahmins are described as having power over local revenue assessments in a letter of Thomas Munro, dated 1794, who was an early officer of the Company in the Salem District and later a famous governor of the Presidency. Cf. G. R. Gleig, *The Life of Major-General Sir Thomas Munro, Bart. and K.C.B., Late Governor of Madras with Extracts from His Correspondence and Private Papers* (3 vols.; London: Henry Colburn and Richard Bentley, 1830), Vol. III, p. 93. On the Brahmin in the royal court of Mysore, see Mark Wilkes, *Historical Sketches of the South India in an attempt to trace the History of Mysore from the Origin of the Hindoo Government of that State to the Extinction of the Mahammadan Dynasty 1799* (3 vols; London: Longman, Hurer, Rees, Orme, and Brown, 1817), pp. 375–376. Wilkes quotes from the Rev. Swartz who served directly at the royal court.

36 The history of this is explained in the chapters titled "The Authorities of the District" and "Legal Reforms and the Zemindars", in James William Ballentyn Dykes, *Salem: An Indian Collectorate* (London: William H. Allen & Co., 1853), pp. 221–225 and 332–358. The village *munsif* (also spelled *moonsif*) was first recognized by Statute in 1816.

37 Cf. *Manual of Administration*, Vol. I, pp. 201–213 under "Civil Justice".

38 His court had no rights of appeal and therefore was not directly linked to the English law. Cf. *Manual of Administration*, Vol. I, p. 213.

39 J. Duncan Derrett, *Religion, Law and the State in India* (New York: The Free Press, 1968), pp. 117–121.

Brahmins in South India were not the dominant force on the level of local politics, nor were they economically powerful,[40] they did possess that important power to lend a more universal perspective to local laws and rulers. As mediators between the hard facts of daily politics and the world of the sacred order, their presence in government was termed "indispensable" even by the British.[41]

The community of Brahmins from which C. Rajagopalachari descended produced, therefore, a very special kind of priest. The patronization of their special learning through land grants could legitimize royal authority. The presence of such Brahmins at court in the legal system sanctified local law and made it known that the king's justice fully acknowledged orthodox standards. Through the power of their knowledge of the sacred word, they harmonized local events, leaders, and customs with the universal dharmic order. The verbal power of Brahmins, of course, was not from a spontaneous gift of poetry. Rather the *agrahāram* Brahmins controlled the power of the word collected and codified in numerous Sanskrit holy books which they had the special right to study, recite and teach. However, the importance of these Brahmanical words rested in the king's simple acknowledgement and patronization of the holy order they represented. Legitimation of the state came through formalized subservience to the Brahmanical order within which the Brahmins co-existed alongside other political realities.

Rajaji's family, therefore, lived in a local world that was rooted within the older Brahmanical-royal authority based upon knowledge of Sanskrit law and lore. Such "knowledge" was not a matter of university degrees or formal schooling in a Western sense; instead, it rested in a tradition that was maintained and exemplified within the family through its upbringing.[42] But this traditional style of knowledge and power was now limited by C.R.'s time to the local level. The direct lines of power from the *agrahāram* to the royal

---

40 It has been pointed out in recent discussions in Madras of 'Brahmin dominance' in South India that before the British the "Brahmin domination – so far at any rate as Tamilnad is concerned – was only in the field of religion and priestcraft and the Brahmin community exercised little direct influence in the political or economic spheres. The Brahmins were notoriously poor and the ruling classes were always drawn from the non-Brahmin communities." A. Subbiah, "The Caste System: Vested Interest of the High Castes", *Quest* (Bombay), April/June, 1963, p. 44. I would also agree that the Brahmins had little power with general administration system, which may account for their great rise during the British era when administrative power became equal to, if not more important than, the control or ownership of land.

41 The British often viewed the Brahmins throughout India as a necessary evil. They saw the Brahmin as almost the sole true representative of the Hindu religion and learning and felt compelled to deal with him, while they viewed the Brahmin also as the arch promulgator of "superstition". An excellent example of this is the description of "the Brahman" given in M. A. Sherring, *Hindu Tribes and Castes as Represented in Barnares* (London: Trubner and Co., 1872), pp. 3–5.

42 The *Laws of Manu* declare that the law can be observed from custom or by the model presented by righteous men; the Brahmin family is considered the model *par excellence*. Cf. Derrett, *Religion, Law and the State*, pp. 118–119.

court were severed by the new British legal system. If a young Brahmin wished to rise higher in the central authority, he had to learn a new law and excel within a new system of legal education. Rajaji took this latter route, like so many other young Brahmins who eventually came to dominate the British court system of the Madras Presidency from the late 1800's onward.

C.R.'s ancestral background was closely connected to the state, the law, and the courts. But for Rajaji they remained the silent tradition – it never appeared specifically in his writing or thought. This should not be surprising, for the force of this particular tradition is not in facts, ideas or philosophies, but instead in an environment close to the daily talk of family life. Its strength is in the unstated, but acknowledged fact that one is a Brahmin and hence the living storehouse for traditional scripture and learning. That one can add another tradition to this knowledge is not unthinkable, for that involved the use of yet another "foreign" language and the memorization of more "scriptures".[43] C.R.'s early religious tradition did not lie in a formal code or theory but in the consciousness of a duty which bound his family to the power of the state and the right functioning of society.

The Theoretical Brahmin: Varna Duties in a New State

In his middle years C. Rajagopalachari led the life of a prosperous lawyer in Salem. He entered political life in the city and became Municipal Chairman, gaining notoriety for his stands on behalf of untouchables. He wrote on educational reform, demanding the use of Tamil as the medium of instruction.[44] At the same time, while a nationalist and social reformer, his life style resembled those who had prospered under the new economic opportunities of the British system.[45] The royal Brahmin patronage may have ended, but the British legal system had its rewards.

In 1919 C.R. left Salem, presumably intending to enter the legal profession in the capital of the Madras Presidency. He had just settled temporarily in a house owned by Kasturi Ranga Iyengar when Mahātma Gandhi came to Madras to survey the potential for a new type of political agitation. As fate

43 In a personal interview (Madras, November 28, 1973), Mr. K. Santhanam told me: "Had Rajaji been born fifty years earlier, he would have been a great scholar in the Vedas", but then explained that he like other Brahmins was born at a time when English education was necessary. Mr. Santhanam felt that the legal profession "came naturally" to the Brahmins; the other castes had their trades. So the Brahmins were left to be teachers, lawyers and priests.

44 See an article by C.R., reprinted in *Tamil Culture*, V (January, 1956), p. 16ff. The original article was published in *Commonweal*, edited by Annie Besant, in September, 1916.

45 C. R. Vasudev, in a personal interview (Madras, February 22, 1974), mentioned that as a boy he saw his grandfather's old house in Salem and it seemed then like a palace. Mrs. Lakshmi Devadas Gandhi, remembers her father's home as "a big old, Western-style bungalow" ("A Daughter's Reminiscences", *93 Souvenir* p. 69.).

had it, Gandhi ended up as C.R.'s house guest and it was in this house that Gandhi had the dream which he credits with inspiring the style of his first mass resistance movement.[46] As for C. Rajagopalachari, this meeting with Gandhi changed his life. C.R. left his law career and joined Gandhi's movement. By 1920 this once very promising lawyer was in jail for civil disobedience. He could no longer stand to see his "own people so busy at the behests of that authority as if it were God's law and *Dharma* that they carry out."[47] The law that he had once practiced was now the "foreigner's law" and was thus morally wrong to obey.

For the former Salem lawyer, practice of the law no longer accorded with *dharma*. The source of law itself was questioned and that source was found to be wrong. This was a crucial change in C.R.'s life, for he could no longer act as a legal functionary in society. Something disrupted the seemingly easy transition from the son of a Hosur hereditary functionary to an English lawyer. The "new" order was no longer seen as legitimate; resistance became *dharma* itself.

> Non-cooperation is not a means to a political end, but a Dharma by itself. To abstain from co-operating with wrong is an absolute duty. This is so, not *formed* because thereby we shall evict the Englishmen. It is an absolute duty to release oneself from the net of wrong in which one is entangled... To refuse to co-operate in the process of reducing ourselves to foreign rule and in the maintenance of it is the natural law and instinct ...Now that we have discovered the rule of life, it is our duty, absolute and for all time, to obey it.[48]

This language of "natural law" and "rule of life", the language of *dharma*, brought the nature of society itself into question. An important step occurred from matters of family traditions and hereditary state connections to a conscious theory of social obligation and a self-conscious questioning of one's rightful place in society.

In *1920 Jail Diary*, C.R. remains conscious that he is a Brahmin by birth and caste,[49] but he does not connect his caste function to his present position. Though keenly aware of being among the "educated", a "gentleman",[50] he now follows the *dharma* of disobedience – of disorder – with Gandhi as his

46 Mohandas K. Gandhi, *An Autobiography: The Story of My Experiments with Truth*, translated by Mahadev Desai (Beacon paperback edition; Boston: The Beacon Press, 1957), pp. 458–460.

47 C. Rajagopalachari, *Rajaji's 1920 Jail Life: A Day to Day Record of Sri C. Rajagopalachari's Life in the Vellore Jail in 1920* (2nd ed.; Madras: Rochouse & Sons, Ltd., 1941), pp. 7–8. This work was originally published as *A Jail Diary*, and covered his time in jail (21 Dec. 1921 to 20 March 1922), but it is known as and referred to hereafter as *1920 Jail Diary*.

48 *Ibid.*, p. 53.

49 *Ibid.*, p. 58.

50 *Ibid.*, p. 85. C.R. says, "As I am engaged in spinning, the thought strikes me that perhaps many friends, if they saw me, would wonder how I could thus waste my time over work which girls and illiterate persons may well do, but which surely is not meant for me with brains and a high degree of education."

"master".[51] After release from jail, Rajaji becomes the editor of Gandhi's paper (*Young India*), fights vigorously against the faction of Congress which wanted some form of constructive co-operation with the British,[52] and later establishes his own *āshram* in Thiruchengode. From 1920 to at least 1935, he was essentially a disciple of Gandhi, leaving his profession behind during this period of national crisis. But when C.R. emerged from the independence movement to be Governor-General of a free India, once again he was the promulgator of law and order. He could announce to his people:

> ...We must restore the unqualified reverence, reverence to the State that our ancients cultivated... reverence for law and discipline equivalent to the reverence for Dharma that was insisted upon in the old days. In fact, we want a revival of feudal manners and chivalry but in terms of modern democracy.[53]

The rule was now legitimate and nothing less than reverence defined the citizen's relationship to the state. The *dharma* of disorder had been for a short time only; as Governor-General, C.R. became once more a functionary of the state – indeed, its very symbol.

From 1920, when his conscience allowed him no place within the government, to 1936, when he parted from Gandhi's stance on non-cooperation and accepted his first public office, C.R. developed a style of leadership and a recognized place within Indian political life. Alongside his role in changing political events, he also experienced a gradual unfolding of his religious posture. In *1920 Jail Diary* he mentions praying and attempts at mental concentration. He regrets having no knowledge of Sanskrit, "without which life of quiet devotion appears almost impossible to a Hindu".[54] Though he read devotional books such as the *Kural*, the *Rāmāyana*, the *Mahābhārata*, and the Bible,[55] he considered the intellectual habit of reading as "mere self-indulgence", declaring that there is "a time in life when you know for certain that additional learning will only make you die more learned, and not enable you to *do* anything further useful to mankind or to correct your character in any

51 *Ibid.*, p. 106. C.R. calls Gandhi "my master."

52 The fight throughout the 1920's between those who wanted to maintain Gandhi's position against any form of cooperation with the British administration (the "no-changers") and those who sought so-called "council-entry" is told in detail in Pattabhi Sitaramayya, *The History of the Indian National Congress* (2 vols.; 2nd ed., Bombay: Padma Publications Ltd., 1946), Vol. I, pp. 185–336. Although C.R. led the fight for the no-changers in the South, he is only mentioned in passing by Sitaramayya. C.R., in fact, is mentioned very little in this semi-official history of the Congress. C.R. as a real "personality" in national politics was recognized only after his break with Gandhi in 1943 and his assumption of Government office from 1946 onwards.

53 In a speech at Banares Hindu University (December 2, 1948) printed in C. Rajagopalachari, *University Addresses* (Bombay: Hind Kitab Ltd., 1949), p. 92.

54 C.R., *1920 Jail Diary*, p. 11.

55 *Ibid.*, pp. 83–84.

manner."[56] C. Rajagopalachari, B.A., B.L., asked, "Why should one who cannot compose any song, poem, good or otherwise, add to the world's stock of knowledge or mental or moral wealth, keep reading and reading forever simply because it is the habit of the educated class?"[57] In 1920, C.R. tried to pray, to meditate, and to turn his reading only toward devotional works, seeing his former education as useless.

While in prison, C.R. began writing his first book, ironically a translation into Tamil of the martyrdom of Socrates. He intended to include a sequel on the death of Christ but never completed it.[58] Clearly, C.R. saw Western learning not as useless but only as a deviation either from devotion or from clear mental productivity. His work on Socrates was followed by numerous short stories intended for children or for the semi-literate.[59] By 1930, when he was again imprisoned for civil disobedience, his new prison work, *Chats Behind Bars*, contained no personal statements whatever. It was rather the notes taken by a fellow prisoner on short discourses C.R. delivered to the inmates on such topics as "Trees and Plants", "Bolshevism", "Social Reforms", "Stars and Atoms", and "Religion".[60] C.R. had become both a writer and a teacher.

This intellectual style of leadership increasingly defined his activities. Even in his *āshram* in Thiruchengode from 1925 to 1930 C.R. assumed the role of a teacher. He opened an elementary school, gave informal talks to villagers on religion and morality, and was sought to arbitrate their disputes.[61] Although leading a simple life in the *āshram*, he personally undertook no fasts, no self-purges, none of the disciplines associated with Gandhi's saintly style.[62] Judging from his jail "chats", C.R.'s style involved teaching a wide range of subjects, all aimed at the moral and mental growth of the masses. By the late 1930's, in fact, his teaching constituency had expanded from the villagers of Thiruchen-

56 *Ibid.*, p. 85.

57 *Ibid.*, p. 86.

58 *Ibid.*, p. 97.

59 Selections from C.R.'s stories beginning in the 1920's were translated by his son and published as *The Fatal Cart and Other Stories*, translated by C. R. Ramaswami (New Delhi: The Hindustan Times, 1946). More recent stories, later translated and added, were published as *Stories for the Innocent* (1st ed., rev., Bharatiya Vidya Bhavan, 1967). C.R.'s Tamil short stories are extremely simple in style.

60 See the complete list in the table of contents to *Chats Behind Bars*.

61 C.R. later told the story during a sermon by Sri Anantharama Dikshitar of how he fought for prohibition in the village near his *āshram* and how he made a cobbler admit to breaking the prohibition pledge by forcing him to swear on a pair of sandals. Khasa Subba Rau, *Sidelights on Rajaji* (Madras: Vyasa Publications, 1961), pp. 42–43. K. Santhanam, in a personal interview (Madras, November 28, 1973), also mentioned that while C.R. was at the *āshram* the nearby villagers thought of him as a "guru" and brought their problems to him. And sometimes C.R. would talk to them on morality and religion. While at the *āshram*, he also began a primary school and was the chief teacher.

62 From the conversation with Mr. Santhanam (footnote 43) I gained the impression that C.R. was more of a campaigner, teacher and reformer. He did not put his energy into personal self-purification and in this sense was not a saint or Mahātma but rather a religious moral teacher.

gode and the literate and semi-literate Tamil reading public to a wider, all-India audience. In 1936, he published in English an "abridged and explained" version of the *Bhagavad-Gītā* for university students.[63] And, by 1946, he felt himself prepared to define for the Indian public "the basic culture of India".[64]

C.R.'s role as teacher assumed greater proportions: he increasingly took upon himself the task of preserving and propagating the ancient traditions of India, directly through translations of the scriptures and indirectly through short stories in which he intended to illustrate traditional values modified by his perception of needed social reform.[65] He also attempted to reconcile the teachings of Western science with Indian values.[66] And, finally, he sought to bring politics, science and religion into proper harmony:

> ...if we desire to secure a firm basis for human progress, all maladjustments either between science and religion or between religion and statecraft must be rectified so that integrated thought and feeling may be established.[67]

C.R.'s teaching role became, therefore, an ordering role. His religious writings and talks could not exclude statecraft or science. What was needed was a new order – Mother India had to be seen again. As he says in his capacity as Governor-General:

> For a long time we failed to see Bharat Mata (Mother India) though she was standing all all around us. Gandhi taught us how to see Bharat Mata, but he has gone away a little too prematurely, before we took the lesson fully. To see Bharat Mata, we must be industrious in our habits, and wise in our activities. If you go to a temple, you will only see stone and not God. If we want to see Bharat Mata really, we will have to be upright in our conduct and good in our mind.[68]

---

63 C. Rajagopalachari, *Bhagavad-Gita: Abridged and Explained* (1st ed; New Delhi: The Hindustan Times Ltd., 1936).

64 C. Rajagopalachari, *Vendanta: the Basic Culture of India.*

65 See C. Rajagopalachari, *Stories for the Innocent* (Bombay: Bharatiya Vidya Bhavan, 1967). These stories were translated by C.R.'s son and others from Tamil versions dating back to the twenties.

66 This is one of C.R.'s favorite points, i.e., that "real" Hinduism is not "unscientific". Cf. *Vedanta*, p. 4. C.R. used the term "Vedānta" at this time rather than "Hinduism" for his particular idea of the core of Indian religion. Interestingly, when *Vedanta* was revised and republished twenty years later, it was then titled *Hinduism: Doctrine and Way of Life.*

67 *Vedanta.*, p. 3.

68 From a speech given at Bangalore, August 20, 1948, printed in *Rajaji's Speeches* (Delhi: Government of India, Ministry of Information and Broadcasting, 1948), p. 10. Hereafter cited as *Rajaji's Speeches* (G.O.I.). Speeches have been printed and edited in several different volumes. To allow cross-references, I have always given the date of the speech. The other volumes of speeches are *Rajaji's Speeches* (2 vols., Bharatiya Vidya Bhavan, 1948), cited as *Rajaji's Speeches* (B.V.B.); *University Addresses*, already cited; and *The Speeches of C. Rajagopalachari, Governor-General of India, June, 1948-January, 1950* (New Delhi: The Governor-General's Press, 1950), cited hereafter as *Governor-General's Speeches.* The last volume gives speeches in chronological order, while the others are edited according to topic.

What was the state's role in this? What were the roles of religious teacher, moral teacher, and political office holder therein?

Rajaji's role as a teacher was a religious function, but it was also a state function because he perceived his audience as the mass of Indians not in their religious role but in their civic capacity. His style as teacher was didactic, mass-oriented and eclectic. His intention was first to establish indigenous rule, then to reconstruct the state; his message was order and harmony in national life; his media were storytelling, lectures, and classic scriptures. Is there any precedent for such a role in state life? Could this not be a new form of Brahmin priesthood, one closely akin to his ancestral profession?

The function of the *agrahāram* Brahmins in Salem had been to sanctify and legitimize the state by providing a bridge between the present rule and the ancient image of the perfected state. The Brahmins represented this legitimation through their mastery of the ancient scriptures, their ability to harmonize local law with ancient *dharma*, their duty to instruct the king in righteous rule, and their right to educate the public. For C. Rajagopalachari, his ordering, preserving, sanctifying and teaching became a national role. His task, as he put it, was to restore this "feudal chivalry" in terms of "modern democracy". As India reached Independence, C.R. presented both to the Indian people and the new Indian legislators an image of India as the new sacred state – reordered on *dharmic* principles, yet totally in harmony with modern democratic thought.

By 1948, when Governor-General C. Rajagopalachari spoke, he recognised that a fundamental change had taken place in the very nature of authority. India was to be a democracy; the final sovereignty was "to be transferred to the bottom".[69] Rajaji, the democrat, was intensely worried, however, about the legitimation of this new society. If everyone were free, who was to rule and on what authority? Rajaji provided a metaphor:

> The clay, the earth upon which you are walking, can be made into Sri Ganesh and people fall prostrate before it. After the worship is over, they throw the clay into the water. We make ministers. You must respect them as you respect the great officers who proceeded the ministers. The ministers are Sri Ganesh. If we do not worship Ganesh, our state will crumble to pieces.[70]

The people of India must obey what they themselves had created; they must certify a system which ultimately is of their own making. This is a difficult but traditional order – to think of the state as sacred but at the same time as man-made, to imagine a leader as "God" but also as "clay".

C. Rajagopalachari had always been singularly unwilling to accept the idea of a purely secular state as part of his belief in democracy. It was not enough that the doctrines of religion might guide the state as in the democracies

---

69 Speech at the Janapada Sabha Bhavan, Nagpur, August 28, 1948, in *Rajaji's Speeches* (G.O.I.), p. 25.
70 *Ibid.*, p. 10.

of Europe; order in India depended upon the state and leaders retaining sanctity. From the British, Rajaji had been willing to accept the idea of democracy, but not the notion of government by contract alone. Democracy did not simply mean balance of power or of competing interests. India was both to be democratic and to retain a sense of its organic wholeness in the minds of all citizens. Rajaji expected this "spiritual life" to operate as the cohesive factor in the new state. Behind all the practical laws there was to be a sense of national consciousness, which ultimately sanctified the man-made state.

> We want a wise allotment of work to individuals as well as groups in accordance with the demands of the general interest in place of laissez-faire and divine right to make profit. If we want society to control individual life so as to produce this result, we cannot depend only on the spy and the policeman watching over citizens. We must build up a spiritual life which makes joy out of discharge of duty and acts as a law from within, making execution of State imposed laws easy.[71]

While India had elections, it also had a national religious life – an unchanging sense of order within the exigencies of political life.

Since C.R.'s spiritual India operated as a law from within, he could combine seemingly conflicting terms such as "individual" and "private" with the language of ordained duty. Democracy depended deeply upon individual character and effort.

> This experiment is truly an experience in the fundamentals of democracy. The fundamental of devotion is character. If authority is to be transferred to the bottom, it depends entirely on individual character. If the character of the people is bad, then democracy will fail.[72]

However, individual character again depended upon the individual's ability to see his place within the new organic state.

> We have to work hard, every one in his job. Every weaver, every peasant, every trader must make up his mind to do his best, *each in his own sphere*, avoiding deceit, avoiding idleness. Public affairs are only the sum total of private lives.[73]

Anyone familiar with classical Indian thought will recognize the language of *varnāshrama dharma*, "caste duty", here combined with words such as "private" and "individual".

Individual growth and individual discipline in duty constitute the spiritual state. But C. Rajagopalachari advanced the process one step further: the moral and spiritual growth of the individual was the irrevocable link to the future progress of the state.

---

71 C.R., *Vedanta*, p. 6.
72 Nagpur (August 28, 1948), in *Rajaji's Speeches* (G.O.I.), p. 25.
73 Broadcast to the nation on August 14, 1948, in *The Governor-General's Speeches*, p. 9.

According to the law of cause and effect with its extension over future births, if we live the Vedantic life, the growth of evils will be stopped, and the souls that will inhabit the future world will progressively rise to a higher state. The object of right living is therefore two-fold: one's own happiness and one's contribution to a better world irrespective of the disconnection in memory. The appeal of Vedanta is based on responsibility for the future world; social and civic co-operation permanently benefit the town or village wherein one is a citizen. Patriotism benefits the future generations of the country to which we belong. Vedanta seeks the welfare of the future world of which we are all the present builders.[74]

Again, C.R. has combined two diverse languages: national moral progress and the *karmic* law of spiritual development. *Karma* in the traditional sense meant "deeds" and the accumulated merit of a lifetime determining the state of an individual's next birth. *Karma* was purely a matter of personal progress. C.R. admitted that his theory was not in perfect accord with the Shāstras.

I will tell you about Karma – it may be only my doctrine of Karma – perhaps may be different from what the Shastras have told you, but later on you may find that there is no difference.[75]

C.R. added his own interpretation of *karma* to that of Shāstric law, seeing this *karma* as the very essence of Hinduism: i.e., the center of Hinduism was the law of *karma*, the law of social-moral progress, whose end product was to be a moral world in which the citizen's duty to the state, even the progress of his soul, was linked to the welfare of the Indian nation.

C.R. did not simply provide theories for his reinterpretation of Hinduism for the modern Indian state; he allowed for sacred scripture to frame and guide religious understanding. Rational thinking alone did not lead to religious understanding.

Things within the domain of human reason can be defined and proved. But for the understanding of things beyond, faith and meditation have to function. The scriptures and holy books may be looked upon as helps to assist reverent meditation, by which alone the human mind can get glimpses of the truth beyond...[76]

But C.R.'s definition of "holy books" was considerably expanded from the classical Hindu scriptures. Religious books from the West could also aid this meditation.

When straying from the studies prescribed for me when I was young, I read Bunyan's *The Pilgrim's Progress*, and Chapters in the Old and New Testaments of the Bible, and later I acquainted myself with the thoughts of Socrates, Marcus Aurelius and Brother Lawrence, and although no one incited me to it, the joy and reverence which these things induced, turned me towards the *Upanishads*, the *Gita* and the *Mahabharata*. All spiritual search is one and God blesses it wherever and by whomsoever it is done. If I am

74 C.R., *Vedanta*, p. 40.
75 C.R., *Chats Behind Bars*, p. 88.
76 C.R., *Bhagavad-Gita*, p. 18.

> today a devoted, though very imperfect Hindu Vedantin, it is no less due to my contact with some of the sacred books of other people, than to the contemplation of what our own great ancestors have left us.[77]

C.R. used Western works, but these essentially led to a confirmation of Hinduism. No matter what book he used he felt free to appropriate its contents. The law of spiritual understanding upon which he operated was founded on "deep thinking" and "meditation", but not in any traditional school of thought. Holy books were the only real guide to religious understanding, because they contained the thoughts of men who were disciplined in that special kind of "scientific investigation" which crowned human reasoning:

> ...but there are a few people like those who sang the *Upanishads*, and like those who are carrying on scientific researches in the West. Both belong to the class of mad men, who light their lamps at night and go on bothering with knowledge and dying for it. It is their work we call religion, their work we call science...[78]

Religion was the work of thoughtful men; scripture was in the hands of those who had the reason to use it.

This stress on the thoughtful men of society led Rajaji away from a democracy based upon the compound character of masses only. In his vision of the "real Government of India", there was room for the enlightened few, those who "go on bothering with knowledge and dying for it". Rajaji had his models for such special souls. His first book was on Socrates; later, he wrote on Marcus Aurelius and intended to write on Christ. But, underneath these figures, the living Mahātma always came to mind:

> He (Aristophanes) ridiculed him and an important section began to note Socrates like some people who believe that Mahatma Gandhi is encouraging and creating violence and bloodshed. The Times of India, The Madras Mail, and other Anglo-Indian papers misunderstand and make fun of Gandhi and readers of these papers may hate Gandhi. One day they may even sit and try and hang Gandhi – as Socrates was tried in Greece...[79]

Rajaji places Gandhi in a long succession of great souls:

> Don't think that Mahatma Gandhi is the inventor of Satyagraha, don't think that Tolstoy invented it, don't think that it was new when Christ stated it or even when Buddha stated it. In the earliest books of the world, you will find this truth, and I suppose we can claim that our Vedas are the oldest books in the world. The oldest knowledge in the world handed down through Buddha, Christ, Tolstoy, and Mahatma Gandhi of our time has this truth namely, that we should not resist evil.[80]

India had its mass character, but it also had its special messenger who restated and reenacted the old truths for modern times.

---

77 *Rajaji's Speeches* (B.V.B.), pp. 19–20.
78 C.R., *Chats Behind Bars*, p. 88.
79 *Ibid.*, p. 9.
80 *Ibid.*, p. 14.

C.R.'s view of the relationship between Gandhi and the new Indian state is important here, for in Gandhi he found a new model – a *dharmic* ideal who had lived perfectly in and through the modern world. For Rajagopalachari, Gandhi's life confirmed the entire structure of the modern Indian state.

> If we live a good life within our family we can be true to Mahatma Gandhi's teachings. If we run a little shop, selling the necessities of life to poor people in a proper way and tidily and usefully serving society, we can live up to Mahatma Gandhi's desire... there is no branch of human activity which alone can be considered as being associated with Mahatma Gandhi or his teachings, because he has lived a full life. He has taught in every manner and you will have to remember him in all the thoughts that we think...[81]

Gandhiji confirms the action of daily life, the family, small business, but also the law itself. Rajaji, in a speech unveiling a portrait of Gandhi to the Madras State Legislative Assembly on August 23, 1948, came close to equating Gandhi's way with *dharma* itself as the foundation of Indian society.

> Earnest men who serve in the Legislature make laws by the sense of right or wrong which they feel in their inner being. Whatever the context or proposals, they have to go finally through this test in their own minds, "Does this proposal fit in with the pattern of law in the abstract and not merely law with a capital 'L'"? Law in the abstract is what you have in your mind. Dharma you may call it in our own phraseology. You must make laws which are constant with Dharma. Mahatmaji is a symbol which you may keep before you mind whenever you make laws.[82]

If Gandhi was a symbol of *dharma*, then *dharma* itself had undergone considerable change and synthesis in Rajaji's mind.

In a much later, but very revealing work on Gandhi, Rajaji clearly pictured the Mahātma as the living synthesis of East and West. The passage is worth quoting in full.

> On the whole my view is that modern influences made the man, although certain basic elements were a permanent acquisition from early life, which was of course the conformist Hinduism of his caste. But as his work was among the masses and no reform work is possible unless you belong to them, he found valuable confirmation for all his tenets of thoughts and conduct in Hinduism and had no difficulty in convincing himself and the masses that he was a Hindu... His anchor was in God and His Grace, which is enough to make anyone a conformist Hindu despite any heterodoxy. It is difficult to refute the claim made by many that on the whole Gandhiji's moral doctrines were accrued from Christianity and the ethics of the modern West and that he found confirmation, not source, in his Hinduism. But it is equally difficult to refute the thesis that he was brought up as a Hindu in his earliest years, the influence of Hinduism must be deemed predominant... Gandhi was by no means a fundamentalist Hindu. He was rather modernist than orthodox although he would like to clothe his modernism in orthodox clothes and raise a smoke-screen of ancientness about it.[83]

---

81 Speech at Trivandrum, laying the foundation stone for Mahatma Gandhi College, August 22, 1948, in *Rajaji's Speeches* (G.O.I.), p. 38.

82 *Ibid.*, pp. 33–34.

83 C. Rajagopalachari, *Gandhi's Teaching and Philosophy* (Bombay: Bharatiya Vidya Bhavan, 1963), pp. 31–32.

Gandhi's life seemed to summarize the redirection of Western ideas into Hinduism. It is clear that Gandhi's approach was both "modernism" and "the great synthesis" in India. This life itself reflected the renewed law, so that India could go about the business of order and harmony once again. India was to have at the same time rationality and idols, both Law and a new exemplar of Law.

What then is the structure of this new Indian state in Rajaji's terms? What is this revival of feudal chivalry in the terms of modern democracy? And, most important, what is the role which a man of Rajaji's sort can play in such a resanctified state?

First, his views of the state's contrasting elements are illuminating. The state is both a creation of the masses, yet it is to be sanctified; the state is to work as an organ, yet it is to be constituted by the fruit of individual character; the citizens of this state are free to develop, but their development takes place within specific limits – their "duty", their job. The education of the masses is to be founded on "holy books", but these books may include all works which are truthful. The authority of the state is trust in a great Mahātma. There can be laws made in legislatures, but these laws must still conform to *dharma* – a *dharma* based on West as well as East. This state, in short, is democratic – "of the people"; yet it is clearly a religious state – a highly ordered world in which law cannot be perceived outside the framework of Bharat Mata. India as a modern nation has become the new definition of a *dharmic* world, and citizenship is a religious act in which personal spiritual development affects the very progress of the state. This new state has its own ideal spiritual and political leader, although it has no king. This is *varnāshrama dharma* without caste; *dharma* through legislation; a Hindu social order without any mention of ritual order; and, kingship without a king!

C.R. attempted to provide a view of the new Indian state which was at once political and religious. His "Hinduism" was almost a definition of citizenship and his image of the Indian state was a religious model in itself. In his harmonizing and teaching roles, C.R. imagined an India totally in tune with the past, ordered along sacred lines, with its own special *dharmic* hero and with a new inner law which operated to affect the character of the people. He had assumed the role of the *agrahāram* Brahmin, bringing a new image of the perfected state to the historical confusion of the emergent democracy. All elements of the *agrahāram* Brahmin were there: the harmonizing of law, the sanctification of new authority, the renewal of scripture, and the constant stress of human models of *dharmic* order. But, C.R.'s Brahmanical role took on aspects which went beyond the Salem *agrahāram*. The needed link between perfection and history was not a matter of hereditary rights to ancient scripture. Instead, he restored creativity to the Brahmanical role and hence reconstituted that important element of a much older priestly tradition: i.e., legitimation of authority through creative use of the power of the word. This leads any study of C.R.'s leadership into examining styles older than the royal Brahmanic tradition. In its broader context his leadership followed the pattern of the royal bard – the *sūta*. But, that thesis is beyond the scope of this present paper.

Religion and the Legitimation of Nehru's Concept of the Secular State

ROBERT D. BAIRD

ALTHOUGH IN ANCIENT India distinctions were made between the responsibilities of king and priest, the primary aim of the state was to promote *dharma*. Hence, "the Hindu kings built temples, granted them large endowments, and exercised strict supervision over their affairs" (Smith, 1963: 57). Under governments claiming Muslim norms, Aurangzeb destroyed Hindu temples and schools. Akbar, as part of his religious quest, supported the Persian translations of (among others) the *Atharvaveda*, the *Mahabharata*, and the *Ramayana* (Smith, 1963: 64). During the British period, in addition to attempts at religious neutrality, there were occasions when the state assumed responsibility for the administration and patronage of South Indian temples. Hence, although the modern distinction between religion and the secular (so important for the thought of Nehru) was known in principle, the two realms were distinguished but not separated. It was frequently the case that government considered itself responsible for the religious well-being of its subjects. This responsibility was implemented directly or indirectly, and with varying conceptions of the nature of religious well-being.

In this setting, Nehru's notion of the secular state carries with it the necessity for political and social change.[1] The purpose of this paper is to determine in what sense and to what extent religion can be said to be a means whereby Nehru legitimated his concept of the secular state. This determination requires some prior methodological considerations.

Religious Legitimation: Sacred and Profane

To speak of religion as a means of legitimating power or justifying the directions of political and social change is to understand religion as distinct from the power to be legitimated or the political or social change to be justified.

1 Although social reformers, using the categories of religion and the secular, call the change social, there are cogent reasons for admitting considerable religious change as well. For a discussion of this, see Baird (1975).

Failure to make such a distinction would require one to show how a given use of power or political or social change is legitimate without recourse to any principle outside of itself. Power would then be justified because it was power, and a given political or social phenomenon would be legitimated because it was indeed that political or social phenomenon.

For this reason it is not uncommon to find that in such discussions religion is understood in terms of the "sacred" over against the "profane".

> The dichotomization of reality into sacred and profane spheres, however related, is intrinsic to the religious enterprise. As such it is obviously important for any analysis of the religious phenomenon. (Berger, 1967: 27)

Peter Berger intends to take the "sacred" in the "sense understood by *Religionswissenschaft* since Rudolph Otto..." (1967: 178). The three characteristics of the experience of the holy for Otto are summarized by W. Richard Comstock as follows:

> First is the sense of the *tremendum* that refers to a feeling of awefulness, and *majestas* or overpowering might that includes the sense of urgency. Second, *mysterium* refers to the uncanniness and mysteriousness that also pervades the experience. Finally, there is the element of *fascinans* as the experience seems to participate in an aspiration toward some ultimate value. (1972: 22)

In terms of the legitimation of power, this means that one is attempting to discover how the dimensions of the sacred are utilized to legitimate dimensions of the profane. Under these categories, secularization, or the profanization of the world, poses a problem for religious legitimation.[2] In terms of these categories, to the extent to which secularization has occurred, to that extent religious legitimation will cease to be a logical possibility. Hence, the topic under consideration in this symposium remains a real topic only to the extent to which secularization has not been complete. For the problem to be phrased in terms of these categories, some sense of the sacred must remain.

Closely related to these categories is the approach found in Donald Eugene Smith's *Religion and Political Modernization*. Here religion is seen in terms of "the religions", i.e., the sacred traditions of "Hinduism", or "Buddhism", or "Islam". The question of religious legitimation in the modern world is then framed as follows:

> The question that engages us here is this: Despite their traditionally conservative role, can the major religious systems be reformulated to provide positive ideological support for largely secular political systems committed to rapid socioeconomic change? Can reformulated Hinduism, Buddhism, Islam, and Catholicism significantly reorient the motivation and behavior patterns of large numbers of people and help to mobilize them for the tasks of development? (Smith, 1974: 23.)

---

2 Chapter 7 of *The Sacred Canopy* shows how this has unfolded in "Western religions."

In this vein Miriam Sharma and Jagdish P. Sharma show how the Sarvodaya movement utilized traditional religious terminology and concepts to justify social change. Bhoodan became the moral duty of good Hindus. Indeed, all good human beings should give one-sixth of their land to the landless.

> Expressed almost exclusively in a religious idiom, Sarvodaya uses a reinterpreted Hinduism to legitimize revolutionary change toward a utopian society. (Smith, 1974: 223)

To examine Nehru's concept of the secular state under the categories of "sacred" and "profane" will abort an attempt to understand Nehru's thought. It might show us what he did not believe, but would not show how it was that his concept of the secular state was legitimated. There are at least two reasons for this. *First*, Nehru was not firmly committed to any religious or sacred tradition. Hence, he could not be expected to attempt the type of reformulation to which Smith refers. Many of his statements about "the religions" indicate that rather than reformulate them Nehru would prefer to see their scope compressed. If this compression is considered a type of reformulation, it is a reformulation which made "the religions" irrelevant to the social or political systems which they might be thought by others to legitimate. Religion as sacred tradition had no hold on Nehru. It does not, therefore, come as a surprise that he does not attempt to justify his concept of the secular state by appeals to a sacred tradition. There were moments in Indian religious history which Nehru appreciated, but he did not use them for legitimation.

Second, and closely related to the first, for Nehru there is no relationship between the realm of the "secular" and "religion". One of the things which most disturbed Nehru about Gandhi was his religious interpretation of the freedom movement.

> Gandhiji was continually laying stress on the religious and spiritual side of the movement. His religion was not dogmatic, but it did mean a definitely religious outlook on life, and the whole movement was strongly influenced by this and took on a revivalistic character so far as the masses are concerned... (1941: 71)

> I used to be troubled sometimes at the growth of this religious element in our politics, both on the Hindu and the Moslem side. I did not like it at all. Much that Moulvies and Maulanas and Swamis and the like said in their public addresses seemed to me most unfortunate. Their history and sociology and economics appeared to me all wrong, and the religious twist that was given to everything prevented all clear thinking. Even some of Gandhiji's phrases sometimes jarred upon me – thus his frequent reference to *Rama Raj* as a golden age which was to return. But I was powerless to intervene, and I consoled myself with the thought that Gandhiji used the words because they were well known and understood by the masses. He had an amazing knack of reaching the heart of the people. (1941: 71–72).

Nehru was willing to submerge his feelings about the intrusion of the sacred tradition into what he considered a purely political quest for at least two reasons. First, he was aware that he was powerless to do anything about it.

Furthermore, although he did not agree with Gandhi's interpretation, nor with his theory, his method did get results.

The commonly used categories of "sacred" and "profane", then, have limited use for an analysis of the stance of one whose thought is predominantly "profane". But one is not bound to these commonly used categories in this analysis. Peter Berger does not intend to suggest that "sacred" and "profane" are the only legitimate terms for religious analysis.

> Definitions cannot, by their very nature, be either "true" or "false," only more useful or less so. For this reason it makes relatively little sense to argue over definitions...
>
> In the long run, I suppose, definitions are matters of taste...[3]

Religious Legitimation: Ultimate Concern

It is possible to study religion as ultimate concern. Religion, then, is studied as that which is more important than anything else in the universe to the individual or group involved.[4] Its application to the study of Nehru's thought would be to ask what Nehru considered of ultimate importance for man. If it was not the performance of puja, or sacrificial rites, or the achievement of some non-dual moksha, then what was it? In view of the topic of this paper, two subordinate questions then present themselves. What place does the secular state have in relationship to that ultimate goal, and, how did Nehru attempt to legitimate his view?

It was in contrast to the approach of organized "religion" that Nehru revealed his own approach to reality, and the ultimate goal for man. "Religion" is emotional and merges with mysticism. Although some insight might come from it, there is an equal likelihood of self-delusion.

> Religion merges into mysticism and metaphysics and philosophy. There have been great mystics, attractive figures, who cannot easily be disposed of as self-deluded fools. Yet mysticism (in the narrow sense of the word) irritates me; it appears to be vague and soft and flabby, not a rigorous discipline of the mind but a surrender of mental faculties and a living in a sea of emotional experience. The experience may lead occasionally to some insight into inner and less obvious processes, but it is also likely to lead to self-delusion. (Nehru, 1946: 14–15)

Gandhi's use of "religion" in his 1932 "fast unto death" angered Nehru. It was the introduction of emotion and sentimentality into politics (Nehru, 1941:

---

3 Berger (1967: 178). Also see Baird (1971) where the same point is made.

4 I have discussed this definition and the method employed in this paper at greater length in Baird (1971). From this point onward in this paper, when the term religion appears it should be understood in the sense of ultimate concern. When "religion" appears it should be understood in terms of Nehru's use of the word as referring to the institutional sacred traditions of "Hinduism," "Buddhism," "Christianity," "Islam," etc., and the traditional practices and values usually associated with these traditions.

237). Over against "religious" emotionalism, Nehru opted for reason and clear thinking.

> Again I watched the emotional upheaval of the country during the fast, and I wondered more and more if this was the right method in politics. It seemed to be sheer revivalism, and clear thinking had not a ghost of a chance against it. (1941: 240)

"Religion" also has a tendency to sponsor superstition, magic, dogmatic beliefs, and unthinking credulance and reliance on the supernatural. This was true even when practiced by "thinking minds" (Nehru, 1946: 14). During his prison stay in 1933, a friend sent him books on Catholicism and copies of some of the papal encyclicals. He realized the hold that Catholicism had on many people and the safe anchorage from doubt and mental conflict which it and other "religions" offered their adherents. But to Nehru, the "religions" had no appeal. "I am afraid it is impossible for me to seek harborage in this way. I prefer the open sea, with all its storms and tempests" (Nehru, 1941: 242). Over against this, Nehru chose what he considered a "more or less scientific" view of things (Nehru, 1946: 13).

Moreover, "the religious outlook does not concern itself with the world" (Nehru, 1941: 242). It has engaged in metaphysics and vague speculation which has often had little relevance to modern problems. Nehru's approach is decidedly this-worldly.

> Essentially I am interested in this world, in this life, not in some other world or a future life. Whether there is such a thing as a soul, or whether there is a survival after death or not, I do not know; and important as these questions are, they do not trouble me in the least. (Nehru, 1946: 15)

Perhaps most important of all, Nehru was not concerned with God nearly as much as he was with man. "A kind of vague humanism appealed to me" (Nehru, 1946: 13). God did not take up his attention, for the very concept seemed odd.

> What the mysterious is I do not know. I do not call it God because God has come to mean much that I do not believe in. I find myself incapable of thinking of a deity or of any unknown supreme power in anthropomorphic terms, and the fact that many people think so is continually a source of surprise to me. Any idea of a personal God seems very odd to me. (Nehru, 1946: 16)

But if God did not take up his attention, man did. "No, one may not lose faith in Man. God we may deny, but what hope is there for us if we deny Man and thus reduce everything to futility" (Nehru, 1946: 477)?

At this point Nehru's religious goal becomes clear. Committed though he was to "the scientific spirit" (Nehru, 1946: 571), Nehru recognized the limits of science. "Science does not tell us much, or for the matter of that, anything, about the purpose of life" (Nehru, 1946: 14). Hence he could not settle for a mere scientific approach, but held out for "a kind of scientific humanism" (Nehru, 1946: 571). His ultimate goal, his religious goal was to create

> *a fully integrated human being* – that is, with what might be called the spiritual and ethical counterpart of the purely material machinery of planing and development being brought into the making of man. (Karanjia, 1960: 34 *emphasis in Text*)

It was this goal of "a fully integrated human being" that gave meaning to Nehru's struggle for freedom: political, economic and social. A planned economy and a secular state were not ends in themselves, but were the most adequate means to his religious goal (Karanjia, 1960: 56). Convinced that people were not equal in abilities, he nevertheless held that they should be granted every opportunity to develop to their fullest potential. This was the goal of socialism.

> I am trying to search for the correct solutions, keeping before me certain objectives, *the broad objectives being human welfare and human development, providing opportunity to every human being to develop to the fullest measure possible...*
> Now when you ask for a definition of Socialism, what you mean presumably is a definition of an *economic policy* which would lead to the desired goal. This is a means to an end: *the end being, basically, as I have said, human betterment, everybody having the chance to concrete betterment.* (Karanjia, 1960: 37 *emphasis in Text*)

Nehru's ultimate goal, then, is humanistic and scientific, it is rational, and, unlike antiquated "religious" superstitions, it is modern. It includes a higher material standard of living while retaining an ethical and spiritual approach to reality. It is, in his terms, "a fully integrated human being".

The Religious Goal and Freedom

In order for this growth into a fully integrated person to take place, people had to be free. Not only did the Indian people need independence from British domination, but national strength and national unity were also required.

> Some fissiparous tendencies have sprung up, as they were bound to, in a country of so many diversities, but I am confident that these will be conquered so as to have all the strands harmonized into a central unity.
> What is needed is education and culture, a common education and culture which makes every citizen of this vast land *think, feel and act the Indian way.* (Karanjia, 1966: 27)

It is wrong to think that individuals can grow by pressing for communal advantages. Communalism weakens India and a weakened India threatens individual well-being.

> The one thing that should be obvious to all of us is this, that there is no group in India, no party, no religious community, which can prosper if India does not prosper. If India goes down, we go down, all of us, whether we have a few seats more or less, whether we get a slight advantage or we do not. But if it is well with India, if India lives as a vital, free

country then it is well with all of us to whatever community or religion we may belong. (Nehru, 1950a: 360)

On his return from Europe, Nehru had enlarged his outlook so as to add social and economic freedom to political freedom. Of what use, he held, was freedom from foreign domination if Indians remained bound by poverty and antiquated social restrictions (1941: 128)? The only justification for national freedom is a real freedom for the Indian masses.

> The only real justification for Indian freedom is the promise of better government, of a higher standard for the masses, of industrial and cultural growth, and of the removal of the atmosphere of fear and suppression that foreign imperialist rule invariably brings in its train. (Nehru, 1941: 300)

In a broadcast from New Delhi on August 15, 1947, Nehru reiterated the theme that the freedom that was gained when Indians lost the yoke of foreign domination had to be preserved and enlarged. What that enlargement entailed was indicated when he continued by expanding his theme in terms of the basic needs of food and clothing, economic production, industrialization, and the equitable distribution of goods (1950a: 7–8). In a speech on the anniversary of independence, on August 15, 1948, he made freedom a matter of the heart, an internal matter.

> For freedom is not a mere matter of political decision or new constitutions, not even a matter of what is more important, that is, economic policy. It is of the mind and heart and if the mind narrows itself and is befogged and the heart is full of bitterness and hatred, then freedom is absent. (1950a: 5)

Freedom also entails equality, for it implies that all persons should be free. But equality in turn requires a limited freedom (Nehru, 1950a: 362). Otherwise, the unlimited freedom of one citizen might hamper or unduly limit the freedom of another. In a 1949 speech in San Francisco, he addressed himself to this issue of freedom and equality.

> Take equality. I am not quite sure if ultimately the concept of equality can be co-ordinated with freedom, because when you bring equality it may interfere with someone's freedom. So there is a slight conflict – not a final conflict, but there is a conflict. Perhaps in understanding the problems of the world today, you might put it in this way: that while in the nineteenth century, and later, the concept of freedom was given considerable emphasis and very rightly, in this middle-twentieth century the idea of equality is gaining more force. Until you balance the two ideas of freedom and equality, both of which are important, and each of which has to be limited to some extent in order to co-ordinate with the other, you will not solve the problems of today. (1950b: 136)

The limitation of religious freedom should be seen in this light. Nehru would concur with *The Constitution of India* where religious freedom is subject to public order, morality and health, and is not to be used as an obstacle to social reform (Karanjia, 1960: 60). Freedom must be expanded to the fullest extent possible.

But this requires the conscious limitation of freedom so that the overall scope of freedom can be maximized.

Freedom and the Secular State

The secular state is the means of maximizing freedom and hence enabling each individual to fulfill himself or herself in keeping with his or her optimum potential. Individual progress depends on national progress and strength. In a country like India, only the secular state will enable this to occur.

> The Government of a country like India, with many religions that have secured great and devoted followings for generations, can never function satisfactorily in the modern age except on a secular basis. (quoted in Smith, 1958: 154)

But, the secular state involves certain limitations and one is the limitation of "religion". This means that Nehru operates with the categories of "religion" and the secular. It also means that in the secular state "religion" has its own sphere which is to be separated from other legitimate and important spheres of life. These spheres which have traditionally been closely related to "religion" must be secularized, that is, made distinct from the sphere of "religion" and purged of "religious" elements. This is all ultimately related to Nehru's religious goal. For the secularization of these endeavors is a necessary part of the secular state. The secular state maximizes human freedom and hence provides the opportunity for persons to achieve a fully integrated existence.

The Secularization of Politics

Part of what it means to be a secular state is that each citizen, regardless of his other associations, is to have equal rights and obligations as part of that citizenship. The citizen must be free to practice "religion", but "religious" association neither grants him special rights nor deprives him of any. Nehru drafted the Congress Election Manifesto of July, 1951, which stated that "As India is a secular State, every citizen has the same duties, rights, privileges and obligations as any other. He has full freedom to profess and practice his religion" (quoted in Smith, 1958: 152). Citizenship, then, is determined on an individual basis, quite apart from one's status in a "religious" community. It was this secular basis for citizenship which made Nehru so much opposed to the Pakistani solution to the Kashmir question. The idea of two nations, each based on a "religion", was against the secularity upon which the Indian state was established.

> India is a secular nation which guarantees equality of citizenship to people of all religions. We consider our Muslim population – we have some fifty millions of them – as part of our nation, the Indian nation, and not some other Muslim nation. We have Hindus, Muslims, Sikhs, Christians and other religious communities, and we obviously cannot consider them as different nationalities. Such an approach would be absolutely fatal from our point of view. If we concede this two-nation theory which Pakistan is sponsoring,

what happens to our vast Muslim population? Do we have to consider them as a different nation just because they have a different religion? The very concept is fantastic. It might lead to further trouble, division and disruption of the nation. (Karanjia, 1966: 128–129)

Since citizenship is secular, so is politics. The individual's citizenship in the secular state is not dependent on "religious" affiliation, and "religion" is irrelevant to politics in the secular state. Indeed, the introduction of "religion" into political issues angered Nehru. Gandhi's announcement of a "fast unto death" in 1932 was interpreted as the introduction of "religious" means to achieve a purely political end. In the secular state, politics must be secularized.

I felt angry with him at his religious and sentimental approach to a political question, and his frequent references to God in connection with it. He even seemed to suggest that God had indicated the very date of the fast. What a terrible example to set! (Nehru, 1941: 237)

Although Nehru was pleased with the way Gandhi seemed to be able to mobilize the masses, his introduction of "religion" into the realm of politics was unacceptable. Moreover, he was concerned lest this bad example encourage others to mix "religion" with politics.

The threat to the secularization of politics was ever present in India in the form of communalism – the attempt to gain political power through alliances of a "religious" nature. Nehru spoke frequently against the communalist view that "religion" could serve as a national bond (1941: 292). Communalism was undemocratic and was seen to go against the concept of citizenship found in the secular state.

Our State is not a communal state, but a democratic state in which every citizen has equal rights. The Government is determined to protect these rights. (Nehru, 1950a: 45)

In a speech delivered before the Constituent Assembly on April 3, 1948, Nehru addressed himself to the dangerous alliance of "religion" with politics in the form of communalism.

...The combination of politics and religion in narrowest sense of the word resulting in communal politics is – there can be no doubt – a most dangerous combination and must be put an end to. It is clear, as has been pointed out by the Honourable Mover, that this combination is harmful to the country as a whole; it is harmful to the majority, but probably it is most harmful to any minority that seeks to have some advantage from it. I think even the past history of India will show that. But in any event a minority in an independent State which seeks to isolate and separate itself does some injury to the cause of the country, and most of all it injures its own interests, because inevitably it puts a barrier between itself and others, a barrier not on the religious plane but on the political plane – sometimes even to some extent on the economic plane; and it can never really exercise the influence which it legitimately ought to aspire to exercise, if it functions in that way. (1950a: 48)

Ultimately, not only does communalism go against the secular concept of the state and weaken the state's solidarity, but it weakens the group which is seeking to strengthen itself through "religious" alliances. By placing a barrier between its members and other citizens, it hinders its members from achieving self-fulfillment and the extent of personal development which the secular state makes possible.

The exclusion of "religion" from politics would exclude all forms of communalism. Ideally, it would eliminate the reservation of seats along communal lines. Seeing that some reservation of seats might be in the offing, Nehru urged moderation. In response to the discussion about joint or common electorates, he urged:

> I hope personally that the less reservation there is the better, and I think that is so mostly even more from the point of view of the group or the minority that might have that reservation than from the point of view of any other group or majority. (1950a: 49)

Not only does the concept of the secular state exclude "religion" from politics, but it also makes it an irrelevant consideration for social and economic planning.

Secularization and the Social Order

Regardless of the extent to which the caste system has been justified on "religious" grounds, within the context of the secular state, social order and social change must be decided on modern and "non-religious" grounds. Nehru spoke approvingly of the position of Vivekananda in which "caste was a form of social organization which was and should be kept separate from religion" (1946: 339).

Nehru recognized that simple equality was impossible, for people's capacities and talents, the Government notwithstanding, were dissimilar.

> You cannot make everybody equal for the simple reason that people are different, intellectually and physically different. There are clever people, there are stupid people, and there are all types of people. But what you can do is to equalize opportunities for all and apply the same standards for everyone. (Karanjia, 1960: 38)

Equality of opportunity is an inference from the secular state's notion of citizenship which is granted equally apart from religious status or affiliation. But the caste system, which served a purpose in the past, had come to be in conflict with such equality.

> In the context of society today, the caste system and much that goes with it are wholly incompatible, reactionary, restrictive, and barriers to progress. There can be no equality in status and opportunity within its framework, nor can there be political democracy, and much less, economic democracy. Between these two conceptions conflict is inherent, and only one of them can survive. (Nehru, 1946: 254)

It was indeed the tendency for Hinduism and Islam to order society and give their ordering "religious" sanction.

> Thus Hinduism and Islam, quite apart from their purely religious teachings, lay down social codes and rules about marriage, inheritance, civil and criminal law, political organization, and indeed almost everything else. In other words, they lay down a complete structure for society and try to perpetuate this by giving it religious sanction and authority. Hinduism has gone farthest in this respect by its rigid system of caste. (Nehru, 1949b: 736)

But the social order cannot be "religiously" determined. The social and economic changes which are to take place must be governed by the secular goal of equality of opportunity. Fortunately, reformers arose whose work led to "increasing secularization of the State and of many institutions – that is to say they were separated from religion" (Nehru, 1949b: 736). A secular state requires the secularization of society and a caste-dominated society cannot be secular.

> Thus, a caste-ridden society is not properly secular. I have no desire to interfere with any person's belief, but where those beliefs become petrified in class divisions, undoubtedly they affect the social structure of the State. (quoted in Smith, 1958: 151)

Secularization and Law

Article 44 of *The Constitution of India*, as part of the Directive Principles of State Policy, stated that "The State shall endeavour to secure for the citizens a uniform civil code throughout the territory of India." At the moment of Independence, Muslims and Hindus were governed by different laws regarding inheritance, marriage, divorce and other matters of personal law. Nor was Hindu law unified. In 1954, Nehru stated that he thought a unified civil code was inevitable, but that the time was not ripe to push it through in India (quoted in Smith, 1958: 165). This was in support of the "Hindu Code Bill" which had floundered as a unified bill, but was being passed in sections. Supporting the separate bills, Nehru argued from his understanding of Hindu history. In the past, he stated, Hindu society evidenced a capacity for change. Furthermore, the attempt on the part of any religion to support practices in conflict with modern trends would only weaken the credibility of that "religion". This was not an attempt by Nehru to offer religious legitimation for the Hindu Code Bill. The uniform civil code of which the Hindu Code was the first step was validated on the grounds of the secular state. That being settled, if a reminder of past Hindu flexibility could be used to get Hindus to take the first pill, that would be utilized. But the movement toward a unified civil code was based on the nature of citizenship in the secular state.

Religious Legitimation of the Secular State

With the categories which we have been using, religious legitimation of the secular state asks what ultimate values are appealed to in support for the Indian secular state. By the nature of the case, ultimate values are not defended, for such argumentation would necessarily appeal to other values which are "more" ultimate. Ultimate values are those which the thinker cannot justify by an appeal to something beyond. They are themselves the ultimate appeal. It might well be that the very values which are ultimate and hence not called to the bar of justification by a given thinker are only penultimate and hence in need of further justification for another. But that is only because ultimate values are not uniform or universally shared. What we want to know in the present instance is what ultimate values does Nehru use to give force or justification to his views of the legitimacy of the secular state for modern India?

We have found Nehru's religious goal to be a fully integrated human being, and that in his conception the secular state is the most effective means for reaching that goal. Nehru also offers some characteristics of his view which are clearly valued but never defended. These valued characteristics are that his view is *rational and scientific*, *Indian*, and *modern*. When a debate over his position actually arises, it is not an appeal to a sacred tradition, but these values which are offered to clinch the validity of his approach. They are ultimate or religious values because they are inseparable, in his view, from his ultimate or religious goal.

Not infrequently in his speeches, Nehru will settle a point by indicating that he does not see how any sensible person could possibly hold to anything else. In his speech moving the Objectives Resolution at the Constituent Assembly in 1946, he stated:

> ...We adhere to certain fundamental propositions which are laid down in this Declaration. These fundamental propositions, I submit, are not controversial in any real sense of the word. Nobody challenges them in India and *nobody ought to challenge them*, but if anyone should challenge them, well, we shall accept that challenge *and hold our position*. (1950a: 351 *emphasis added*)

The reason why Nehru's fundamental position ought not to be challenged is that it is the only possible modern, scientific, and Indian approach that can be taken. Nehru does not defend modernity, he does not argue for science over superstition, and he does not buttress his appeal to it as being Indian. All of these are self-evident. No one should disagree with them, and if they do, then, "we shall accept that challenge and hold our position." These three qualities or characteristics of his position are brought together in an interview.

> But on the whole I think that Congress is infused not with anything like a Nehru ideal or any other individual approach, but what is basically and fundamentally the Indian approach, the modern approach, the scientific approach, that is, the Socialistic approach – the only possible approach in the modern world. (Karanjia, 1960: 59)

These three qualities are interrelated. Sometimes Nehru refers to his approach as rationalistic, and the rational is frequently coupled with scientific. Nehru presents his approach as one which is opposed to dogmatism, and he thereby distinguishes his from traditional "religious" approaches. The Indian approach is not an appeal to past authority, but the assumption that in modern India with its varied "religious" traditions, the only possible Indian approach is that of the secular state.

Those who want to make "religion" the basis of statehood are less than modern. Pakistan's approach is "antediluvian".

> Pakistan, of course, thinks otherwise. She calls herself a Muslim State, that is a religious and theocratic state. And the conflict over Kashmir arises from this different approach of theirs. They insist that because Kashmir has a Muslim majority it must go to Pakistan. We cannot agree to such a theory. *We consider it an absurd, obnoxious and antediluvian theory to divide people into nations on a purely religious basis.* (Karanjia, 1966: 129 *emphasis added*)

This last statement is not an argument, but an assertion of basic values.

To introduce "religion" into politics as the Swatantra party wants to do is a "throw-back to the past".

> You may call it counter-revolution. And as you see, as usual, it covers both our domestic and foreign policy. It is, if I may say so, a *complete throw-back to the past... Dharma* is good so long as it does not get into conflict with a rational and scientific outlook – but don't you see that is exactly what these Swatantra gentlemen want to do! (Karanjia, 1960: 60 *emphasis in text*)

If, in London, Nehru denounced South African apartheid, it was also because it was an "evil development opposed to the whole concept of modern thinking" (Karanjia, 1960: 91). Socialist objectives were considered an important and necessary consequence of the goals of freedom and equality. Hence socialism can be argued for as a means to reach the goals of the secular state. But socialism too is modern, and is commended on that ground.

> I am not embarrassed about being a Socialist or our objectives being Socialist. That should be the ideal of every sensible nation or society or individual. Modern thinking all over the world is increasingly becoming Socialist and only people who have lost touch completely with contemporary trends can think otherwise. (Karanjia, 1960: 57)

In 1964, Mr. R. K. Karanjia asked Mr. Nehru to what he would attribute the success of the past "golden decade" of Indian freedom? His answer was that his policies of democratic socialism and non-alignment for peace have been based on a correct ideology which reflects the "genius of our own country" and is "in step with our times" (1966: 38). But what if some future regime, following Nehru, were to get out of step, what then? Nehru held that such would not be possible in the long range for it would go against the natural evolution of history and those who seek to break this will only break themselves. His position, then, is modern (in step with the times), it is rational and scientific, and it is historically guaranteed.

> Our philosophy and ideology, as I have always maintained, are not some private fad or creations of mind. They belong to the *ethos* of our nation and people. They arise from the spirit of our times. If we accept this premise, there is no getting away from them. Any

person or regime that tries to divert the course of our freedom and its natural evolution, will succeed only in injuring itself. I do not think our parliamentary democracy will permit any such reversal of our basic policies. (Karanjia, 1966: 38)

The secular state as a political solution for modern India, then, is based on the argument that it affords the optimum freedom for people to develop into fully integrated human beings. The goal of fully integrated human beings is a modern goal, a rational and scientific goal, and an Indian goal. These ultimate values should be apparent to all, and it is because of this that they are for Nehru both ultimate and the final legitimation for the secular state.

REFERENCES

Baird, Robert D.

1971 *Category Formation and the History of Religions.* The Hague: Mouton & Company.

1975 "Religion and the Secular: Categories for Religious Conflict and Religious Change in Independent India". *Journal of Asian and African Studies* XI, 1–2, pp. 47–63.

Berger, Peter

1967 *The Sacred Canopy.* Garden City: Doubleday & Company, Inc.

Breecher, Michael

1959 *Nehru: A Political Biography.* London: Oxford University Press.

Comstock, W. Richard

1972 *The Study of Religion and Primitive Religions.* New York: Harper & Row.

Das, M. N.

1961 *The Political Philosophy of Jawaharlal Nehru.* London: George Allen & Unwin Ltd.

Karanjia, R. K.

1960 *The Mind of Mr. Nehru: An Interview with R. K. Karanjia.* London: George Allen & Unwin Ltd.

1966 *The Philosophy of Mr. Nehru: As Revealed in a Series of Intimate Talks with R. K. Karanjia.* London: George Allen & Unwin Ltd.

Nanda, B. R.

1962 *The Nehrus: Motilal and Jawaharlal.* Chicago: The University of Chicago Press, 1974. First published in 1962.

Nehru, Jawaharlal

1941 *Toward Freedom: The Autobiography of Jawaharlal Nehru.* Boston: Beacon Press, 1958. First published in 1941.

1942 *The Unity of India: Collected Writings 1937–1940.* London: Lindsay Drummond Ltd.

1946 *The Discovery of India.* New York: The John Day Company.

1949a *Jawaharlal Nehru's Speeches*, Vol. I. Government of India: The Publications Division.

1949b *Glimpses of World History.* London: Lindsay Drummond Ltd., 1934. Using 4th edition, 1949.

1950a *Independence and After: A Collection of Speeches, 1946–1949.* New York: The John Day Company.

1950b *Visit to America.* New York: The John Day Company.

1954 *Jawaharlal Nehru's Speeches*, Vol. II. Government of India: The Publications Division.

1958 *Jawaharlal Nehru's Speeches*, Vol. III. Government of India: The Publications Division.

SINHA, V. K. (ed.)
1968 *Secularism in India.* Bombay: Lalvani Publishing House.
SMITH, Donald Eugene
1958 *Nehru and Democracy: The Political Thought of An Asian Democrat.* Calcutta: Orient Longmans Private Ltd.
1963 *India As a Secular State.* Princeton: Princeton University Press.
1974 *Religion and Political Modernization.* New Haven and London: Yale University Press.

Religion and Legitimation in the Mahar Movement

ELEANOR ZELLIOT

THE MAHAR MOVEMENT, more than any other Untouchable caste's effort to achieve upward mobility, may be seen as Western in its orientation. My own writings convey this impression (Zelliot, 1966, 1970a, 1970b, 1972). It is easy to see why: the methods used by Dr. B. R. Ambedkar, unquestioned leader of the movement and Western-educated, seem modern: governmental petitions and testimony, organized political parties, parliamentary procedures, mass contact through conferences and newspapers. The institutions created by the Mahars can all be named in English: the People's Education Society, the Republican Party, even the Buddhist Society of India. The rhetoric used also seems universal to all low-class movements: claim equality! unify! agitate! educate! However, as I have turned my attention recently from the actions and the organizations of Dr. Ambedkar and the Mahars to what might be described as the inner aims of the movement, to its poetry, and to the mythic elements which bound the highly educated Ambedkar to the Untouchable masses, I have come to have new respect for the purely Indian (or purely Maharashtrian) and traditional elements of the movement. I now want to look from inside the movement, through its own documents, to see in what ways it attempted to legitimize higher status and new functions through religious sanctification or traditional legitimation.

I will focus on six moments in time in the eighty-five years of the modern recorded history of the Mahars of Maharashtra. The first is the 1894 petition of Gopal Baba Walangkar, a retired Mahar British army soldier, whose work is the first written record of new Mahar ambition in the 19th century. Its very existence indicates a change in the economic status of the caste, i.e., the fact that some Mahars had left the traditional position of Untouchable servant of the village for non-traditional occupations. The second document repeats the theme of the first: a plea for recruitment into the British army and the lower ranks of administration; it is the 1910 petition to the Government written by Shivram Janba Kamble, a Mahar butler in the Masonic Hall in Poona.

The next three documents are from the Ambedkar period of leadership. The Mahad Conference of 1927, which is seen by many Mahars as the moment of their mass awakening, was called by Ambedkar after ten years of work through conferences, newspapers and parliamentary action. The Conversion speech of 1935 announced Ambedkar's rejection of Hinduism and an end to Mahar efforts to force entrance into the institutions of Hinduism, although conversion to another religion was set aside for twenty years in favor of intense political, educational, and social activity. At the time of the third of Ambedkar's documents, the Buddhist conversion speech of 1956, such unity had been achieved that 75% of the Mahars and a number of smaller groups outside Maharashtra followed Ambedkar into Buddhism, resulting in three million new Buddhists.

The final documents are current and consist of literature, the poetry and short stories of the *Dalit* school. This is the writing of the now-educated, highly politicized, still radical Mahar-Buddhist left; it constitutes both a new level of Mahar achievement and a restatement of their basic aims.

From the very beginning of the Mahar movement, its leaders seem to have searched for legitimacy for a change in social position in five ways which could be classified as religious, or, more broadly, traditional:

1. Brahmanical approval of new status and function. In the Maharashtrian context, Brahman must be seen as elite, as cultural and social arbiter, as well as ritual specialist.
2. Societal acknowledgement of a right to a place in religious activities on a level with clean castes.
3. Recognition of religious knowledge and purity of life.
4. Scriptural sanctification.
5. Justification by mythic history.

In examining the six documents, I have added the briefest of notes on the historical context of the material and have stressed the ways in which the document illumined the quest for legitimacy in one or another of these five ways.

The Walangkar Petition

Toward the end of the 19th century, recruitment of Untouchables from Maharashtra (Bombay Presidency) into the British army was stopped in favor of a "martial race" (chiefly from the Northwest) pattern of recruitment. For Mahars, who had been employed in British forces for a hundred years, this blocked one of their chief paths of advancement. A retired Mahar Havaldar, Gopalnak Viththalnak Walangkar, known as Gopal Baba, prepared a long petition for re-entry into the army and circulated it among the Untouchable pensioners. They were not ready for such unified action, however, and the petition was never signed and sent to the British Government. A handwritten copy which is bound together with a long poem by Pandit Kondiram, evidently a Mahar religious figure, is in the Khairmode Collection of Ambedkar material in the library of the University of Bombay. (Ambedkar was a distant relative of Walangkar's and from the same Mahar army family background.) Newspapers of the 1890's period confirm the authenticity of the document and report similar sentiments from Walangkar's public speeches.

Walangkar's main plea for the re-admission into the army of Mahar, Cambhar, and Mang castes (all Marathi-speaking Untouchables) was on the basis of the proven worth of the "anarya" (non-Aryans) as military men. His rhetoric, however, also suggests an interesting pattern of legitimizing devices, and the accompanying poem further develops the Mahar position. Walangkar deals with the five legitimizing points listed above in the following ways:

1. *Brahmanical approval.* Although there was high caste criticism of the treatment of Untouchables at this time and even the possibility that a sympathetic Brahman helped Walangkar write his petition (Shinde, 1958: 214), Walangkar's main effort is to question the origin of the high castes, and hence their right to discriminate, rather than to note the approval of the reformers among them. His sweeping judgments reflect a view of India's history as one of great mobility and change: Why should the opinion of the high castes count for so much, asks Walangkar, when the high caste people of the South were originally "Australian-semitic non-Aryan and African Negroes", when the Chitpavans were "Barbary Jews" shipwrecked on the coast who married low caste women and became Brahmans when they became rulers, when the Marathas themselves came to India as Turks? God has sent the British to rule, Walangkar claims, as punishment for these peoples' persecution of the Untouchable. In the tough language of 19th century Maharashtrian reformers, Walangkar by-passes the need for Brahmanical approval by disparaging Brahmans, a position possibly only so long as the British controlled the opportunities wanted.

2. *Rights in religious activities.* Walangkar does not concern himself with this. A newspaper report of another of his public protests (*Iṇdu Prakāsh*, Bombay, May 5, 1890) notes his protest that Untouchables were not allowed to stay in *dharmsalas* (pilgrims' guest houses), but there seems to be no protest of the disbarment of Untouchables from temples and religious processions at this time.

3. *Recognition of religious knowledge and purity of life.* Walangkar notes that even if a group stops eating beef for generations, they are still Untouchables. Sanskritization (Srinivas, 1966) evidently brought no social reward. The poem attached to Walangkar's petition indicates why Walangkar did not belabor this point. In bitter, reproachful tones it notes the social consequences of the deprivation of the Untouchables: lice in women's hair, children playing in rubbish and dancing in *tamasha* (folk drama), men eating carrion, ignorance, humble faces, knowledge only of the demon gods, immoral *gosavis* (holy men). No claim to higher status on the basis of religious knowledge and purity of life among the masses could be made at this time. Internal reform must come first.

4. *Scriptural sanctification.* Walangkar asked the Brahmans, his petition states, five years before to prove the lowness of the Untouchable by religious scripture and to show how by religious remedies this lowness could be removed, but "none of the caste-proud of their priests up to now have proved our lowness". The poem of Pandit Kondiram is more radical. It ends starkly: "Burn these Brahmanical scriptures".

5. *Mythic history*. Walangkar presents two contradictory myths in casual form to underwrite his plea for re-entrance into the army. The name of the group in whose name the petition was written is, in English, the Non-Aryan Group for the Removal of Wrongs. The position that Untouchables were the pre-Aryan peoples of India was accepted by movements in the South (*Adi-Dravida*, the first Dravidians) and in the North (*Ad-Dharm*, first religion). Such a concept legitimizes social protest by assuming that Aryan conquest, not inherent polluting qualities, reduced the Untouchable to low status. However, in Maharashtra, this mythic history rationale was little used. Walangkar himself counters his own claim by asserting that the Mahars were former Kshatriya, demoted during the Great Famine for eating forbidden food. A consistently satisfying mythic history was not developed in the Mahar movement until Ambedkar's Buddhist conversion speech of 1956, but the *need* for such a mythic history is apparent at all levels of the Mahar movement.

The Walangkar petition and Pandit Kondiram's accompanying poem cannot be read as evidence of mass Mahar thought. Both were obviously far more radical statements than the majority of Mahars were prepared to make publicly. However, one can draw some general conclusions about the movement from these early protests.

First, Mahar leadership was more concerned about *function* than about ritual status. The right to have an opportunity to leave the traditional village Mahar duties of watchman, scavanger, message-bearer, etc. demanded that the ruling power provide opportunity to make that move. The right to have a new function, however, did involve legitimizing arguments both to the Government and to fellow Hindus. In the Walangkar petition, we see the Mahar avoiding a claim based on ritual purity to stress the view that high status groups have been low themselves in the past, that change has taken place in many periods of India's past, that the Mahar has just as much a right to change function as have high caste peoples. What is needed is good performance of that function and some sort of legitimizing mythic history to explain present low status and hence allow change!

Later documents are more concerned with ritual status as the mass of Mahars reaches toward the life styles and values of the clean castes. This initial view of change in function as basic remains constant, however. It was the Mahar who had left the village function of, in British legal terms, "inferior village servant", who began the Mahar movement. As the movement progressed, not only did more Mahars enter non-traditional occupations (the mills, dock-work, construction, the railroad), but also those remaining in the village were urged to drop that aspect of their village function which was most polluting – the eating of the carrion beef which it was their duty to drag from the village. The Mahar traditional occupation could not modernize, although it could be stripped of polluting elements. It was up to the "new" Mahar, the Mahar who had left the village, to legitimize his new function, and then to try to extend that legitimacy and its consequent higher status image to his brethren still in the village.

Shivram Janba Kamble's Petition of 1910

The position of Kamble as butler in the Masonic Hall in Poona illustrates still another new Mahar occupation – that of servant of the British. This kind of service allowed the Mahar to learn English as well as to secure economic independence from village work, and, low as such service seems now, produced a number of Mahar innovators in the past. Kamble's group were those who had become urbanized and worked at semi-skilled labor, as well as a few old retired soldiers of Walangkar's breed. His petition, although it is also a plea for re-admittance into the army and opportunities for service in the lower reaches of Government administration, is far more sophisticated than Walangkar's. It was sent to the Earl of Crewe, Secretary of State for India, London, from the Conference of the Deccan Mahars and may have helped, along with wartime necessity, in the creation of a Mahar labor force as an adjunct to the army during World War I. Looking at the Kamble petition through the same five foci as we did Walangkar's petition indicates that the basic matter of *function* still predominates (Navalkar 1930).

1. *Brahmanical approval.* Kamble notes the anti-untouchability stance of several Brahman reform-minded political leaders. Here the elite status rather than the ritual status of the Brahman is important, but it must be remembered that in the Maharashtrian context, social elite are Brahman, thus inextricably mixing ritual and social status. Kamble also rests his case on the fact that the British parliament now contains groups who, "only a quarter of a century ago, were regarded as but Mahars and Paryas by the more educated and affluent classes of their nation", thus extending the concept of radical change in history from the Indian to the European milieu.

2. *Right to religious activities.* Since Kamble's petition is directed very consciously to the British, this element does not enter into the document. Kamble's own activities, however, included a sustained, organized attempt in 1929 to enter the Parvati Temple in Poona. This *satyagraha* failed completely in the face of obdurance and violence, but Kamble's efforts to force entrance of Untouchables into tea shops in Poona indicated that an attack on this aspect of ritual pollution in the urban area could be successful.

3.4.5. *Purity of life, scriptural sanctification, mythic history.* Kamble's position on these matters cannot be gleaned from the petition. A suggestion that Kamble attempted to use mythic history is in the title of a newspaper that he founded in 1909, *Somwaṇshiya Mitra* (Friend of the Somwanshi). Somwanshi is a sub-caste division among the Mahars; it also is a major mythological division of Hindus into "the race of the moon" in contrast to "the race of the sun". Kamble used the word Mahar in calling caste conferences as early as 1903 and was far more caste-based in his activities than either Walangkar before him or Ambedkar after him. It seems to me that in his use of *Somwaṇshiya* he is linking the Mahars to a mythic past, important chiefly to Rajputs, and hence suggesting a Kshatriya linkage. Kamble worked with a retired Mahar army man in his various campaigns in Poona and he often held meetings at the foot of the Koregaon monument, a pillar erected to commemorate the war dead during the British defeat of the Peshwa in 1818 which lists many Mahar names. Kamble's stress on the militant Mahar past indicates a basic Kshatriya mythic history.

The Mahad Conferences of 1927

B. A. Ambedkar appeared publicly on the Bombay scene in 1918, when he testified at length to the Southborough Commission on the necessary franchise for the new Montagu-Chelmsford reform measures elections. This testimony, however, was mid-point in his advanced education. After graduating from Elphinstone College, he had studied at Columbia University with the financial aid of the reform-minded Gaikwad of Baroda, a non-Brahman prince, and he went on to England to do a D.D.S. from the London School of Economics and to pass the Bar. Returning in the early 1920's, he used the same methods as had Kamble, conferences and newspapers, to build group unity, served as a legislator (as a nominated Untouchable representative) in the Bombay Assembly, and began to push at a much greater pace the demands for opportunities for employment in British administration, the schools and the police. The Mahad conference of 1927 was one of many he called, but its drawing power and its actions created the numbers and the news which made it a landmark (Keer, 1962: 68–79, 89–93, 97–108; Zelliot, 1969: 100–107).

The Kolaba District Depressed Classes conference (note that the name Mahar is not used) met at Mahad, a small town south of Bombay. The site was chosen on the basis of an invitation by the caste Hindu reformer who headed the Municipality and who was a friend of Ambedkar's. The speeches and resolutions of the first conference were similar to those of other conferences. However, at the conclusion of the meeting, several thousand conferees marched to a pond in the high caste area of Mahad and the first arrivers drank water, an act which incited town violence and sent Untouchables hastily on their way in fear of their lives. A second conference was called later in the year to protest the ritual cleansing that the Mahad pond had undergone, and at this meeting the Mahar path of radical protest was begun and the ancient law book *Manusmriti*, which condoned untouchability, was burned.

In terms of the five point rubric used previously, the conferences' speeches and actions yield these positions:

1. *Brahmanical/elite approval*. A number of reform-minded Brahmans and high caste non-Brahmans were among Ambedkar's followers. One had invited Ambedkar to use Mahad as a site for a conference; a Brahman proposed the resolution to condemn the *Manusmriti*. Ambedkar did not ask for Brahmanical sanction for change in any ritualized way. He did, however, use all the support he could muster from the elite for his program, maintaining his hold on the reins of power and delegating certain responsibilities to these radical reformers. In addition, Ambedkar himself *appeared* as one of the elite; his speech, dress, presence, educational background and aggressive temperament were all similar

to those of the Maharashtrian Brahman elite. It might be said that by the time of Mahad, Ambedkar himself had assumed elite function also – as teacher, writer, legislator – without, of course, elite or clean-caste ritual status. Using what radical Brahmanical approval was available to him, Ambedkar was beginning to reject any sort of orthodox legitimization. His functioning himself as one of the elite both served as a source of charisma for his own caste and as an enabling device in governmental circles. Ambedkar's "westernization" could also be called "brahmanization" in a broad cultural sense, and this met some ideal goal current among his people, binding them to him.

2. *Right to religious activities.* The Mahad satyagraha was for the right to water, not temple-entry, but it was the fear of the townspeople that the Untouchables would enter the temple that triggered the attack, according to reports. (Keer, 1962: 73.) Temple-entry was in the air and the Mahars were soon to make three organized attempts at Amravati, Poona and Nasik. They had already attempted to enter a Ganapati Procession in Bombay unsuccessfully. Ambedkar was never especially concerned with ritual rights, but it is clear that those who followed him expected that participation in institutionalized Hindu activities would be a consequence of their activities and self-improvement.

3. *Recognition of religious knowledge and purity of life.* Ambedkar did not try to claim that the heterodox religious practices of the Mahars were worthy of respect, nor did he encourage sanskritized religious practices. As a student at Elphinstone College in Bombay he had attempted to study Sanskrit, but objections by the teacher forced him to take Persian as his second language instead. I have no doubt but that had he been able to master Sanskrit, he would have added that source of religious knowledge effectively to his own elite image. Deprived of that basic skill, he devoted his energy to encouraging "purity of life" among his followers. At the Mahad Conference he asked all attenders to take a vow to renounce the eating of carrion and reinforced this attempt to remove the basic root of Mahar pollution by asking caste Hindus to bury their own dead cows and the Government to prohibit by law the eating of carrion! He also told his listeners to "improve the general tone of our demeanour, *re-tone our pronunciations* and revitalise our thoughts." (Keer, 1962: 70) (italics mine). Women in a special meeting were asked to dress like caste Hindu women, to send their children to school, not to feed their husbands if they were drunkards. Internal attempts at reform, now much stressed by the Mahar movement, fit very well into M.N. Srinivas' rubric of Sanskritization (Srinivas, 1966), but note here that the emphasis is on elements which are social rather than ritualistic.

4. *Scriptural sanctification.* The high point of the second Mahar Conference of 1927 was the ceremonial burning of the *Manusmriti*, a gesture re-called with shock by caste Hindus even today. Within a few years, Mahatma Gandhi was to challenge anyone to find justification for Untouchability in the scriptures, but the Mahars had already asked the question, had found evidence of scriptural legitimization of their untouchability, and rejected it.

5. *Justification by mythic history*. Ambedkar used neither the pre-Aryan nor the former-Kshatriya myths. Possibly he felt that a pre-Aryan claim would set the Mahars aside as a separate race, and he had seen permanent racial divisions in America during his student years. As for claiming Kshatriya status, the clean-caste Maratha community had fought that battle for years with a much more viable argument of past kings and Rajput linkages. During his Mahad speech, Ambedkar hinted at a time when "we, who are condemned as Untouchables, were much advanced, much ahead in education compared with communities other than the advanced classes. This part of the country was then pulsating with the action and authority of our people" (Keer, 1962: 69–70). His reference is not clear but could be his own reading of the early army days of the British period. The need for a mythic past, however, is clear, and when Ambedkar had developed a view of the Mahar past which would both explain the caste's low position and justify its current struggle for empowerment, it became a vital part of his message.

The Conversion Speech of 1935

By the mid-thirties, the Mahars had been involved in six years of futile temple-entry struggle; they had also been involved in agitation for political rights which had won them reserved places in the legislature which would insure representation even beyond their numbers. It seems to me that the conversion speech can be seen in two lights: one is the genuine anguish which Ambedkar felt as a Hindu who polluted other Hindus; the other is the glow of political success and the hope that the threat of conversion, which would cut down the numbers of Hindus in the numbers game of separate electorates vis-a-vis Muslims, would act as a catalyst to force Hindus to open up in the religious field from political motives. The mood of the speech is best expressed by a short quotation:

> Because we have the misfortune of calling ourselves Hindu, we are treated thus. If we were members of another Faith, none would dare treat us so. Choose any religion which gives you equality of status and treatment. We shall repair our mistake now. I had the misfortune of being born with the stigma of an Untouchable. However, it is not my fault; but I will not die a Hindu, for this is in my power. (*The Depressed Classes*, 1935: 41)

To capture some of the power of Ambedkar's imagery and oratory, I have placed the concluding passages of his speech at a Mahar Conference in 1936, at which the conversion idea was accepted by the caste, as an appendix to this paper. The analysis of this speech and the first conversion announcement in the previous year involves only one of my five points, that of the need for an acknowledgement of religious rights. It is this element of legitimation that Ambedkar is trying to force. The religious rights he saw as necessary to underwrite the Mahar claim to equality must be gleaned not only from these speeches but also from his reaction to the responses which followed.

Although individuals among the Mahar community protested, no Mahar group rejected the idea of conversion. The *Manusmriti* was burned again, this time near Nasik, the site of a five-year temple entry satyagraha. Groups from outside Maharashtra, chiefly in the North and in the Kerala area, picked up the conversion refrain, but Ambedkar did not use this response to organize a massive movement. Caste Hindus also responded. Pandit Madan Mohan Malaviya offered to fund a special ritual "with which all disabilities would go except dinner and marriage" (*The Depressed Classes*, 1935: 37–58). Dr. Kurtakoti, the Sankaracharya of Karwar Math, offered to found a new sect with equal status to other sections of Hinduism (Sharma, 1957: 89). To these overtures, Ambedkar answered with a clear view of what he meant by religious equality: K. K. Sakat, an Untouchable who was an exemplary Hindu, should be elevated to the position of Sankaracharya for a year and so acknowledged by Chitpavan Brahmans (Keer, 1962: 40); Hinduism should be changed from a "religion of rules" to a "religion of principles", and the necessary changes would involve: (1) one standard book of Hindu religion, (2) no hereditary priesthood, but an examination system open to all, (3) state permits required for priests, (4) a limit by law on the numbers of priests, (5) state supervision of the priest's morals, beliefs and worship (Ambedkar, 1945: 74–5). No Hindu, however reform-minded, indeed no realist, could accept these dicta. Hinduism would have to entirely change its character. But Ambedkar's point is that the Mahar here himself claims the right to earn Brahmanhood.

Ambedkar dallied with the Muslims, Christians, Sikhs, Buddhists and Arya Samajists who were interested, for one reason or another, in the possibility of a Mahar conversion to their numbers. He seemed to lean toward Sikhism, and then dropped the whole matter when it became clear he could not carry the new political privileges of the Untouchables into a new religion. The Mahars, however, never returned to a group movement for Hindu religious rights.

The Buddhist Conversion of 1956

Twenty years after the Mahar conference on conversion, Ambedkar was at last ready to announce a new religion. An old man, sick with diabetes and with less than two months to live, he took *diksha* (conversion) from the hands of the oldest Buddhist monk in India under the hot October sun in Nagpur. The following day he converted the half-million of his followers who had come at his call to convert. Ambedkar had been interested in Buddhism since the early 1930's; by 1956 Buddhism had become not only an intellectual passion but a more viable new religious home for those who had not found Hindu sanction for their new role and function. In Buddhism, Ambedkar had found an Indian, not a foreign, religion which could legitimize the claims of the Mahar. The nature of the Buddhism which he initiated may be seen in his conversion speech (Ambedkar 1956); in *The Buddha and His Dhamma* (1957), Ambedkar's rationalized life of the Buddha and explanation of his teachings;

in the twenty-two "Buddhist Oaths" which constituted part of the conversion ritual (see Appendix II); and in the small number of practices Ambedkar was able to develop before his death.

Opting out of Hinduism might seem to obviate the need to legitimize through the five ways I have used to analyze all other documents. Looking at the conversion through these lens, however, does show that the acceptance of Buddhism in some ways tracks closely with previous Mahar efforts.

1. *Brahmanical or elite approval.* By choosing Buddhism, Ambedkar lept over the necessity of eliciting approval. Buddhism itself was egalitarian, and by 1956 Buddhism as a religion was respected although not much practiced in India. The symbols of independent India, the wheel on the flag and the lion pillar, were Buddhist or from Buddhist times. Two important neighbors, Burma and Ceylon, which Ambedkar had visited to inspect living Buddhism, were Buddhist countries. Several important Buddhist scholars, chief among them Dharmanand Kosambi, a Maharashtrian, had appeared in India and a few Indian intellectuals (Rahul Sankrutyayana, Anand Kausalyayan, Kashyap) had become Buddhists out of conviction. Ambedkar stressed the respect in which Buddhism is held in the world in his conversion speech: "Even today, 2500 years afterwards, all the world respects the principles of Buddhism." "Only one name is proclaimed throughout the world, and that name is Buddha."

2. *Religious rights.* Ambedkar made it clear that the Buddha's message was equality. "In the Buddhist religion, 75% of the Bhikkhus were Brahman; 25% were Shudra and others." Ambedkar set in motion no way to develop a Sangha; he actually only began the institutionalization of the conversion. It is as if he made a gift of Buddhism to those who had followed him along the educational and political paths he opened, wiping away the stigma of religious inequality by presenting a way to say with inner certainty, "I am equal; I do not pollute." The Buddhist's Oaths which are reproduced in the Appendix illustrate the way in which Ambedkar combined the rejection of specific Hindu beliefs with an acceptance of Buddhism. The rather crude negative oaths seem to have been essential to inculcate the sense of psychological freedom from pollution that the Mahar had never been able to gain within the confines of Hinduism.

3. *Recognition of religious knowledge and purity of life.* Throughout his conversion speech, Ambedkar told homey little stories which reinforced all the long years of striving to purify Mahar practices. A Brahman had asked him, "Why do you throw away 500 rupees profit every year from hide, hoof and meat when you are so poor?" and Ambedkar had told him, "You have many dependents. Why don't you remove the dead cattle and get the profit? I myself will give you 500 rupees on top of that." He used another homily to re-stress the need to maintain the dignity of women: In the locality of prostitutes in Bombay, the women rise in the morning and say, "Suleman, bring bread and a plate of minced meat." The Depressed Class sisters do not even get ordinary chutney-bhakri. However, Ambedkar said, they live with dignity; they live piously. The point is clear; the Mahar, now Buddhist, life is to be pure by

both Hindu and elite standards. The Buddhist newly converted, said Ambedkar, must bring honor to Buddhism, whether he is an educated or an illiterate man.

Ambedkar's conversion speech simplifies Buddhism. It is in no way a scholarly analysis of the religious knowledge Mahars would then be expected to exhibit. It must be understood, however, that education had been a major tenet of the movement from its earliest days. In his speech Ambedkar assumes that the Mahar will value education; he refers often to his own school days and his own learning. He states that it is his duty to lead his people "to a stage of full knowledge" and that he is writing a book to teach them. The speech of 1956 stresses behavior. For the more sophisticated audience of the students in the colleges he had established, Ambedkar had already instituted Pali departments and it is clear that he expected those who became highly educated to master the source of religious knowledge. At this time the emphasis is still on gaining religious knowledge and establishing purity of life, not on securing acknowledgement of those accomplishments.

4. *Scriptural sanctification.* Obviously the scriptural sanctification required here is in Buddhism. In his speech, Ambedkar tells of an argument with Mahatma Gandhi over the *chaturvarna* (four-fold caste hierarchy) in which he asked, "Who created the *chaturvarna* and who will end it?" and Gandhi gave no answer. Ambedkar then added that Marxism is not enough to remove suffering. No "scripture" sufficed for Ambedkar save the Buddha's teaching of equality.

5. *Justification by mythic history.* Ambedkar had already developed his theory that Untouchables had been Buddhist peoples, cast aside as India became re-Hinduized, in his book *The Untouchables: Who were they? and why they became Untouchables* (1948). In his speech at the time of conversion he stated that during the Aryan harrassment of the Nag people, Agasti Muni helped one Nag man to escape. "We spring from that man." The Nag people then met Gautam Buddha and "spread the teaching of Bhagwan Buddha all over India." The city of Nagpur was chosen for the conversion because it was the city of Nags. In his speech, Ambedkar does not fully develop his theory or belabor this point. In the Mahar mind, however, the idea was quickly assimilated. The Mahar as former Buddhist, persecuted because he had clung to his Buddhism, was now returned to his old faith. Ambedkar had given a fully satisfactory explanation of low status and a justification for a claim to a respected place in Indian society.

The analysis ought to end here with a note comparing Walangkar's original statement of Mahar aims and Ambedkar's concluding message for his people. The Mahar, now Buddhist, movement is still dynamic, however. Buddhism has not proved to be a panacea. *Bauddh,* in Marathi, means Mahar. As a Buddhist, he has a sense of psychological freedom, a satisfying mythic history, and full rights within a respected world religion. But although many of the old practices of untouchability are gone, the Buddhist still suffers from poverty, from some discrimination, and from the violence which erupts when he oversteps his place in the village. In the last years another new phase to the movement has developed, that of *Dalit* politics and *Dalit* literature. *Dalit* means broken, "reduced to pieces", oppressed or low. It avoids the ritual pollution connotations of the word Untouchable but unmistakably refers to that group.

Dalit Panthers, Dalit Literature

Dalit literature, that is, writing which is considered genuine literature rather than folk-protest poetry and "movement" literature, may be said to have begun in the late 1950's with the short stories of Shankarrao Kharat, who wrote movingly and sorrowfully of his childhood as a village Mahar (Miller & Kale, 1972: 317–359). A lawyer and now Vice-Chancellor of Marathwada University, Kharat produced books within the movement: an edition of the letters of Ambedkar, the story of the Buddhist conversion. He also produced short stories which had to be considered as genuine evidence of creativity in the strong Marathi literary tradition. Since that time, a fairly steady flow of short stories and poetry and a series of Buddhist Literary Conferences have resulted in what must be called a significant new school of Marathi writing, that of Dalit Literature. Acknowledgement of the worth of this writing is evidenced in the November 25, 1973 supplement of the *Times Weekly*. Dileep Padgaonkar's introduction to this special issue on Dalit Literature states:

> Its immense merit is to have effectively rebelled, in life as in letters, against the middle-class Hindus who have monopolised cultural expression.

Accompanying the tough, realistic, unorthodox literature, a new socio-political movement has surfaced; it was organized in 1972 as the Dalit Panthers. The first of the new Mahar/Buddhist writers, Shankarrao Kharat, is not part of this movement, but most of the recently acknowledged young writers are. The Dalit Panthers reject the compromising ways the political party Ambedkar had established came to adopt. Their methods (calling for a boycott of an election, marching on a village where a caste Hindu who raped a Buddhist girl was not brought to justice) are outside normal politics. The Panthers, however, do not reject Ambedkar or Buddhism, and although their loyalty to his teaching, if not his organizations, is mixed with a vague Marxism, they feel themselves the new thrust of his movement.

The rhetoric of the Dalit Panthers returns to the days of Ambedkar's exhortation of his followers to be defiantly strong, even to the time of Walangkar's disparagement of Brahmans, of belief in the possibility of radical change. Ambedkar once told his people, "Become the ruling community," a slogan I have seen painted on the walls of a tiny library built in the 1930's in a Mahar city slum. A pamphlet of the Dalit Panthers states, "We do not want a little place in the Brahman Alley. We want the rule of the whole land." The poetry returns to the tough, bitter tone of the poem of Pandit Kondiram which lay, unpublished, in the personal library of Ambedkar along with the Walangkar petition of 1894. One example is Arun Kamble's *The Life We Live*, translated by Gauri Deshpande in the *Times Weekly Supplement*, November 25, 1973:

If you were to live the life we live
(then out of you would poems arise).
We: kicked and spat at for
  our piece of bread
You: fetch fulfilment and
  name of the Lord.
We: down-gutter degraders
  of our heritage
You: its sole repository
  descendants of the sage.
We: never have a paisa to scratch our arse
You: the golden cup of offerings in your bank.
Your bodies flame in sandalwood.
Ours you shovel under half-turned sand.
Wouldn't the world change, and fast,
If you were forced to live at last
This life that's all we've ever had?

Another poem by Kamble, *Speech*, translated by Gauri Deshpance in the same *Times Weekly* supplement, also contrasts the Mahar – Brahman images:

Bone-chewing granpus
at burning ghat
permanent resident
of my own heart
with weight of tradition
behind his back
yells, "sadding bastard, I tell you,
Stutter with *our* tongue!"
Picking through the vedas
buttering his queue
Brahmin teacher at school
bellows, "speak my pure tongue,
whoreson."
Now, you tell me which
  speech
am I to tongue?

Here is the Mahar defiant, the Buddhist free from the psychological burden of pollution, bitter about both past and present but still proud of being what he is, and proclaiming both bitterness and pride in the Brahman's own tongue: sophisticated literature.

What dimension does the new school of Dalit Literature add to the Mahar movement? What new demands are made and what sorts of legitimation are sought for them? Walangkar's petition to re-enter the army was met in 1942 by the establishment, at Ambedkar's urging, of a Mahar Regiment which still bears that name as a proud unit of the Indian army. Kamble's urging that the Mahar be accepted into the lower ranks of administration and police was met by the legal provision that a percentage of all governmental positions be reserved for the Scheduled Castes. Ambedkar's secular demands have been met, at least in theory, by the constitutional outlawing of any act of discrimination against Untouchables; his religious demands were obviated by the Buddhist conversion, and for those who did not convert there has been a general opening of Hindu temples, at least in urban areas. What still burns is the general poverty level of most Scheduled Castes; sporadic but often intense enforcement of traditional subservience, at times violent, in the rural areas; subtle indications of inferiority in the cities – and something that can only be described as a lack of recognition of *manuski*, the full humanity of the Untouchable.

Looking at the Mahar story, it seems as if religious legitimation of their upward movement has been unimportant; the great changes wrought have come by secular governmental fiat or economic opportunity. But Hinduism is more than a religion, and its hierarchy of social groupings has been correlate with not only status but *function*. When one studies the Mahar movement as a group change in function, it becomes clear a simple view of education and urbanization equaling modernization is not good enough. One must look at the nature of the function the Buddhist leadership now performs not only in terms of occupation but in terms of the traditional caste structure of Maharashtra. And one must consider this caste structure in order to understand why all Ambedkar's efforts, and those following him, failed to build a class movement, an organization of the Depressed Classes and the exploited in general, and has remained limited to the Mahars (and to smaller groups of other castes in areas outside Maharashtra).

Given this view, one asks: what new function could a Mahar Untouchable have whose traditional role was to serve the village as remover of pollution, low-status functionary in the bureaucratic system, entertainer in folk-music and folk-drama, and of course agricultural labor? When he becomes highly educated, urbanized, politicized, he does not yearn for the land (which he has never owned in viable quantities); he has no artisan skill; he has no instinct for trade (no Marathi-speaking caste of any size has entered this field); he can only fill the traditional social role of the Maharashtrian Brahman: the administrative echelons and the cultural establishment. Entering government service has been encouraged by special-privilege acts of the Government of India; filling a cultural role has been on the Mahar's own initiative.

What seems to be happening now is that the Mahar as "Brahman" is seeking and winning societal approval for a cultural *function*: the creation of literature, which is a meaningful high status value in Maharashtrian society. And the approval must come from the cultural establishment, which is still largely Brahman. In the words of Padgaonkar quoted earlier, the Dalit writer has "effectively rebelled, in life as in letters, against the middle-class Hindus who have monopolished cultural expression." The village enemy may well be the Maratha, the caste that dominates the land agriculturally and politically. The ideological enemy, the "mirror-image" in Arun Kamble's poems, and in many others, is still the Brahman. And yet, the very poets who translated the Dalit literature in the Special Issue of the *Times Weekly* are Brahman!

But all the years of effort have still left the bulk of the Mahars, now Buddhists, in the village. What is especially interesting throughout the Mahar movement is that its leadership, however elite they themselves become, have sought to extend the legitimacy won in the exercise of their new functions to those still caught in the lower reaches of society. This cohesiveness is what has made the Mahar struggle in Maharashtra a movement of a different quality than other Untouchable efforts toward higher social status. The tie of the Dalit poets with the Dalit Panthers is not coincidence. The new Mahar, the Buddhist, the poet, with his new "tongue" proclaims the human worth of all his fellows.

APPENDIX

Ambedkar's 1936 Conversion Speech

(Note: the excerpt below is the end of the speech, arranged as free verse to stress its rhythmic qualities.)

Religion is for man; man is not for religion.

If you want to gain self-respect*, change your religion.
If you want to create a cooperating society,
    change your religion.
If you want power, change your religion.
If you want equality, change your religion.
If you want independence, change your religion.
If you want to make the world in which you live happy,
    change your religion.

Why should you remain in a religion that does not
    value your manhood?*
Why should you remain in a religion that does not
    let you enter its temples?
Why should you remain in a religion that does not
    give you water to drink?
Why should you remain in a religion that does not
    let you become educated?
Why should you remain in a religion that bars
    you from good jobs?
Why should you remain in a religion that dishonors you
    at every step?

That religion which forbids humanitarian behavior*
between man and man is not religion
but a reckless penalty.
That religion which regards the recognition of man's self respect*
as sin is not a religion
but a sickness.
That religion which allows one to touch a foul animal
but not a man
is not a religion
but a madness.
That religion which says that one class may not gain knowledge,
may not acquire wealth,
may not take up arms,
is not a religion
but a mockery of man's life.
That religion which teaches that the unlearned should remain unlearned,
that the poor should remain poor,
is not a religion
but a punishment.

Do not say: men who treat animals with more respect than humans
and who respect all Brahmans as Gods
are religious.
Do not say: men who feed ants with sugar
and let men go without water
are religious.
Do not say: men who embrace another religion
and push their own far from them
hate society.

(Ambedkar: 1936)

Buddhist's Oaths

1. I will not regard Brahma, Vishnu and Mahesh as Gods
nor will I worship them.
2. I will not regard Rama and Krishna as Gods
nor will I worship them.
3. I will not accept Hindu Deities like Gauri, Ganapati, etc.
nor will I worship them.
4. I do not believe that God has taken birth or incarnation
in any form.

* The Marathi word *manuski*, a key word in the Mahar movement literature, is used four times in this segment of Ambedkar's address. It may be variously translated as humanitarian attitude, self-respect, manhood, humanity. Its literal meaning is "of man."

5. I do not believe that Lord Buddha was the Incarnation of Vishnu. I believe this propaganda as mischievous and false.
6. I will never perform any Sharaaddha* nor will I offer any Pinda**
7. I will never act against the tenets of Buddhism.
8. I will never get any SAMSKAAR performed by Brahmins.
9. I believe in the principle that all are equal.
10. I will try to establish equality.
11. I will follow the Eight Fold Path of Lord Buddha.
12. I will follow all the ten Paramitas of The Dhamma.
13. I will have compassion on all living beings and will try to look after them.
14. I will not lie.
15. I will not commit theft.
16. I will not indulge in lust or sexual Transgression.
17. I will not take any liquor or drink that causes intoxication.
18. I will try to mould my life in accordance with the Buddhist preachings, based on Enlightenment, Precept and Compassion.
19. I embrace today the Bauddha Dhamma discarding the Hindu Religion which is detrimental to the emancipation of human beings and which believes in inequality and regards human beings other than the Brahmins as low born.
20. This is my firm belief that the Bauddha Dhamma is the best religion.
21. I believe that today I am taking New-birth.
22. I solemnly take oath that from today onwards I will act according to the Bauddha DHAMMA.

Sabbe Satta Suknee Hontu

Note: this English version of the 22 oaths has been taken, without correction, from a pamphlet published by the Buddhist Society of India, New Delhi, no date.

REFERENCES

AMBEDKAR, Bhimrao Ramji
1936 *Mukti Kon Pathe?* (*What Path Freedom?*). Bombay: Bharat Bhushan Printing Press.
1945 *Annihilation of Caste with a Reply to Mahatma Gandhi.* 3rd ed. Amritsar: Ambedkar School of Thought. (1st published 1936).
1948 *The Untouchables. Who were they and why they became Untouchables.* New Delhi: Amrit Book Co.
1956 "Report of Dr. Babasaheb Ambedkar's Speech in Nagpur", in *Prabuddh Bhārat* (27 October). Translated by Rekha Damle and Eleanor Zelliot from the Marathi.
1957 *The Buddha and His Dhamma.* Bombay: Siddharth College.
The Depressed Classes
1935 "Bombay Depressed Classes Decision", in *The Depressed Classes: a Chronological Documentation.* Part I: Ranchi: Rev. Fr. J. Jans S.J., Catholic Press. Part II–Part VII: Kurseong: St. Mary's College. Published in one volume, 1935–1937.

* A ceremony after the death of the man in Hinduism.
** Handful rice offered in the name of the deceased.

KEER, Dhananjay
1962 *Dr. Ambedkar, Life and Mission*. 2nd ed. Bombay: Popular Prakashan.
MILLER, Robert J. and Pramod KALE
1972 "The Burden on the Head is Always There", pp. 317–359, in J. Michael Mahar (ed.), *The Untouchables in Contemporary India*. Tucson: University of Arizona.
NAVALKAR, H. N.
1930 (petition) "To The Right Honourable The Earl of Crewe", pp. 142–157, in *The Life of Shivram Janba Kamble and Brief History of the Poona Parvati Satyagraha*. Poona: S. J. Kamble.
SHARMA, Nalin Vilochan
ca. 1957 "A Biography (of Jagjivan Ram)", in Vishwanath Verma and Gyaneshwar Prasad (eds.), *The Working Man*. Patna: Jagjivan Ram Abhinandan Granth Committee.
SHINDE, Viththal Ramji
1958 *Mājhyā Aṭhvaṇi va Anubhav (My Memories and Experiences)*. Poona: R. B. Andre.
SRINIVAS, M. N.
1966 "Sanskritization", pp. 1–45, in *Social Change in Modern India*. Berkeley: University of California.
Times Weekly Supplement
1973 "Special Issue on Dalit Literature" (November 25). Bombay.
WALANGKAR, Gopalnak Viththalnak
1894 "To His Excellency the Commander in Chief of Bombay Presidency, at Poona, from the Anarya Doshpariharakham at Dapoli." *Ms* with accompanying *pad* by Pandit Kondiram in the Khairmode Collection of the University of Bombay Library. Translated by D. R. Maheshkar.
ZELLIOT, Eleanor
1966 "Buddhism and Politics in Maharashtra", pp. 191–212, in Donald E. Smith (ed.), *South Asian Politics and Religion*. Princeton: Princeton University.
1969 *Dr. Ambedkar and the Mahar Movement*. Unpublished Ph. D. dissertation. University of Pennsylvania.
1970a "Learning the Use of Political Means: the Mahars of Maharashtra", pp. 29–69, in Rajni Kothari (ed.), *Caste in Indian Politics*. New Delhi: Allied Publishers.
1970b "The 19th Century Background of the Mahar and Non-Brahman Movements in Maharashtra", pp. 397–415, in *The Indian Economic and Social History Review*, VII: 3 (September 1970).
1972 "Gandhi and Ambedkar: A Study in Leadership", pp. 69–95, in J. Michael Mahar (ed.), *The Untouchables in Contemporary India*. Tucson: University of Arizona.

The Legitimation of Religious Policy in Tamil Nādu

*A Study of the 1970 Archaka Legislation**

FRANKLIN A. PRESLER

In the early 1970s, the Tamil Nādu government initiated two policies which, had they been fully implemented, would have altered significantly the character of worship in Hindu temples and the position of temple priests. One policy would have opened the priesthood in any temple to qualified persons irrespective of caste and birth. The government at this time was under the control of the Dravida Munnetra Kazhagam (D.M.K.), a political party which, historically, had espoused a distinctly anti-Brahmin ideology. It was widely believed that the policy regarding the priesthood, though articulated in general terms, was in fact intended to end the hegemony of the Brahmin temple priest (*archaka*) in the large, orthodox temples, and to encourage lower castes, particularly *Harijans*, to enter the priesthood in large numbers. Another policy would have changed the language of the *archana pūjā*, a popular form of private worship, from Sanskrit to Tamil. Together, these policies, the former a legislative act and the latter an administrative order, would have affected the daily religious practices of millions of Tamilians. Most immediately affected were Brahmin priests, forced by government order to abandon sacred Sanskrit and to re-learn a ritual in a new language, and with their job tenure no longer secure. Despite the obvious significance of these measures, however, they did not result in significant political protest from the general public. On the contrary, both policies would probably have been implemented without serious political disruption had the Supreme Court of India not intervened. The priests and their sympathizers, having failed to achieve their ends politically, took their case to the legal arena. Here, in separate actions, the Supreme Court removed much of the "teeth" from both measures on narrow constitutional grounds.

The question, then, with which this essay begins is: Why was there so little political opposition to these measures from society generally, and why

* The research on which this paper is based was conducted in Madras in 1973–74 and was made possible by the Social Science Research Council, whose support is gratefully acknowledged.

was the opposition which did exist so unsuccessful politically? In more general terms, the question being asked is: What is the nature of the legitimacy enjoyed by the Indian state in religious matters, such that governments can act in ways which appear to affect fundamentally the character of Hindu worship?

In the length of this essay it is not possible to deal in detail with both the *archaka* legislation and the *archana* order. Therefore, we will concentrate on the *archaka* legislation, the 1970 law which abolished the hereditary priesthood. But the analysis is intended to suggest more general relationships between the state, on the one hand, and social groups and religious institutions, on the other.

The analysis will focus on legitimacy as a political outcome, a process, rather than on symbols and concepts taken in isolation. This approach follows naturally from a case-study, but there are also theoretical reasons for it. Symbols, concepts and normative orientations to politics are certainly important. Focusing on them alone, however, tends to suggest that a society's political values form an interdependent and internally consistent system, stable over time and shared equally and in the same sense by all groups of the polity. Such uniformity may exist in a very general and abstract sense. But it does not seem to be a very useful vantage point from which to approach modern India, where the polity is an amalgam of local, regional and national institutions with diverse historical and cultural origins.

Accordingly, here I shall assume that legitimacy is a more historical and time-bound product. It is a political outcome, structured by formal governmental institutions, and shaped further by conflict among groups and individuals attempting to enhance particular interests and to pursue particular goals. There are two implications of this approach which I should mention briefly.

First, as I have indicated, this approach assumes that the proximate political values in a society do not necessarily form an internally consistent and interdependent system. A plural and complex society has a plurality of political values, with the same problematic relationships among them as have the groups which hold them. As we shall see, this plurality does not preclude the existence of abstract legitimating principles for the whole polity, such as those enshrined in national constitutions or deriving from local and regional histories. But the fact that these abstract principles are held seriously and in their own right by almost everyone does not mean that they are understood in the same sense by everyone. Indeed, it is precisely because of their generality that abstract principles are subject to a variety of interpretations and uses. Part of the process of legitimation can be analyzed as the struggle among contending groups to establish as "correct" their respective interpretations of the general principle shared or at least appealed to by all.

Second, in viewing legitimacy as a political and historical outcome, this approach recognizes that legitimation occurs in contexts of inequality, of unequal power, status and resources. What is in the final analysis legitimate depends in part on who says it is legitimate, and here the weak have less of a say than the strong. Examining the legitimation process, then, requires that we look at political inequalities: at the relative advantages enjoyed by more powerful, superordinate groups and institutions, including governments and bureaucracies, and at the disadvantages faced by less powerful, subordinate groups, those with fewer choices and with less capacity to move in and manipulate the public arena.

This last point structures the way in which the material here is presented and how the argument will proceed. We shall look first at the state and its resources, and at how it interprets the widespread notion that the state must in some way "protect" religious institutions. Next, we shall look at the priests and their organization, the South India Archaka Sangham, in an attempt to understand why the political opposition to the government policies was so weak and ineffectual. Finally, we shall look at the broader political context in which the *archaka* law was initiated. As we shall see, there is a disjunction between the political and legal arenas in respect to legitimation. Policies may be legitimated politically along principles quite different from and in tension with the principles governing judicial decision-making in the courts.

I

I begin with the fact that it was the government which sought to initiate the radical changes in temple worship, not the temple priests (*archakas*) or the general worshipping public.

The *archaka* bill was presented to and passed by the Tamil Nadu legislature in late 1970.[1] In the "Statement of Objects and Reasons" attached to the bill, the D.M.K. government urged that the law be seen as a social reform measure, yet another of the many steps taken in the modern period to reform Indian society. According to the government, in other words, abolishing the hereditary principle of appointment was a fundamentally social, not religious matter. It would bring closer to reality the ideal of a democratic, egalitarian society, since the priesthood would be "open to candidates irrespective of caste, creed or race". Looking further into the future, the "Statement of Objects and Reasons" also envisioned a day when an "ecclesiastical organization" would be set up, although the bill itself contained no provisions in this direction.[2] Presumably established under the state's supervision, such an ecclesiastical

1 See Tamil Nadu Hindu Religious and Charitable Endowments (Amendment) Act, 1970. The bill was introduced in the Tamil Nadu Legislative Assembly on Nov. 30, 1970, and was passed by that body on Dec. 1, 1970. For an account of the debate, see *Hindu*, Dec. 2, 1970. Circulars relating to the language of *archana* were issued from the offices of the Commissioner and Deputy Commissioner, Madras, of Hindu Religious and Charitable Endowments (Administration) Department. Copies of these circulars may be found with the *writ petitions* filed with the Supreme Court of India challenging the orders.

2 Quoted in the judgment of the Supreme Court of India, *Seshammal and Ors. etc., etc., etc. v. State of Tamil Nadu.* (1972) 3 S.C.R., p. 820.

organization, hitherto absent in Hinduism, would provide for all priestly candidates a formalized educational training in religious scriptures and rituals.

Technically, the *archaka* act abolished the hereditary priesthood simply by re-defining the legal classification of temple personnel. The unamended Hindu Religious and Charitable Endowments (Administration) Act, 1959 (hereafter H.R.C.E. Act) had classified *archakas* separately from other temple personnel, recognizing they had special rights to their office. An effect of this special classification was to give *archakas* special privileges in relationship to state authority. Along with the separate appointment procedures resulting from their hereditary status, the H.R.C.E. Act also included provisions whereby, for example, *archakas* (and other hereditary personnel) had special rights of appeal to the Commissioner of Hindu Religious and Charitable Endowments against disciplinary action or dismissal by temple trustees.[3]

The 1970 *archaka* act simply deleted these special provisions. In the amended act, all "office-holders and servants" of the temple, without further distinction, are made subject to the temple trustees in matters of appointment and discipline, with limited right of appeal. The word "hereditary" no longer appears. Indirectly, but effectively, this abolished the hereditary priesthood. The temple *archaka*, who until this time had been legally considered a special sort of person in the temple, was now re-classified and placed within the general category of persons called simply "office-holders and servants". To ensure that there be no doubt about this, the bill's framers added a special explanatory clause: "The expression 'Office-holders or servants' shall include *archakas* and *poojaris*."[4] As we shall see, the mere fact of being re-classified was the issue of over-riding importance to the *archakas*. Though the loss of hereditary rights and privileges would be felt in immediate, material ways, re-classification posed threats of a deeper and far more significant nature.

India's state and national governments profess to follow secular principles. Outsiders sometimes express surprise that any government professing secularism would initiate changes such as the D.M.K.'s *archaka* and *archana* policies, the former regulating the recruitment of central religious functionaries, and the latter altering the language of religious worship. But both these policies are merely dramatic examples of a general pattern which must be appreciated if we are to understand how these policies are legitimated politically. In Tamil Nadu, the state dominates the day-to-day administration of most important temples. Because of this dominance, the state has been responsible for more

3 See Hindu Religious and Charitable Endowments (Administration) Act, 1959, (hereafter, H.R.C.E. Act) Sects. 55, 56. Copies of the H.R.C.E. Act may be found in B. K. Mukherjea, *The Hindu Law of Religious and Charitable Trusts*, 3rd ed. (Calcutta, 1970); and in V. Rajasikhamani, *The Tamil Nadu Hindu Religious and Charitable Endowments Act XXII of 1959*, 2nd ed., (Madras, 1971). The latter volume includes extensive notes and commentary on the act.

4 These sections, in their original and amended versions, are contrasted in (1972) 3 S.C.R., pp. 821–22.

than one initiative profoundly affecting temples' internal affairs. What are the bases of the state's power in this area?

There is, first, the legal base. Since 1925, Hindu temples in South India have been legally under the supervision of a central administrative body, now known as the Hindu Religious and Charitable Endowments Department (H.R.C.E.). Originally consisting of an autonomous Board of Commissioners, the H.R.C.E. since 1951 has been a regular department of the government, headed by a cabinet minister. The jurisdiction of the H.R.C.E. has been gradually expanded over the years since the original legislation in 1925.[5] Today, the department is able to control, directly through its own personnel and indirectly through temple trustees and other functionaries, the financial and administrative affairs of most temples, a control which inevitably touches on matters customarily regarded as religious.

Most temple trustees, for example, are appointed by the H.R.C.E., and are bound by law to obey H.R.C.E. instructions. Moreover, the day-to-day management of a temple is seldom in the hands of priests or traditional religious personnel. Instead, most temples are administered by Executive Officers (E.O.) who are civil servants posted and paid by the H.R.C.E. Through E.O.s and members of its immediate bureaucracy, the H.R.C.E. is able to give close attention to the internal affairs of the temple. Department leverage is enhanced by the legal provision that all temple budgets must be submitted annually to the H.R.C.E. for approval.[6]

The Supreme Court of India has upheld the constitutionality of this legislation which sets this pattern for state-religion relationships. In the early 1950s some provisions of the H.R.C.E. Act, 1951, then in effect, were challenged in the court on the grounds that they interfered with religion and were contrary to the Indian Constitution. Although the Supreme Court did strike down several of the Act's provisions, it affirmed that the basic outlines of the legislation were constitutional, and since then the fundamental legality of the H.R.C.E. has not been seriously questioned.[7]

Legally, then, there exists considerable scope for state initiative in the affairs of temples. But the *archaka* and *archana* policies are more complex than this. Here were public policies which were apparently accepted as legitimate by wide sections of the public, but which were in fact eventually robbed of their force by the Supreme Court on constitutional grounds. To look at the legal aspect alone, then, is not sufficient. The legitimation process operates on

---

5 For a detailed account of the background of the legislation and the early history of the department, see Chandra Y. Mudaliar, *The secular state and religious institutions in India: a study of the administration of Hindu public religious trusts in Madras* (Wiesbaden, 1974).

6 For relevant provisions, see H.R.C.E. Act, Sects. 27, 49, 53, 54 (on trustee appointment and responsibility); Sect. 233 (on Executive Officers); Sects. 86–90 (on audits and annual budgets).

7 A major case in this connection is *Commissioner of Hindu Religious Endowment, Madras v. Lakshmindra Thirtha Swamiar of Sri Shirur Mutt* (1954) S.C.R. 1005. The implications of this and other cases are dealt with in Mukherjea, *op. cit.*, pp. 306–20.

levels other than the legal, and to understand the *archaka* law we must look more closely at the history of the religion-state relationship in South India, at the ideals in terms of which that relationship is articulated, and at the political context in which the 1970 policy was enunciated.

The foundations for the H.R.C.E.'s authority were laid in the 19th century and before. Historians of the 19th century have not yet explored fully the extent to which the British government maintained an active role in religious institutions throughout the period. Although direct supervision as an explicit public policy ended in the 1840s, indirect interference by the government was never entirely terminated. For example, the Revenue Department exercised considerable leverage through its administrative jurisdiction over temple lands held on *inām* tenure. Towards the end of the century, the jurisdiction of the civil courts became increasingly important. Section 539 of the Civil Procedure Code empowered courts to prescribe mandatory "schemes" which would govern how a temple should be managed and how the relationships of temple personnel should be structured.[8]

Throughout the 19th century, British administrators generally pressed for increased government interference. Characteristically, the defence of interference was joined to a theory of the state as a protector. The state, it was argued, had to interfere with temples in order to protect them. Temples were frequently very wealthy, and experience had shown that without state supervision this wealth was exploited for private gain. Temples became enmeshed in political intrigue and conflict, and their property ended up being used for the personal gain of local notables. The religious function of the temple suffered.[9]

Historical arguments were also used to defend the notion of state protection. It was pointed out that South Indian rulers normally had been intimately associated with religious institutions. The larger temples were built and endowed by local rulers. Their successors had felt a responsibility to protect these endowments, adding to them if possible. Indeed, it was noted,

8 See Sect. 539 of Act XIV of 1882. This section corresponds to Sect. 92 of the later Civil Procedure Code (Act V of 1908). For the text, see Sir Ernest John Treveleyan, *Hindu Law as administered in British India* (Calcutta, 1912), pp. 545–46. On the role of governmental supervision after 1843, see my forthcoming dissertation, "State, Religion and Politics in India: A Study in Administrative History and Political Culture in Tamil Nadu" (University of Chicago).

9 British administrators were not the only ones to make this argument. In their report of 1893, the T. Muttusami Aiyer Committee recommended much stronger state intervention:

> We deem it our duty to state that there exists a widespread feeling among the Hindu community that the duty of providing effectual remedies against the crying abuses existing in the administration and management of temples is one which has devolved on the British Government from former Governments, and that religious and charitable endowments, founded and augmented by many generations of wealthy and pious Hindu rajahs and noblemen and dedicated to objects held dear and sacred by every section of Hindus, will gradually deteriorate and eventually be absorbed into private property, unless the further progress of evil is arrested by altering the existing law.

See G.O. 72–74 Legislative, May 26, 1894.

even the Muslims and early British had continued this tradition, donating funds to finance specific rituals and festivals. Finally, this historical argument was buttressed by an analysis of current public opinion. Discontinuing state supervision would be politically dangerous, according to some administrators. The public expected the British government, as the present ruler of South India, to protect the temples actively. If it did not, an important cornerstone of political legitimacy could be undermined, particularly if, as the theory predicted, the temples deteriorated once the government had withdrawn its supervision.[10]

In the post-Independence period, protection remains a central concept in the discussion of the relationship between temple and state. During my research in 1973–74, state protection was mentioned repeatedly by most groups and individuals concerned with temple affairs. As we shall see in a moment, the *archakas* rely on the concept heavily, as do H.R.C.E. and government officials, although in different ways. Also, the interest group most actively concerned with temple matters incorporates the word in its name, the Hindu Temple Protection Committee. In short, in discussions where legal or constitutional issues are not raised explicitly, protection overshadows the concept of secularism as the basic frame of reference.

Historically, then, the concept of protection has expressed a widely shared understanding regarding the relationship of temple and state. But the concept of protection is also very abstract and non-specific, sufficiently vague to admit of diverse interpretation. It prescribes some sort of association between the state and temples, but is not specific regarding the details of that association. Precisely because of this vagueness, the concept has proven to be important politically and ideologically. It has been appealed to – by government, by opposition groups, by *archakas* – in order to justify policies moving in quite different directions. I will now outline the meanings which the state has given to protection in the modern period, and indicate the implications of those meanings concretely, especially as they affected the interests of *archakas*.

Because of the legal, administrative and historical facts we have just discussed, the state has been in a strong position to advance its own interpretation of protection. It has also been able to change this interpretation over time as the overall direction of state policy has changed. The government's relative control of the public definition of protection has been a resource of considerable importance, particularly with regard to justifying new policies.

---

10 In 1840, Governor Elphinstone of Madras strongly argued this point in an attempt to dissuade the London authorities from pursuing the policy of withdrawal:

> It cannot be doubted that if the right of summary interference was abandoned, the property of the Pagodas would be speedily embezzled and alienated. The Government, it is true, would be no losers by this, but the people would look upon such a state of things with deep dissatisfaction, and would justly consider that they were denied that protection which Government is assuredly bound to afford them.

See Minute by the President June 9, 1840, in *Revenue Consultations*, Vol. 497, pp. 2674 ff.

Nineteenth century British administration was shaped by a concern to preserve and stabilize the organization of temples. One reason, as we have seen, was the conviction that this was a traditional responsibility of government in South India. More immediately, local administrators found their work threatened constantly by disputes within temples over management, property, and the relative rights and prerogatives of groups and individuals. Also, temples were classified in Anglo-British law as "trusts", which gave the state authority to ensure that the intentions of the original donors of temples were continued, if possible.[11]

For *archakas* as a whole, there were three especially important results of the government's concern to preserve and stabilize temple organization. First, in many temples, formal recognition was given to the existence of hereditary rights to some temple offices, such as the priest's office. Second, an attempt was made to fix permanently the land rights of religious service *ināmdars*, many of whom were *archakas*. Third, a firm rule evolved in both the courts and bureaucracy that "ancient custom and usage" would be the criteria when disputes emerged over the rights of individuals and groups to temple offices, rights and honors.[12]

State administration at this time was also relatively decentralized. Temples varied immensely in their organization, the nature of their land tenures, and the rights of individuals and groups within them. Under a decentralized system, governmental decisions were shaped significantly by the customs of the locality, as reported by local people, and by the structure of local power, as determined by the government official on the spot. When added to the policies mentioned in the paragraph above, this decentralization gave *archakas* (and other members of the locality) a greater leverage over the direction of administration than they would have later under the H.R.C.E.

In contrast to the 19th century, the H.R.C.E. in the 20th century has stressed the bureaucratic goal of efficient centralization and the modernizing value of social reform. It has also, somewhat more cautiously, tried to further its interpretation of the temple's religious function.

(i) *Efficient centralization.* As is often remarked, centralizing the locus of decision-making means that persons in the localities typically have less influence over the direction and implementation of policies intimately affecting their interests. Another less well-noted result of efficient centralization involves the way in which phenomena are to be classified. Centralized bureaucracy tends to reduce the diversity and multiplicity found in reality into a few basic classifications. This has the virtue of simplicity and may increase efficiency, but it is seldom neutral in human terms. On the contrary, important social and political consequences almost always follow administrative re-classification.

---

11 Useful discussions of this aspect are found in B. K. Mukherjea, *op. cit.*, and in E. J. Treveleyan, *op. cit.*

12 For a discussion of the criteria of "custom and usage," see P. V. Kane, *Hindu Customs and Modern Law* (Bombay, 1950).

Individuals (or groups or institutions) long understood as distinct from one another are suddenly placed within a common rubric. This process alters identities and identifications. It also makes individuals (or social groups or institutions) suddenly subject to new regulations and procedures, some of which may be incompatible with past practices. For some, long accepted rights and immunities are threatened; for others, new rights and advantages are created.

This pattern applies to the H.R.C.E. Since it began work in the 1920s, the department has progressively reduced the number of categories into which it classifies temples and temple functions, and has struggled to create a common structure of management for as many temples as possible. This re-classification has affected the *archakas*. Repeatedly, the H.R.C.E. and other government departments have moved to make as little distinction as possible between priests and other temple functionaries. The 1970 law, under which *archakas* were re-classified and included in the general designation "office-holders and servants", is the most recent of these efforts, and we will deal in the next section with the severe social and psychological threats which this categorization has posed. But the basic link between efficient centralization and re-classification, and the political implications of this link, are nicely illustrated by an earlier instance involving temple priests, the "vexing problem", as the H.R.C.E. perceived it, of the northern Āndhra *archakas* in the 1930s.

Soon after it was established in 1925, the H.R.C.E. discovered that *archakas* in some districts of present-day Andhra Pradesh performed two roles. Apparently, this region of the Presidency, unlike others, did not adhere to the custom of having a separate office of trustee, and the *archakas* combined in themselves the functions of priest and trustee. They conducted the rituals as elsewhere, but also looked after temple lands and finances, responsible to no one but themselves. The situation gave the *archakas* unusual power, wealth and prestige.

In the H.R.C.E.'s view, this was unacceptable, an "anomalous and unjustifiable" combination of two offices. The department undertook to alter the situation. Over the next several years, in a process that involved great expense, threats and incentives, the H.R.C.E. gradually forced the Āndhra *archakas* to renounce their claims to the trustee function. New trustees were put in overall charge of the temples, and the *archakas* were demoted to "their legitimate place as servants of the institutions", as one H.R.C.E. report put it.[13] This re-classification was achieved in order to "improve the general management" of the Āndhra temples. Essentially, for the H.R.C.E., improving temple management meant making management in Āndhra look like management elsewhere. Change was a necessary consequence of this view. Rather than

13 G.O. 1455 Local and Municipal, March 25, 1929: *Third Annual Report, The Board of Commissioners for Religious Endowments, Madras* (1927–28) para. 10. The Board's reports for the years 1926–36 include detailed accounts of the Board's dealings with the *archakas*.

preserving local "custom and usage", the H.R.C.E. called custom "anomolous", and abolished it.

(ii) *Social reform.* Protection in the 20th century has also come to mean social reform. For example, according to the D.M.K., the *archaka* law was a social reform measure designed, like temple entry in the 1930s, to further the ideal of an egalitarian democratic society.[14] Here as with bureaucratic efficiency, protection can mean change, rather than preservation of the status quo. But social reform is often joined to an interpretation of Indian history according to which the change re-establishes ancient practices and ideals; it is not fundamentally innovative. Thus, in defending the *archaka* law, D.M.K. spokesmen and others argue that caste restrictions in temples are of relatively recent historical origin and constitute a falling away from the medieval South Indian ideal of open worship with each individual approaching the deity on his own behalf. The order changing the language of *archana pūjā* from Sanskrit to Tamil was accompanied by a similar sense of recapturing the past, a past when each individual could hear prayers uttered and hymns sung in his own language.[15]

(iii) *Temples' religious function.* H.R.C.E. administrators have also given a more conservative meaning to protection: the protection of temples' religious and spiritual integrity. Because it exists at the borderline of interference with religion, this meaning is seldom stated explicitly in public, but is nevertheless a significant component in H.R.C.E. administration. Along with the values placed on bureaucratic efficiency and social reform, the concern for a temple's specifically religious function is an essential element in the background of the *archaka* legislation.

In their conversations with me, H.R.C.E. officials were distinctly negative and skeptical about most temple priests. Indeed, they expressed cautious approval of the *archaka* legislation precisely because, in their view, *archakas* have performed their job of preserving the purity and efficacy of Hindu ritual rather poorly. This feeling seems to be shared widely by the public. Repeatedly, I heard the complaint that priests are ignorant, dishonest and self-serving, and pay inadequate attention to their priestly functions. Too often, it is maintained, *archakas* do not really understand the significance of the rituals they perform or the meanings of the Sanskrit phrases they recite. They mutter unintelligible but impressive sounding phrases, often leaving out crucial parts of the ritual. The result is that, unbeknownst to the public and often even to themselves, priests are constantly making "mistakes". Some H.R.C.E. officials consider

---

14 This view was expressed in numerous conversations with D.M.K. leaders in 1973–74. For an early defense of the measure, see the speech by the Minister for Religious and Charitable Endowments, reported in *Hindu* Jan. 31, 1971.

15 The 1971 H.R.C.E. circulars from the Deputy Commissioner, Madras, argue, for example, that "...for many years this method of *Thirumurai archana* existed in many temples...", and that "...the Tamil Nadu people desire that in all temples *archanas* should be performed in Tamil..."

themselves more knowledgable, and have not hesitated on occasion to order priests to modify details of rituals in ways the official knows are "correct".

This concern about mistakes is not simply a matter of pedantry on the part of the official, or a show of his bureaucratic power. A mistake in ritual or in speech is very serious because the power and efficacy of the entire ritual may be lost. Ironically, then, the H.R.C.E. is protecting the temple from the functionary at its very center, the priest. In making this point, one official added to it another sense in which governments must be especially concerned with temples:

> This matter of not saying the rituals properly is very important, for we believe that if they are not said properly, the state is damaged. The temple, in fact, is intended for prayers for the general welfare of the community and the world at large.[16]

In summary, the 1970 *archaka* legislation received impetus from at least three directions, each suggesting a dimension of the meaning which the state imputes to the concept of protection. Reclassifying the *archakas* to include them in a common category "temple office-holders and servants" would increase the control and efficiency of bureaucratic administration, particularly in terms of recruitment and discipline. Opening the priesthood to all castes, particularly to *Harijans*, would promote the modern social goals of egalitarianism and equal opportunity, while at the same time evoking complementary strands in medieval religious history. Finally, abolishing the hereditary priesthood would enable the H.R.C.E. to think along the lines of a more systematic religious training for *archakas*. By some, it was hoped that an ecclesiastical organization regulated by the state would eventually develop.

II

So far, we have discussed the setting of the *archaka* legislation: the legal jurisdiction of the state over religious institutions, the roots of and justifications for this jurisdiction, and the present-day meaning given by the government to the concept of protection. In this section we will turn to the political reaction to the 1970 law, and focus particularly on the handicaps *archakas* face in representing their interests effectively. We can begin by re-phrasing the initial question of this essay: Although the *archakas* were the group most intimately

---

16 Interview with author. This concern on the part of government officials has been a recurrent theme during the history of the department. For example, the 1941 Administration Report noted:

> The question of framing rules under the Act or introducing suitable provisions in the Act to empower authorities of temples to preclude persons not properly equipped from officiating as priests may soon have to be tackled; so as to enable priests to acquire the required knowledge the Board has been desirous of establishing institutions for imparting instruction in rituals and agamas.

See *Sixteenth Annual Report, The Board of Commissioners for Hindu Religious Endowments, Madras* (1940–41), p. 10.

affected by the 1970 law abolishing the hereditary priesthood, they were unable to mobilize an effective political opposition to the law. Why was this so?

Archakas in South India have been nominally organized for three decades. The South India Archaka Sangham was founded in 1948 when the bill which was later enacted as the H.R.C.E. Act of 1951 was under consideration. The Sangham submitted memorials to the government dealing with those parts of the bill of particular concern to temple priests.

The Sangham's records of its early years through the 1950s give a fairly vigorous picture of its activities.[17] Numerous petitions were sent to the government; attempts were made to get more representation on governmental bodies dealing with temples; and a long-term project was undertaken to have sacred *āgamic* texts printed so that they could be distributed to *archakas* fairly inexpensively. The focal point of the Sangham's activities was the annual conference, usually held during the winter months in Madras. Meetings were held for two or three days, and were addressed by government ministers, members of the Legislative Council, newspaper editors and trustees of prominent temples.

But this picture of organizational vigor, drawn from the files of the Sangham, is probably more appearance than reality. Few of the Sangham's projects met with success: representation on government bodies was not achieved, and though a few *āgamic* texts were printed they have remained for the most part undistributed. The patronage given by government officials who attended the Sangham's conferences was indeed impressive. Since an organization in South India is measured in part by the stature of the guests who honor it at its conferences, the Sangham must at least by this measure be deemed a "success". But this success did not carry over to its other activities.

In recent years, even the Sangham's ability to attract prominent guests to its annual conferences has declined. Records at my disposal do not enable me to determine whether this change was gradual or sudden, but certainly D.M.K. legislators and ministers did not attend in the same numbers as did those of the Congress party in its days of power prior to 1967. Equally significantly, and probably a related phenomenon, there has been a drop in attendance by the *archakas* themselves. In 1974, only about seventy-five priests came to the meetings, and these were mainly from Madras city and its nearby districts. And, in contrast to the two and three day sessions of earlier years, the 1974 conference lasted for one day.

Measured by its energy and persistence in furthering *archaka* interests, or by the extent to which *archakas* sense themselves a part of a cohesive association, the South India Archaka Sangham has been even less successful. Dominated by a few office-holders, usually enjoying re-election each year, the Sangham

17 I would like to express my appreciation to the officers and members of the Tamil Nadu Archaka Sangham, particularly to its Secretary, Sri Swaminatha Gurukkal, and its President, Sri Ganesa Gurukkal. This section relies heavily on the files and historical records of the Sangham.

has not developed into a channel for on-going communication among geographically and socially isolated Brahmin priests. With few exceptions, the Sangham has not provided any special services to its members. Like so many other *sanghams* and *sabhas* in South India, the Archaka Sangham basically surfaces once a year, at its annual conference, at the conclusion of which resolutions are passed directed primarily at the government.

Strong, vital interest associations are of crucial importance for achieving effective representation in pluralist political systems, particularly for the representation of smaller groups lacking some other, usually economic, base of power. For our purposes, three dimensions of interest groups deserve special mention. First, an interest group is based on a strong sense of shared (usually material) interest, to which often is added a sense of identity as a social community. Second, and especially important here, the group must have a sense of its own integrity. It must perceive that its concerns and priorities are distinct and defensible on their own terms, however much they may be in tension with those of other groups and institutions, including those of the state. Third, and related to this, an interest group must have confidence in its own interpretation of what public policy should be.

It seems clear that the *archakas* in South India do not constitute an interest group in this sense. *Archakas* are profoundly insecure, individually and collectively, regarding their social and political status; they lack a sense of unity and independence from the state; and they are uncertain regarding the proper direction of public religious policy. A central reason for this is that, throughout the modern period, *archakas* have been radically dependent on the state. This dependence, in the first instance of a material kind, has had important intellectual and psychological ramifications. Especially, this dependence expresses itself in a subjective identification with the state, rather than alienation from it, even when *archaka* interests are clearly at variance with state policies. Vertical identification with the state is strengthened by the weak bases for horizontal, collective identification with one another. *Archakas* are socially, geographically and economically isolated from one another, and also lack effective supporters in society generally. Dependence on the state also shapes the manner in which priests articulate the concept of protection, an articulation which in the final analysis complements rather than contradicts that of the state. Let me elaborate these points, starting with the issue of material dependence.

Historically, the material support of temple priests has been based chiefly on two sources: offerings and *pūjā* fees, and land. Aggregate data is not available on the relative importance of these two at any given time, and the position undoubtedly varied from temple to temple and region to region. But there is no doubt that land has always been the more highly prized. Today, *archakas* believe firmly that, unlike themselves, priests in the past enjoyed a secure income from land. In this case, the belief is as important as the actual historical facts, which remain unclear.

When *archakas* talk, as they do repeatedly, about the extensive land holdings they believe their forebears enjoyed they are talking primarily about land held on *inām* tenure. *Ināms* are tax-free grants by the state, giving the holder a right to cultivate a parcel of land, or a right to a portion of the land's produce. The fact of central importance here is that in this tenure the state has a discretionary power to take away, as well as to give, *ināms*. Religious *ināms*, granted to individuals, are not given outright or permanently, they are conditional grants made in return for certain services. Thus, when an *inām* is given to a priest in return for his service to a temple, his possession of the *inām* is secure only so long as that service is continued. If he fails to maintain his religious service, his *inām* can always be revoked and resumed by the state.

Such, at least, was the interpretation of *inām* tenures worked out by the British in the 19th century.[18] As part of a general attempt to introduce certainty and security in property, a Commission was established in 1859 to go into the whole question of *inām* tenures, classify the kinds of *ināms*, and settle just who possessed what rights in each category. The Inam Commission's inquiries extended through the next decade, during which it confirmed the titles of thousands of *ināmdars* (holders of *ināms*).[19] But the Commission was not able to settle once and for all the question of what an *inām* "really" is, and controversy has continued within the bureaucracy down to the present. Also, many revenue administrators disliked the *inām* system as a cumbersome and an often unjustifiable drain on state revenues. Suspicious that many *ināmdars* took advantage of their grants without fulfilling the service requirements, the Revenue Department tried to guard the state's interests closely. Since it was felt, until fairly recent times, that abolishing *inām* tenure would be an unjustifiable expropriation, this meant that the Revenue officers had to act as watch-dogs to see that *ināmdars* were keeping up their service.

The point here is that, in principle, priests did not control the crucial decisions affecting their livelihood. Nor, for that matter, did the temple trustee or the worshipping public. *Ināms* originated from the state, and the state continued to exercise its prerogative over them.

In practice, two areas turned out to be of particular importance, both decided by government bureaucrats: the precise nature of *inām* rights, both in general and in each case, and the definition of adequate "service". The Inam Commission left many unresolved questions concerning both of these areas, and in subsequent years they were the subject of strong disagreement within the bureaucracy. These disagreements have never been resolved. Over time,

18 The literature on *inām* tenure is extensive. For a relatively short and precise description of *ināms*, see B. H. Baden-Powell, *The Land Systems of British India*, Vol. III (Oxford, 1892), pp. 81 ff. In 1913, a thorough review of the intra-governmental disagreements regarding the nature of *inām* tenure and of the important shifts in policy taken in the nineteenth century was undertaken by Mr. T. E. Moir of the Madras Revenue Department. See G.O. 2133 Revenue, July 16, 1913.

19 The major assumptions and procedures of the Inam Commission are outlined in Mr. Moir's report, in *ibid.*

the result has been a proliferation of complicated rules and regulations.[20] Based sometimes on legal distinctions, sometimes on procedural precedents, and sometimes on historical reconstruction, these rules have seldom been comprehended in their entirety even by administrators with years of experience, much less by priests uninitiated into the mysteries of bureaucracies. Moreover, the rules have always been subject to change. Sometimes, change occurs because of changed policy priorities in the government, which are publicly stated and legislated, and at least relatively easy to understand. Usually, however, the change results from new twists in judicial rulings, or from a turn-over in bureaucratic personnel leading to new interpretations of past policy.

The long-term effect has been to create in *archakas* a pervasive sense of uncertainty, insecurity and a psychology of dependence. The implications of a new law or regulation are seldom entirely clear. This has been true, for example, in recent years with land reform legislation, some of which has in fact affected priests and some of which merely threatened to do so. *Archakas* are convinced that their collective material welfare is inexorably declining. Historical comparisons here are difficult since, as already mentioned, many priests never had *ināms* to begin with, but depended instead on offerings. But, for those who do have land, it is probably true that they have become increasingly less knowledgable about how to keep it, about what they must do and what they must avoid doing to ensure that they are not violating a clause on which their tenure is based. Priests also correctly perceive that whether or not they will be able to keep their remaining lands is a matter which is in large measure beyond their control anyway. It is known that recommendations have been made to the government from within the state bureaucracy to replace the bulk of temple lands, on whatever type of tenure, with cash payments made to each temple on an annual basis.

Although *archakas* have for years shared this common threat to their material livelihood, they have not evolved an effective collective strategy to improve their leverage with the government. This is not as paradoxical as it seems. The objective situation is not one which promotes collective action. Each *inām* title-deed has distinct legal and historical conditions surrounding it, and in this sense each *ināmdar* has a relationship with the state which is distinct from those of his fellow *ināmdars*. A single change in *inām* regulations seldom affects more than a small minority at any given time, although together a set of changes may constitute a significant shift in state policy. Additionally, the bureaucracy historically has lacked the resources to apply systematically every regulation change to all eligible *ināms*. In practice, new regulations are

20 For the period up to 1913, these rules and the difficulties surrounding them are described in Mr. Moir's report. Later revisions, through 1948, may be traced in Chapter IV of the *Standing Orders of the Board of Revenue* (Madras, 1931). This volume was kept up to date, subsequent to 1930, by means of "correction slips" pasted in the binding of the relevant page. The multiplicity of "correction slips" on any given page is evidence of the frequency with which *inām* regulations changed – sometimes almost monthly.

implemented on a case-by-case basis, usually occasioned by a particular *inām* having come to a local bureaucrat's attention for some other reason. A premium is thereby placed on keeping a "low profile", avoiding action which might draw the notice of government officials.

Social divisions also inhibit collective action. *Archakas* do not form a social community in a subjective sense. Broad sectarian distinctions exist, such as between Vaiṣṇava and Śaiva, and the sub-divisions within these sects. These divisions are reflected politically and socially, particularly in terms of competing claims of status, prestige and power. That *archakas* come together in the South India Archaka Sangham (to the extent that they do) is more the result of external pressure and circumstance than it is of an enduring sense of fellow-feeling. The individual *archaka*'s sense of himself is shaped more by his sectarian affiliation, his sub-caste and the prestige of his temple.

The work situations of *archakas* also divide them. Each temple is unique; it has its own sacred history, its own customs, economy, sacred calendar and relation to society. To a large extent, an *archaka*'s life and consciousness is circumscribed by the physical and mental isolation imposed by the life-cycle of his temple. Moreover, each *archaka* is subject to the particular directives of his trustee and Executive Officer. The relationships he evolves with these officials are crucial to his security and welfare and, though governed in broad terms by H.R.C.E. regulations, are nonetheless highly specific in character. As with our analysis of the *ināmdar*, here too we can say that each *archaka* has an individualized relationship with the state, since both the E.O. (directly) and the trustee (indirectly) represent state authority.[21]

Returning now to the South India Archaka Sangham, we can begin to understand its difficulties. Economic, social and work conditions tend to separate and divide rather than unite priests. As a result, the Sangham has remained a loose association of mostly inactive members. Its major activity is the annual conference, at which resolutions are passed usually in the form of demands on the state.

Though few of the Sangham's resolutions have led to concrete results, they reveal much about the fears, preoccupations and points of agreement among the *archakas*. As such, they are important for our analysis here. Especially, they indicate how *archakas* handle their dependence on the state intellectually, and how they view themselves.

Protection is central to the *archakas*' notion of their relation to the state.[22] The term occurs repeatedly in Sangham resolutions, as well as in speeches and

---

21 This is somewhat less true, to be sure, in the larger temples with large priest populations, although here my information is only impressionistic. Smooth administration in the larger temples requires that the E.O. establish more formalized and regulated relationships with *archakas* as a group. *Archakas*, in turn, often have leaders to represent them collectively or, at least, to represent their particular faction. But this kind of organization seldom extends beyond the boundaries of a single institution.

22 Protection: *pādukāppu*, *kāppāṟṟu*.

conversations. On more than one occasion, in fact, the Hindu Religious and Charitable Endowments Act is mistakenly referred to as the Hindu Religion Protection Act. Protection here means preservation, preservation of the rights and customs on which the position of *archakas* depends:

> The government should protect the archakas' rights in receiving *prasadam* as instructed by the agamas and sastras of our ancestors.[23]
> Vaisnava and Saiva religious opinions should be made known to the ... H.R.C.E. department in order to protect their rights.

However, the *archakas* also realize that more than ancient custom is necessary to protect them in modern circumstances, and their language changes accordingly. Some resolutions touch on working conditions: they have asked for rights of leave and holiday "...on par with government servants". They have also appealed for formal representation on the Legislative Council and on the Advisory Committee of the H.R.C.E. so as to "...advise in the matter of legislation on religious institutions." More striking, *archakas* want to be included in the "backward classes" list, like so many other groups in India today:

> The *archaka* community should be included in the backward classes list and they should be provided free education in the high schools and colleges, reservation of seats in the public institutions, financial help, employment facility, etc.

More than those above, however, the following resolution encapsulates the issue about which *archakas* feel most threatened and regarding which they believe government policy to be crucial. It is a resolution about status and rank, a subject about which temple priests are profoundly insecure. It protests the treatment of *archakas* as "ordinary" temple servants. The government is petitioned to use its power to support the *archakas*' claim to a higher status than that of their colleagues within the temple:

> Lastly, it is submitted that the position and status of the archakas deserve to be improved. Most of the archakas are thought and in some cases treated (sic) just as ordinary temple servants. Their position in the conduct of daily worship and other matters are almost forgotten. This matter requires earnest and serious consideration at the hands of the government.

With only minor changes in wording, the appeal in this resolution has been made almost every year for which records are available since the Sangham was founded. Moreover, the issue with which it deals is, in the final analysis, identical with that raised by the 1970 *archaka* legislation.

Mention has already been made of some of the reasons that the public holds *archakas* in low esteem: their relative poverty, and their alleged ignorance of the *āgamic* scriptures and inconsistent performance of rituals. To these reasons

23 This and subsequent resolutions are selected from the several dozen Sangham resolutions passed over the years from 1948 to 1973

must be added the fact that the caste position of the Brahmin temple priest in South India is itself ambigious. Although usually classified within the Brahmin *varṇa*, other Brahmins consider the *archakas* inferior to themselves, question their status as genuine Brahmins, and tend to view *archakas* with a mixture of bemusement and contempt. Many are quick to observe that *archakas* "get paid" for worshipping god, the implication being, on the one hand, that the monetary aspect vitiates the meaning of the worship and, on the other, that *archakas* cannot rank highly since they are willing to receive money ritually from all castes, even the most lowly. One Brahmin informant, who was in fact a lawyer employed by several *archakas*, shared this view. He noted, as a "commonplace", that *archakas* are identified as *mattyāna panchamma*, which he translated as meaning that, until he takes his daily bath, the *archaka* is in fact of the fifth and lowest class of the Hindu hierarchy. The uncertain status of the temple priest was also observed in Thurston's ethnography of South India. Of the *gurukkals*, or Śaiva Brahmin temple priests, he wrote:

> They are temple priests, and other Brahmins regard them as inferior, and will not eat with them. Even in temples, the Gurukkals sprinkle water over the food when it is offered to the God, but do not touch the food. They may not live in the same quarters with other Brahmins. No agraharam will ever contain a Gurukkal's house. There should, strictly speaking, be at least a lane separating the houses of the Gurukkals from those of the other Brahmins.[24]

Today, *archakas* have internalized their critics' negative views, a fact which greatly weakens their self-esteem and capacity to form an effective interest group. *Archakas*' sense of dignity is fragile and uncertain. Like their critics, they condemn themselves for being poorly trained and educated, for being ignorant of the scriptures and for making mistakes in ritual. They know that their *varṇa* status is problematic, that others (and not only other Brahmins) view them skeptically, are critical of their habits and behavior, and shun close association with them.

Characteristically, the *archakas* look to the government to bolster their position, and in two major ways. First, the Sangham is interested in professional training, especially schools:

> This conference requests the government, administrative officers, the *dharmakartas* of large temples, and the Religion Protection Commission (sic) to establish *agama* colleges in every district and taluk in order that the *archaka* youth may have *agama* education.
> The government should distribute *agamic* scriptures and pamphlets to the *archakas*.

The H.R.C.E. agrees that schools are needed, but has not pressed the matter vigorously. With government backing, large temples have occasionally sponsored summer refresher courses, but these are scarcely adequate to meet the need. The education which the *archakas* are demanding has associated with

24 Edgar Thurston, *Castes and Tribes of Southern India*, Vol. I (Madras, 1909), p. 347.

it the modern trappings of formal syllabi and diplomas, features which *archakas* apparently feel, as do many others, are essential for respectability. Ironically, in fact, the Sangham passed a resolution in 1953 which comes close, in detail if not in spirit and ultimate purpose, to the D.M.K.'s 1970 *archaka* law itself:

> Some five years or so after the establishment of such schools (for the instruction in *agama* sastras and Sanskrit), no *archaka* should be permitted newly to commence doing *archaka* service *even though he may have a hereditary right* without producing a diploma or certificate that he has undergone the prescribed course of instructions in one of such institutions. (emphasis added)

But education cannot affect fundamentally the fact that the *archakas'* status is problematic and ambiguous in caste terms. And this brings us to the second area in which the Sangham looks to the state for support, i.e., their role classification within the temple, an area which we have already seen was crucial in the 1970 *archaka* legislation.

To support their claim to high status within the Hindu hierarchy, temple priests rely on their highly visible and pivotal role in temple worship. Special dignity and honor are attached to them, they believe, because of their unique privilege in touching the temple idol. They also function as intermediaries between the devotee and god. Because of the frequency and emotional feeling with which this argument is made, it is worth quoting at length:

> The principal functionaries in these institutions (i.e. temples), who have more than any others contributed to the preservation of their sanctity, their glory and their importance are the Archakas, – the Bhattars, the Gurukkals, the Poojaries and the like. Their position in these institutions is unique and at the same time onerous. They alone have the right to enter the Sanctum Sanctorum of the temples. They alone have the right to touch the idol, bathe the idol and bedeck the idol with clothes, ornaments and flowers. They alone have the right to offer worship, offer Naivedyam, and perform the Archana. At the same time, it is they that have to keep care of the priceless ornaments of gold and precious stones worn by the deities and the rich silver ware used in the sannadhies. The Archakas serve as the medium through whom the public make their offerings, or their Archanas to the Deity. This important office is held by selected families whose members acquire the qualifications required by the Shastras by tradition from their ancestors and it is only within these families, from generation to generation, for hundreds of years the office has descended. In the distribution of temple honours, they enjoy certain preferential rights. The Archakatvam office is a spiritual rather than a secular one. Under these circumstances, the holder of the office cannot be treated in the same manner as the holder of other minor or secular offices.[25]

This argument really has two parts. The first part draws a picture from which it is difficult not to conclude that the *archakas'* function is indeed a special and elevated one. But the point of crucial importance to the priests, which is made in the final three sentences, is that this elevated status should have concrete

25 From the Memorandum submitted by the Archakas of Madras and South India to the Select Committee, Madras Hindu Religious and Charitable Endowments Bill, 1949. Dated March 29, 1949.

social and political consequences. In other words, the dignity which comes from touching the idol is in the final analysis empty unless it shapes other, human, relationships. To be meaningful, it must lead to special treatment and special respect, the effect of which will be to rank *archakas* higher hierarchically. Concretely, the memorandum notes, this dignity should result in "preferential rights" in honors and other perquisites, and in special treatment, different from that of other temple functionaries.[26]

But the possession of these special privileges is uncertain and insecure. Temple society is highly competitive, and favored positions are threatened constantly by factional disputes and conflict. To some extent, competitive relationships within the temple can be and are regulated by the H.R.C.E. and by its local agent, the Executive Officer. This is the reason for the *archakas*' enduring concern over the seemingly mundane question of how they are classified legally and bureaucratically. The government has the capacity, through its policies, to shape significantly the status enjoyed by the *archakas*. Obviously, it cannot shape that status completely, but it has a greater potential in this direction than does any other single agency or institution. Thus, the Executive Officer plays a crucial role in the daily making and un-making of status. His influence is felt directly, for example, when he arbitrates disputes among temple factions over various honors and privileges. More indirectly, as the central authority in the temple, the E.O. shapes status through the deference or lack thereof with which he conducts his dealings with temple personnel.

The Executive Officer does not have a free hand, of course. He operates within the broad guidelines set by H.R.C.E. law and regulations, including those regarding the classification of temple functionaries. Here, the experience of the priests has not been a happy one. As we have seen already, the H.R.C.E. has moved consistently in the direction of reducing the number of special administrative categories and regulations. Moreover, in so far as there exists room for discretion in these matters, H.R.C.E. officials and E.O.s tend to share the same negative attitude towards *archakas* as exists in society generally.

In this sense, the 1970 legislation, which abolished the hereditary priesthood by including *archakas* within the common category "office-holders and servants", was not new. Although its specific provisions were unusually blunt and extreme, the act embodied a set of attitudes and policy directions with which *archakas* have long been familiar and which they do not really expect to be able ultimately to reverse. Their counter-arguments have been repeated so often and with such regularity that they have become stale and ritualized. The long quotation above was taken from a memorandum originally sent by the Archaka Sangham to the government in 1949. But it differs little, either in emphasis or detail, from the legal briefs *archakas* filed with the Supreme Court

26 For a recent discussion on the nature and role of honors in South Indian temples, see Arjun Appadurai and Carol Appadurai Breckenridge, "The South Indian Temple: Authority, Honor and Redistribution," in *Contributions to Indian Sociology* (Dec. 1976).

against the 1970 law, or from conversations with me in 1974. The past 25 years have seen very little change in the *archakas*' analysis and pessimistic view of their situation.

Up to this point, I have tried to show that the *archakas*' weakness as an interest group is rooted in economic, social and administrative structures largely independent of and pre-dating the specific political context of the late 1960s and early 1970s, during which the D.M.K. party was in power. But we must also recognize that the particular emphasis embodied in both the 1970 *archaka* law and the *archana* policies of the same period bore the distinctive stamp of the D.M.K.: extreme enthusiasm for the Tamil language, sympathy for egalitarian forms of worship, and lingering anti-Brahminism. It is unlikely that any other major party would have initiated these policies in quite the same form. Many in Tamil Nādu believe, in fact, that the real force behind the 1970 *archaka* law was E. V. Ramasamy, the "grand old man" of the Tamil non-Brahmin movement, whose unrelieved hostility to established religion, to Brahmin dominance and to casteism was well known.[27]

As the government in power, the D.M.K. commanded a majority of votes when the *archaka* bill was presented to the legislature. But the bill's smooth passage was further ensured by the fact that, with one exception, no major opposition party actively made an issue of the legislation. The exception was the Swatantra party, which by this time had only marginal strength in any case. The D.M.K.'s rise to power was accompanied by a gradual expansion of its support base among the non-Brahmin and ideologically mobilized sections of society. From the mid 1950s, this resulted in a gradual shift in the Congress party's strategy such that, in ideological terms, both parties were often appealing for the support of the same constituencies.[28] The *archaka* legislation was presented by the government to the public as a reforming, democratic egalitarian measure. On public platforms, D.M.K. spokesmen stated their intention of appointing *Harijans* as priests in the great orthodox temples hitherto dominated by Brahmin priests, a clear appeal for mass support from the lowest sections of the population. The Congress party had split into two new parties in 1969, and both groups were struggling for supremacy against one another and against the D.M.K. In these circumstances, little was to be gained by championing the cause of the *archakas*, who were few in number and insignificant politically. Individual legislators were free to speak out against the

27 Among the many interpretations of the significance of E.V. Ramasamy and the Dravidian movement, see especially Charles A. Ryerson, "E.V. Ramasamy Naicker and the Dravidian Movement: Identity, Change, and Tradition," (paper read at the Conference on Religion in South India, Bucknell University, 1975); Lloyd I. Rudolph, "Urban Life and Populist Radicalism: Dravidian Politics in Madras," in the *Journal of Asian Studies*, XX (May 1961), Also useful is P. Spratt, *D.M.K. in Power* (Bombay, 1970).

28 For more detailed analyses of this period, see V. K. Narasimhan, *Kamaraj: A Study* (Bombay, 1967); Robert L. Hardgrave, *The Dravidian Movement* (Bombay, 1965); and P. Spratt, *op. cit.*

measure, and some did, but the parties as organizations did not mount vigorous oppositions.

Nor did the *archakas* receive expected support from other organized groups typically concerned with legislation of this kind. Particularly noteworthy was the absence of active support from the Hindu Temple Protection Committee (H.T.P.C.). By the early 1970s, the H.T.P.C. had emerged as the most vocal and persistent critic of temple administration under the D.M.K. government. Primarily, the H.T.P.C. consisted of a loose coalition of smaller groups and individuals who expressed a concern for the fate of Hinduism and who oppose the "atheist" D.M.K. Significant ties existed between it and Hindu revivalist groups, such as the Madras branch of the Rāshtriya Swayam Sevak Sangh (R.S.S.). In the early 1970s, the H.T.P.C. demonstrated frequently against government policies it considered harmful or insulting to Hinduism and temples. Sometimes its agitations were mounted independently, other times in conjunction with the "Hindu Mission", an action arm associated with the R.S.S. One might expect that a group of this kind would be a prime candidate for leading an opposition to the 1970 law and, indeed, the Committee has often expressed a general support for the efforts of the Archaka Sangham.

On the other hand, the Committee's membership and conception of its task had a specific and somewhat narrow character. Membership was drawn almost exclusively from upper non-Brahmin groups, many of whom had seen their political fortunes decline with the rise of the D.M.K. The Madras branch of the Committee, ironically, was headed by former members of the old Justice Party of E.V. Ramasamy. Though they had broken with E.V.R. on the question of atheism, they remained basically unsympathetic to the claims of Brahmin priests for special privileges. Their attacks on the D.M.K. were based rather on allegations that temple administration was corrupt and was being used for political patronage. Similarly, the members of the Madras R.S.S. were not particularly concerned to preserve a hereditary priesthood. On the contrary, in conversations with me they expressed basic support for the legislation, if not for what they perceived to have been its underlying motivation. They pointed out that caste restrictions on physical contact with the idol (on which *archakas* base so much of their case) are the exception rather than the rule in India, and expressed approval of less restrictive North Indian practices.

Thus, in late 1970 and early 1971, the *archaka* law was rather low on the H.T.P.C. action agenda. Its attention was directed at two issues of more transitory importance, but from which the H.T.P.C. hoped to gain in the coming elections. A hue and cry was raised over the "T. Nagar Vinayaka", an idol whose sudden appearance in the T. Nagar area of Madras was surrounded by mystery and for whose equally sudden disappearance the government was alleged to be responsible.[29] An even more prominent focus of controversy was the "Salem Incident", a procession in Salem town in which the

29 The story of the T. Nagar Vinayaka was covered thoroughly by the Madras newspapers *Mail* and *Hindu*, September–December, 1970.

black-shirted followers of E. V. Ramasamy allegedly testified to their atheism and contempt for religion by beating pictures of Hindu deities with their sandals.[30] The great energy expended by the H.T.P.C. over these issues was in marked contrast to its response to the *archaka* legislation. In fact, the Committee made no mention of the legislation in the resolutions of its annual conference in 1970, although the bill had just been passed a few days before.

III

The position we have reached may be summarized as follows. State policy frequently conflicts with the interests of *archakas*. This was certainly the case with the 1970 legislation abolishing the hereditary priesthood. We would expect this conflict to be reflected in the respective interpretations made by *archakas* and by government of the abstract principle of protection, and to some extent it is. But *archakas* have also internalized a portion of the state's point of view. They evaluate themselves and their performance negatively, and agree some improvement is necessary. But they look to the state to initiate that improvement, thereby tending to grant the latter's prerogative to make changes more or less of its choosing. In broad terms, then, the pattern of temple-state relations assumed by *archakas* does not differ from that actually existing today. The state's and *archakas*' respective interpretations of protection tend to complement one another.

As I have stressed, this complementarity has been shaped by the weak political position of the temple priest in relation to government and to society. *Archakas* are unusually dependent on the state and are relatively powerless to affect the course of public decision-making. The result has been a diminution of self-esteem and the acceptance of a relationship to the state which is often disadvantageous to their real interests and to their capacity to take initiative on their own behalf.

This analysis substantially explains the routine pattern of temple administration, the terms in which state policy is ordinarily legitimated, and the difficulties encountered in mounting political opposition to government policy regarding temples. But the analysis is still incomplete so far as the 1970 *archaka* act is concerned. Although opposition of a specifically political kind was notably weak, the act did not go completely unchallenged. On the contrary, several *archakas*, some in their private capacities and some nominally representing the South India Archaka Sangham, did challenge the legislation in the judicial court system.

Some *archakas*, in other words, do not accept unambiguously their dependent relationship on the state. This is particularly true of the more active, articulate priests. They correctly perceive that the underpinnings of the traditional pattern have been eroded in the modern period. The modern Indian state's legitimacy is formally based on constitutional principles, such as

30 On the controversy, see *Hindu*, January–March, 1971.

secularism and democracy, which are different from those which historically governed the state's role as protector. Also, temples are integrated in major ways with the larger political party system. The result, according to *archakas*, is that government policy is often framed less to benefit religious institutions than to further the short-range electoral and patronage interests of political parties. The 1970 *archaka* law could be interpreted in this way, for example. It is also widely believed that the use of temple finances is influenced inappropriately by politicians, frequently for illegal purposes. From this vantage point, the government appears to be an exploiter, rather than a protector of temples.

Until this point, our analysis has not required that we differentiate systematically among the branches of the state, among, for example, the legislature, executive, bureaucracy or courts. Protection has been presented as a function which legitimates state authority *in general*, whatever be the specific agency exercising that authority at a particular time. Hence, we have referred to the state as an undifferentiated whole, sometimes designated by the word "state" or, when appropriate, by "government", by "H.R.C.E." and so forth.

But the modern Indian state is not undifferentiated, and *archakas* who challenged the 1970 law in the Supreme Court recognized and took advantage of this empirical fact. The state is institutionally complex, and in a way such that ends which cannot be achieved through one of its branches may be pursued more effectively in another. Two aspects are especially important. In the first place, representation in at least one of these branches, the courts, does not require the kind of political and organizational strength which the *archakas* so conspicuously lack. To be sure, litigation is expensive, but here the *archakas* were fortunate. They engaged a famous advocate who provided much of his service without charge. A second consequence of institutional complexity is that the branches among which state authority is distributed do not always evaluate policies in terms of the same principles and priorities. Ironically, in appealing to the Court to defend their traditional interests, *archakas* relied on modern constitutional principles, such as the separation of religion and state, and legal recedent, such as the inviolability of custom. The D.M.K. government, on the other hand, though elected on the basis of a modern constitution, defended the 1970 policy ideologically through a reinterpretation of the traditional concept of protection.

To read the Supreme Court's decision on the *archaka* case is to enter a world where the assumptions are quite different from those discussed so far.[31] There is no reference to the concept of protection, nor is there mention of the economic and political dependence of priests on the state. Instead, analysis of the Court's decision suggests that it was shaped basically by three questions: Do the *āgama* scriptures govern the ritual in the temples concerned in the case? Is the hereditary principle of appointment a well-established "usage", and therefore possibly protected, or is it a mere "matter of convenience"? Is the

31 *Seshammal and Ors. etc., etc. v. State of Tamil Nadu* (1972) 3 S.C.R., pp. 814–34.

appointment of a temple priest a religious or a secular act? There is an internal tension in the Court's ruling which results from the fact that its answers to these questions did not suggest a single direction for public policy.

Regarding the first question, the Court found that the *āgamas* indeed regulated who may touch the temple idol and officiate at worship, and that the restrictions which these scriptures imposed were protected by the Constitution:

> ... the Archaka undoubtedly occupies an important place in the matter of temple worship. Any State action which permits the defilement or pollution of the image by the touch of Archakas not recognized by the Agamas would violently interfere with the religious faith and practices of the Hindu worshipper in a vital respect, and would, therefore, be prima facie invalid under Article 25(1) of the Constitution.[32]

Thus, the Court confirmed that only members of particular "denominations" (e.g., those born of Vaikhānasa parents in Vaikhānasa Vaiṣṇava temples, etc.) were competent to officiate in the large class of temples governed by the *āgamas*.

Regarding the second question, the Court found that, legally, the hereditary principle of appointment must be regarded as a usage peculiar to the temple. The government had argued to the contrary that heredity was merely a "matter of convenience", a rule-of-thumb procedure whereby the next qualified person can be easily selected. But the Court found otherwise:

> It, however, appears to us that it is now too late in the day to contend that the hereditary principle in appointment was not a usage. For whatever reasons, whether of convenience or otherwise, this hereditary principle might have been adopted, there can be no doubt that principle had been accepted from antiquity and had also been fully recognized in the unamended section...[33]

So far, the Supreme Court's decision moves in the direction of supporting the *archakas*. It affirms that *āgamic* prescriptions against defilement of the image must be respected, thereby restricting the priesthood to members of a few families. It also affirms that hereditary appointment is an established usage in the temples, a finding which means that heredity cannot be summarily abolished without further investigation.

But the third question remains to be answered: Is the act of appointing a temple priest a religious or a secular act? The 1970 *archaka* law, it must be remembered, did not directly attack the *āgamas*; it only changed the appointment procedure for *archakas* to make it consistent with that for other office-holders. The crucial question in deciding the constitutionality of the act, therefore, was whether the government was competent to make this change. To affirm that hereditary appointment was a usage was not enough:

32 *Ibid.*, p. 826.
33 *Ibid.*, p. 830.

> The real question, therefore, is whether such a usage should be regarded either as a secular usage or a religious usage. If it is a secular usage, it is obvious, legislation would be permissible...[34]

Here, the Court's decision was doubly disappointing to the priests. Not only did it answer that appointment was essentially secular, it also tied this answer to a series of comments affirming that *archakas* were essentially ordinary servants in the temple. Should the *archakas*' status be considered essentially similar to that of a *maṭhādhipati*, the spiritual head of a monastery? Definitely not, in the view of the Court:

> The Archaka has never been regarded as a spiritual head of any institution. He may be an accomplished person, well versed in the Agamas and rituals necessary to be performed in a temple, but he does not have the status of a spiritual head.[35]

On the contrary, the *archaka* is essentially a "servant". The Court quoted prior decisions as well as the H.R.C.E. Act to demonstrate that the *archaka* is subject to the trustee, who can enquire into his conduct and dismiss him for misconduct. From these observations on the status of the priest the Court drew its conclusion regarding the nature of the act of appointment:

> That being the position of an Archaka, the act of his appointment by the trustee is essentially secular. He owes his appointment to a secular authority.[36]

Thus, although the *āgamas* impose restrictions on who can be a priest, and these restrictions are protected on religious grounds by the Constitution, the appointment act itself is nonetheless secular. Apparently recognizing that the resulting position was somewhat artificial, the Court reiterated it several times:

> It is true that a priest or an Archaka when appointed has to perform some religious functions, but the question is whether the appointment of a priest is by itself a secular function or a religious practice...[37]
>
> Thus the appointment of an Archaka is a secular act and the fact that in some temples the hereditary principle was followed in making the appointment would not make the successive appointments anything but secular... That after his appointment the Archaka performs worship is no grounds for holding that the appointment is either a religious practice or a matter of religion.[38]

In summary, the Court upheld the constitutionality of the 1970 *archaka* act, but did so in such a way as to render the act ineffective. While it confirmed that the government could abolish heredity as a principle of priest appointment, it also confirmed that the state was bound not to violate the regulations

34 *Ibid.*, p. 831.
35 *Ibid.*, pp. 831–32.
36 *Ibid.*, p. 832.
37 *Ibid.*, p. 831.
38 *Ibid.*, p. 832.

laid down by the religious *āgamas*. The *āgamas*, in turn, declare that only persons following certain traditions and born of certain parents are competent to perform worship, and this obviously comes to much the same thing as heredity.

In the final analysis, the Court's decision left neither side satisfied. The government's view that the 1970 act was constitutional was confirmed, but confirmed in such a way that its immediate political and ideological purposes could not be carried out. In 1974, the Tamil Nādu legislature passed a resolution expressing to the central government its opinion that the Constitution must be amended so as to ensure the effectiveness of social reform legislation. On the other side, the priests achieved their short-range objectives in that their tenure and the tenure of their sons within the temple was not immediately threatened. But they were also discouraged that once again their claim to having a higher status than that of "servants" was denied.

Conclusion

We have examined two different principles of legitimation. The relationship between them seems contradictory or at least problematic. The first, on which we concentrated in the initial part of this essay, allows the state considerable scope to shape the fortunes of groups such as *archakas*. Important aspects of this principle are: the administrative authority of the H.R.C.E. to oversee temple affairs, the considerable dependence of *archakas* on the state for material welfare and social prestige, and the social and political weakness of the Archaka Sangham. These factors structure the choices open to the *archakas*, and define the manner in which they ordinarily relate to the state ideologically and practically. It is a situation wherein the government is able to manipulate the meaning of protection with little political opposition from the public, at least insofar as the temple priesthood is concerned.

The second principle of legitimation is that institutionalized in the legal system and the Constitution. Important here are: legal training and understanding of the Constitution; a capacity to make what are often very subtle distinctions, such as that between priest appointment as a "religious practice" and as a "secular function"; and the ability to bring to bear on a given issue a wealth of legal precedent. Under the Constitution, the legitimacy of state action does not derive from its being protective, in some sense, but from its being lawful. Among other things, the Constitution ensures the freedom of religious practice, with certain restrictions, and it was because of the relevance of the 1970 law to this issue that it was brought to the Supreme Court for its ruling.

Each of these two principles and the distinctive structures and processes they imply have a separate relevance for the *archakas*. They have had to come to terms with, and have utilized, both structures. On the one hand, the reality of their daily dependence has been translated – sometimes illogically – into an acceptance of the state's prerogatives. On the other hand, the fact that their already fragile position has been, in recent times, threatened further has more than once led *archakas* to challenge state policies in the courts. The discontinuity between their vocabulary of acceptance ("protection") and their vocabulary of challenge ("secularism") is part of a larger discontinuity within political and legal institutions of modern India. This discontinuity has sometimes hindered the effective implementation of policies properly on the public agenda, such as egalitarian reforms. But the roots of this discontinuity lie in the cultural and historical diversity of the agencies which have shaped the modern Indian polity, and it is this very diversity which has often provided channels through which otherwise powerless groups have been able to pursue their interests with some hope of success.

The Sri Lanka Insurrection of 1971: A Select Bibliographical Commentary[1]

H. A. I. GOONETILEKE

"April is the cruellest month, breeding
Lilacs out of the dead land, mixing
Memory and desire, stirring
Dull roots with spring rain".
T. S. Eliot. *The Waste Land* (1922) I. The Burial of the Dead, 1–4.

"We must remember that we are all sitting on top of a volcano today. We are unable to say at what moment this terrible volcano will erupt. Before it erupts and causes a great calamity, we need to take adequate protective measures to save ourselves from impending disaster".
Sirimāvo Ratwatte Dias Banda ranaike, *Prime Minister. (Parliamentary Debates. House of Representatives. Official Report (Hansard))* – Vol. 96, No. 10 (Pt. II), 25 November 1971, column 2211, 19–26.

Introduction

UNTIL THE "cruellest month" produced the tragic spectacle of insurrection in 1971 in Ceylon, political commentators, here and abroad, were united in their praise of the island as Asia's most successful democracy, and a shining illustration of Western parliamentary systems taking exemplary root in an Eastern plural society. The young men and women who took up arms against the government were to assail these rather constricted and ostentatious notions in the most dramatic fashion, and the experience has indeed been traumatic. A down-to-earth and qualified political critic has admitted that "the impact of the revolt was felt in all spheres of national life, and the entire fabric – social, political and economic – experienced a crisis unparalleled in its history".[2] The insurgency was not an instant or spontaneous revolt,

1 Since the manuscript was delivered for publication in May 1976, the Criminal Justice Commission report (see page 138) was issued in January 1977, the CJC Act was repealed by the new UNP Government in October 1977, and all those imprisioned in connection with the April 1971 insurrection set free.

2 W. A. Wiswa Warnapala, "Sri Lanka in 1972: Tension and Change". *Asian Survey* Vol. 13, No. 2, February 1973, p. 217. The author is a Lecturer in Political Science at the University of Ceylon, and presently Counsellor in the Sri Lanka Embassy in Moscow.

though its sudden explosion in April 1971 was unanticipated by imperialists and unexpected by revolutionaries, ageing or otherwise, in Ceylon or elsewhere. Apart from the fundamental lag between political promise and performance since 1956, as well as between booming education and *lumpen* economic development, the pattern of rigid ballot-box politics, with its almost prefigured electoral set-pieces, encouraged the sprouting of a brand of pure radicalism among the young, unenamoured of the existing modes of Marxist revolutionary party expression since the middle nineteen-thirties. It was, in some respects, the untimely interest on the large hoards of misinvested socialist capital in the island since that time.

Most revolutionary movements are mounted in search of an earthly paradise. This one was no exception. As in any revolution, also, it is important to be able to see the essences. The quintessence of this revolt was a fantastic will for change. As in all revolutions, admittedly, there were, also, fantastic disorders, perversions, injustices, extremisms – but the object was to discover a new kind of political order, a new redistribution of economic power, as the old forms were no longer respected or accepted. Neither were old responses accepted or acceptable. The political terms of the past seem to have little meaning when applied to this new convulsion. Ceylonese society has largely reacted with a mixture of stunned bewilderment, abandoned unconcern and beleaguered defiance. But, however inclined, it cannot afford to estrange itself from this tragic failure of an insurrection, lacking an agreed manifesto, social content or clear political direction, and even sadly opportunistic as it was. Contending with revolution, even in the abstract, is the pattern of our times. Everyone agrees that subduing it with military violence or police power is no final answer – the young, whether meek or militant, will, sooner if not later, inherit the earth. Some opportunity to realise itself or to influence power, and even on occasion to seize it, appears a way of containment if not fulfilment. Otherwise, the suppression of the movement of April 1971 may well become a symbolic act of political impotence and regression. The implications of the uprising are, therefore, immeasurable, and by forcing such questions to the forefront, the political leadership and power structures of present-day Ceylon have received their grimmest challenge, up to now. On the entire left movement, the upsurge has had the effect, at the very least, of clarifying problems, pointing out the contradictions, and sharpening the lines, and, in this sense, may well mark a turning point in its hitherto too conventional and cloistered history.

The insurrection embodied in substance the explosive force of an extremely left-oriented nativist militant cross-section of under-privileged rural youth in the upper forms of secondary schools, a minor army of disgruntled and largely jobless school-leavers, plus a sprinkling of university graduates and undergraduates from the forgotten backwoods of Ceylon. This millennial-style movement emerging from the grassroots level in the middle sixties, driven by primitive socialist urges, openly professed its disenchantment with the prevailing political system, riddled and enmeshed by inherent inhibitions, built-in weaknesses and a stratified bureaucracy, and was desperate to alter the shape of Ceylon's society to the romantic egalitarian hearts' desire of its adherents. These young men and women were caught up in a system alien to their lives, and subjected to tremendous pressures to achieve ends with which they could not identify. They assisted, with their crucial support, the birth of a new phase of United Front government in Ceylon in May 1970, but their rising expectations of the promised radical measures which would swiftly transform the economic and social face of the country were to be sharply belied. "Waiting for Socialism" was to become, in their transcendental eyes, as farcical and futile as "Waiting for Godot". To them, indeed, the often narcissistic politics and irrelevant ceremonials of parliamentary democracy had become monumentally marginal. Rejecting the axiom of their avowed mentors – Marx, Engels, Lenin and Mao – that insurrection is an art, and that, without the most careful preparation and planning for insurrection, spontaneous revolutionary action, however high-souled and puritan, is doomed to defeat by the organised violence of the ruling class, they plunged precipitately into open rebellion.

Five years after the blood has dried, the victims buried, the shotguns rounded up, the hand-bombs defused, and 18,000 "misguided terrorists rehabilitated", the winding sheets of parliamentary democracy, now a little frayed and threadbare, begin to be drawn again over the tragic scene. Yet, the events of that year of torment and valour continue to excite the minds of men. The entire drama was reenacted with cool and measured tread, in retrospective slow motion and meticulous cross-examination, in the solemn court of the Criminal Justice Commission in Colombo – an immaculate though bathetic coda to the gory symphony of April 1971. The event, however, has taken its place in the calendar of revolution, as a flash-point of forces that pre-existed, and that project their impact into the future. Certain dominant trends, like the conjunction of politics and culture, Marxism and anarchism, will be recurring themes. April 1971 constituted, however we look at it, an intense and far-reaching critique of the established order, a complex fusion of imagination and action, and an affirmation of a new society. The sense of excitement, and even amazement which it aroused in observers and participants remains to haunt the individual and collective memory.

Paradoxically enough, the whole insurrection – antecedents, development and dénouement – was most inadequately reported at the time in the local and world press. There was less concern with what was happening than why it was happening and later less concern with what had happened than what was likely to happen. This was largely due to the strict censorship imposed by the Government, shortly after April 5th, 1971, of all news pertaining to activities related to the emergency and arising from the insurgency, and the banning of nine newspapers and journals published by the Janata Vimukti Peramuna (People's Liberation Front) and other radical left-wing organisations not allied to any "established" socialist party. Though preventive censorship, according to the book, has now been lifted for almost four years, the intellectual life of the country has not been emancipated, because areas of creativity continue to be surrounded by barriers that hinder unconditional presentation of ideas, and make their full evaluation impossible. Indeed, to judge from the prevailing silence, all comment and analysis on the events of April 1971 appear to be virtually taboo except those, perhaps, which may present views attractive to the current administration.

It is not surprising, therefore, that the bulk of the literature provoked by the insurrection has been published abroad, and most of these contributions to the debate have been written by outsiders, more privileged perversely than Ceylonese to comment on this cataclysmic event. Preconceptions, political prejudices and biases, and the need to produce neat and congenial hypotheses, have inevitably produced many distortions about the basic issues in the encounter between the main protagonists. But they reflect a whole spectrum of opinion, ranging from ecstatic possession to contemptuous derision, in which many valuable and significant strands of appreciation and understanding can be discerned. Whether the writer is proclaiming that the JVP represented the highest form of an autonomous mass uprising in the shape of an unalloyed radical youth movement, or denouncing it as an infantile ultra-left disorder leading to a nihilist romantic adventure, masterminded by crypto-fascist agents, the information and analysis are essential to perceiving even the tip of the iceberg. But, after all the varieties of exultation or condemnation, speculation or interpretation, dire prophecy or many-splendoured vision have been read and digested, one is left irresistibly pondering over the enigma of whether revolutions can be artificially induced and new societies brought into being before the time is ripe and all the signs and portents have been studiously observed. Any attempt, however bold and imaginative, at inducing the premature birth of a new order appears to be, therefore, fraught with peril in that counter-revolutionary neo-fascist societies or dictatorships are likely to arise. These, by their very nature, will vitiate and destroy the dreams and aspirations for which a revolution is undertaken. In the classic socialist strain, the liberation of mankind can only be wrought through majoritarian and democratic decisions and enterprises, whether violent or non-violent.

This abortive revolt, as mentioned earlier, signalises a political and intellectual crossroads in the fractured contemporary history of Ceylon, especially after the formal colonial yoke, disguised in pretentious dominion trappings, began to be eased after 1948. In this period all too familiar neo-colonialist strategies, and sub-imperialist modes of economic conduct were permitted to penetrate a supposedly liberated society, and not even the "social revolution" of 1956 had succeeded in stemming or turning away the political and cultural conditioning resulting from the operation of these subtly powerful agencies. The insurrection, therefore, cast a flare over cardinal aspects of the theory and practice of revolution in what is commonly considered a revolutionary era. Concern in the future must increasingly be with general structural factors and circumstances impacting on a revolutionary situation, and less with personalities, old or young, living or dead, specific circumstances, and a mixture of purely incidental factors. Capitalist systems make use of a wide and devious spectrum of repressive techniques to build up a structure of violence, and it is saddening to observe that self-styled socialist regimes are only too prone to sedulously cultivate the very methods they are pledged to abjure. Revolutions occur when the assorted victims of these repressive structures, through a concerted expression of will and highly conscious mobilisation, attempt to change the structure in favour of those exploited. Revolutions are not conjured up out of some visionary air, reeking with the stale stench of populist slogan-mongering; no inexorable, mechanical processes impel them into the open. On the exploited is cast the burden of strenously and deliberately determining the revolutionary goals which will ensure that there will be progressively less exploitation, less infiltration by irrelevant material, technological and cultural devices, less fragmentation of their unity, and less marginalisation of their outcast strengths. They must equally be prepared to confront the inescapable challenge of a non-verbal language of revolution – violence – when faced with a structure where power has degenerated into forms of violence and oppression in the effort to perpetuate itself. Indeed, to judge from the experience of the last twenty-five years, "revolution" seems, more often than not, to have become an activity studiously designed never to succeed. "Revolutions" and swelling movements for radical change have been talked away by a vociferous dispro-portion between passionate consciousness and intellectual analysis on the one hand, and lack of practical will on the other, or vaporised through the strident rhetoric and clamorous symbolism of para-military street pageants on May Day – an annual public dramaturgy of rising expectations by the deprived in the auditorium of the privileged.

As a bibliographer I have found myself increasingly under siege in the last five years by inquiries about what to read on the insurrection. This select bibliographical essay, therefore, is an attempt to document the main and specific contributions to the literature on April 1971, most of which have been written and published after the events. Its value would have been immeasur-ably strengthened by the inclusion of certain other unpublished material – e.g., the various versions of the seminal "Five Lectures," the hot gospel core of the JVP ideology, but these were unfortunately not available to me at the time of compilation. Another important document is the judgement of the Criminal Justice Commission in the principal trial which ended on December 20th, 1974, but that had not been published up to the end of April 1976 owing to delays presumably in translation and printing. Some of the items were available only in mimeographed or typewritten form for private circulation, but have been included as they constitute essential threads in the overall documenta-tion. Purely descriptive annotations which reflect the writers' views have been provided, at some length in certain cases, to enable the bibliography to bring out the salient features of the crisis, and to serve as a searching commentary in itself. This exercise in the craft of bibliography is a very selective and updated version of the monograph published earlier in two editions in 1973 and 1975, and those interested in a wider range of documentation may consult the second edition.[3] This essay is only intended to provide in convenient form the essential commentarial literature from as many points of view as available. I hope it will help people to appreciate the tragic necessity of understanding the central concepts and subtle inflections of this notable occurrence, which is likely to mark a watershed in the modern history of Sri Lanka. No longer can the breaking of parliamentary wind be mistaken for a political thunderclap.

The end of the April insurrection, it seems plain, was only the beginning of that insurrection's role in Ceylonese history and thought. Despite failing to achieve any of its objectives, it provided fresh and novel viewpoints on problems of development and the economics of the transition from dependence to socialism, free of the seemingly impregnable hold of Western models and modes of analysis, which have, for too long, been permitted to fashion both political and economic impulses. Self-reliance and self-determination were posited as the true means to inward-looking and self-generating development. It threw into confusion those "progressive" forces to whom a mere redistribution of power at the State and bureaucratic levels – without a continuation of mass protest and mobilisation – was the *summum bonum* of socialism. It also stimulated and hastened certain fundamental measures of socio-economic reform, which, it is true to say, are likely to have been delayed if not for the hot breath of this staggering upheaval. But it has further helped to consolidate and strengthen the reactionary forces in the country so that a possible merger of these groups, both within and outside the government, appears likely in the near future. Civil rights, too, have been seriously emasculated and democratic freedoms endangered, so that the supreme task of the radical intellectual or worker in deriving relevant socialist formulae to fit the special circumstances of what must be accepted in a unique society has been further imperilled.

THE BIBLIOGRAPHY

1. Abhayavardhana, Hector. The April insurgency. The rage of a trapped intelligentsia manipulated by foreign and local vested interests. *The Nation.* (Colombo). vol. 6, no. 29, April 7, 1972, p. 4.

A first anniversary article by a pioneer member of the LSSP, and leading theoretician of the former United Front, which sets out to correct all the misinformation, prejudices and false revolutionary criteria on which the periodical articles hitherto written had been based. The author's thesis is that the insurrection was an eruption of anarchic emotion among groups of bitterly frustrated, petty-bourgeois youth, masterminded by a combination of foreign agents and local vested interests. The prominent features of the JVP movement are outlined to pinpoint the roots of the conspiracy. Its antecedents, subjective motivations and economic causes are described in the context of a gravely undeveloped economy and a rapidly disintegrating society. Suggests the social, political and educational fronts on which deterioration of standards and values needs to be checked to prevent a recurrence of the April tragedy and to reverse the economic trends that led to it.

3 *The April 1971 Insurrection in Ceylon. A Bibliographical Commentary.* 2nd ed. rev. and enl. Centre de Recherches Socio-Religieuses, Université de Louvain, 1975. 100 p. + 50 illus.

2. ACHARYA, Gopal. Ceylon: myths and reality. *The Marxist Review. A monthly journal of politics and economics* (Calcutta). vol. 5, no. 8, Feb. 1972, pp. 290–296.

A criticism of a Soviet analysis by V. Tyagunenko in *Soviet Review* (New Delhi), 4th Jan. 1972, that the JVP rebellion was engineered by reactionary forces against a popular socialist government. *See* no. 193.

3. ALLES, A. C. Insurrection. Parts I–III. Pt. I. Re-appraisal of April '71; Pt. II. It could have been more serious; Pt. III. Youth and responsibility. *Ceylon Daily News*. Dec. 22, 1975, p. 4; Dec. 23, 1975, p. 4; Dec. 24, 1975, p. 4.

The author was one of the five Judges of the Supreme Court appointed by the President to inquire into the Insurgency of 1971, and participated in the main case which was concluded on 20 December 1974. Using the findings of the Criminal Justice Commission No. 1 on the basis of the evidence placed before it during the trial of the 41 suspects, retired Justice Alles evaluates the main features of the insurrection and seeks to highlight the impressive nature of the massive youth disaffection with prevailing political authority and economic development which produced this remarkable outburst of radical and armed fervour. He compares the uprising to the October Revolution in Russia in 1917, and this re-appraisal of the April 1971 insurrection was one of the first two contributions by Ceylonese commentators to be published in the major national press, nearly five years after the event. The series by Victor Gunawardena in the *Sunday Times* appeared at the same time.

4. AMNESTY INTERNATIONAL. International Secretariat London. *To whom it may concern*. Letter dated 16th September 1971, signed by Martin Ennals, Secretary-General, given to Lord Avebury setting out purpose of his visit to Ceylon from 18th–28th Sept., 1971. 1 p.

5. ——. *Press statement Ceylon: a statement by Lord Avebury*. September 29, 1971. 4 p.m. London, 1971. 6 pp.

Preliminary findings based on Lord Avebury's oral report. The final report by Amnesty International was published on 15th March 1972, and led to an editorial in the London *Times* of March 16th, 1972, entitled "Change of name, not of problems".

6. ——. *Report on visit to Ceylon, September 1971* [by Lord Avebury]. London, 1972. 9 pp. [+ 11 appendices totalling 38 pp.]

Lord Avebury spent nine days in Ceylon from the evening of September 18th to the morning of September 28th, 1971, conducting a study in accordance with seven terms of reference given on the first page. After an introduction, there are sections on the emergency legislation, the release programme for detainees, trials, rights of detainees, position of families, conditions of detention, rehabilitation scheme, other matters (including atrocities), and a conclusion. There are eleven appendices relating to the matters discussed in the report, of which Appendix I is headed "The JVP uprising" giving in three pages a concise account of the background to the emergence of the J.V.P. and the eventual armed insurrection. The main report is dated 10th October 1971. *See also* nos. 149–151.

7. ——. Report of a Mission to Sri Lanka, 9–15 January 1975, undertaken by Mr. Louis Blom-Cooper, Q. C., and Miss Yvonne Terlingen on behalf of Amnesty International. London, 1975. 19, [4] pp.

I. Introduction, pp. 1–2; II. General observations, pp. 2–3; III. Judicial process, A: Numbers, pp. 4–5; B: Criminal Justice Commission, pp. 5–9 (contains strictures on the procedures available under the Criminal Justice Commission Act to dilute justice in the interests of the political establishment); C: Prisoners held without trial or charge, pp. 9–11; D: Capital punishment, pp. 11–12; IV. Tamil prisoners, pp. 12–13; V. Prison conditions, pp. 13–15; VI. Released prisoners, pp. 15–16; Recommendations, pp. 17–19. There are three Appendices, A–C, on the 4 unnumbered pages, giving statistics.

8. ARASARATNAM, Sinnappah. The Ceylon insurrection of April 1971: some causes and consequences. *Pacific Affairs*. vol. 45, no. 3, Fall 1972, pp. 356–371.

The major post-war characteristics of Ceylonese politics, economics and society are examined in order to understand the distinctly new phenomenon of political agitation and violent revolutionary activity on the part of Marxist-oriented youth groups. The main trends in the drive towards the new-left home-based insurrection, and government responses in the wake of its overthrow are identified. Concludes that the climate is ripe for a recurrence of populist revolutionary movements unless the continuing social and economic problems are solved dramatically. The author, the well-known Ceylonese historian, is currently Professor of History in the University of New England, Australia.

9. "The armed uprising in Ceylon". *Monthly Review. An independent socialist magazine* (New York). vol. 23, no. 8, Jan. 1972, pp. 43–52.

An edited version of a manuscript which reached the editors from friends in Ceylon. Written close to the events in mid-April or a little later, and betraying considerable sympathy for the rebel cause, while decrying the "over-kill" response of the government.

10. ASSOCIATION FOR ASIAN STUDIES. Michigan. Panel on "Radical change in a non-radical society: the 1971 insurgency in Sri Lanka". Annual Meeting of the Association for Asian Studies, April 1, 1973. Chicago.

The chairman was Professor Robert N. Kearney, and there were three papers for discussion by Professors Gananath Obeyesekere, Charles S. Blackton and Agehananda Bharati. The papers by Obeyesekere and Bharati have been revised and published, *see* nos. 38 and 161. For the paper by Blackton, *see* no. 42.

11. BALASOORIYA, Kirthi. *Janatha Vimukti Peramunē dēsapālanaya hā panthi svabhāvaya.* [The politics and class character of the People's Liberation Front]. Viplavavādi Komunist Sangamayē prakāshanayaki, 27, Arethusa Lane, Colombo 6, [1971]. xiv, 74 pp.

A critical exposé of the theory and practice of the People's Liberation Front (JVP) by the Revolutionary Communist League, which also advocated extreme radical measures on less unorthodox Marxist-Leninist lines. The author's preface is dated "11th, December 1970". All publications of the RCL were also banned under the Emergency Regulations of April 1971, and this valuable analysis is, therefore, not as well known as it should be. The Revolutionary Communist League's paper *Virōdaya* was one of the nine papers banned.

12. BALASURIYA, *Father* Tissa. Pattern for Asia? Insurrection in Ceylon. *Commonweal* (New York). vol. 94, no. 13, June 11, 1971, pp. 300–301.

An explanation of why Ceylon's youthful rebels attempted a straightforward capture of power in order to establish a self-reliant Marxist-type socialist regime in Ceylon. Their violence, according to them, was only made necessary by the government's resort to violence to defend its power. Their bid for power, based on the conclusion that only a radical reorientation of the country based on self-reliance and values of community sharing could bring about an effective regeneration, has failed for the present. The author, a well-known Roman Catholic intellectual, was at the time Rector of Aquinas University College, Colombo, the leading Catholic institution of higher education.

13. BANDARANAIKE, Felix R. Dias. *Minister of Public Administration, Local Government, Home Affairs* (and later *Justice*). The recent events in Ceylon. *Ceylon Today*. vol. 20, nos. 5–6, May–June 1971, pp. 1–12.

Text of a press conference in Ottawa on May 3, 1971, when the Minister was in Canada for the Executive Committee Meeting of the Commonwealth Parliamentary Association. A frank and early appraisal of the April events, in which the Minister admitted that, "We have discovered no evidence of any foreign weapons or foreign money or any foreign involvement in a direct sense in the insurgent movement at all from any source... In fact, our little insurrection was essentially a sort of do-it-yourself home-made job". *See also* no. 145.

14. ——. Speech on the "Governor-General's Speech: Debate on the Address". Fourth day. *Parliamentary Debates (Hansard). House of Representatives. Official Report.* vol. 94, no. 6, Tuesday, May 4, 1971, cols. 535–581.

The first official account in some detail of the insurrection as the Government viewed it in the immediate aftermath of its survival.

15. ——. Speech on the insurgency and its aftermath. *Parliamentary Debates (Hansard). House of Representatives. Official Report.* vol. 97, no. 1 (pt. 1), Nov. 30, 1971, cols. 95–109.

An important speech, made on the Prime Minister's instructions, during the discussion on the Prime Minister's vote at the Committee stage of the Appropriation Bill 1971–72. "I must state to this House that there is absolutely no evidence of anyone leading them beyond the Central Committee of the Janatha Vimukti Peramuna. That is where the insurgency begins and ends. There is absolutely no evidence or proof that anybody, a politician or any other person, has been behind it, has helped or assisted or taken part or financed the insurgency in that way".

16. BANDARANAIKE, Sirimāvo Ratwatte Dias. *Prime Minister; Minister of Defence and External Affairs; and Minister of Planning and Employment.* Statement by the Prime Minister on the calling out of the Armed Forces. *Parliamentary Debates (Hansard). House of Representatives. Official Report.* vol. 93, no. 16, March 7, 1971, cols. 2101–2103. Reprinted as "Government ready for any threat to the peace". *Ceylon Daily News.* vol. 55, no. 58, March 8, 1971, p. 1.

17. ——. State of Emergency: statement by the Prime Minister on the declaration of a State of Emergency on March 16, 1971. *Parliamentary Debates (Hansard). House of Representatives. Official Report.* vol. 93, no. 18, March 23, 1971, cols. 2197–2206 (English text, cols. 2197–2201). Reprinted: *Ceylon Daily News.* vol. 55, no. 71, March 24, 1971, p. 1; *Nation.* vol. 5, no. 24, March 23, 1971, pp. 4 + 7; as "Why the Emergency was declared". *Ceylon Today.* vol. 20, nos. 3–4, March–April 1971, pp. 9–16, 10 illus. (of insurrection episodes).

18. ——. "No bloodshed in a Buddhist land". Speech at the prize-day meeting of Kittamahara Maha Vidyalaya in Attanagalla electorate on April 1, 1971. *Ceylon Daily News.* April 3, 1971, p. 3.

19. ——. "If plot succeeded, who would have been in power". Speech at a mass rally of the United Front at Kandy on April 2, 1971. *Ceylon Daily News.* April 4, 1971, p. 3.

20. ——. A threat to democracy in Ceylon. Full text of April 9th broadcast to the nation. *Ceylon Today.* vol. 20, nos. 3–4, March–April 1971, pp. 2–3.

21. ——. Broadcast to the nation [April 24, 1971]. *Ceylon Daily News.* vol. 55, no. 97, April 25, 1971, p. 3; reprinted in: *Parliamentary Debates (Hansard). House of Representatives. Official Report.* vol. 94, no. 6, May 4, 1971, cols. 553–566 (English text, cols. 560–566); reprinted as "Insurgent movement: the facts". *Ceylon Today.* vol. 20, nos. 3–4, March–April 1971, pp. 4–8.

22. ——. *Nomaga giya taruna taruniyan veta kerena rajaye nivēdanayai; A notice to misguided youth.* Colombo, Dept. of Govt. Printing, Ceylon, 1971, 4 pp.

A four-page leaflet, with text in Sinhala only on three pages, containing a special message from the Prime Minister announcing the four-day amnesty and surrender terms ending at 4 p.m. on May 3rd, 1971. It was dropped from the air on April 29, 1971. The English title on the first page is not an exact translation of the Sinhala title which reads "A message from the Government to the young men and women gone astray". The English translation of the text was published in *Ceylon Daily News* April 29, 1971, p. 1.

23. ——. *Nomaga giya taruna taruniyan veta kerena rajaye nivēdanayai; A notice to misguided youth.* Colombo, Dept. of Govt. Printing, Ceylon, 1971, 2 pp.

A two-page leaflet, under the same Sinhala and English titles, containing a second and final appeal to surrender was dropped from the air at Poson and was operative from June 7th–9th, 1971. The English translation of the Sinhala text was published in *Ceylon Daily News* June 5, 1971, p. 1, and the *Nation* vol. 5, no. 33, June 6, 1971, pp. 1 + 8.

24. ——. Reply to Mr. Dudley Senanayake's letter to the Prime Minister of April 23, 1971. The Prime Minister's letter is dated 30th April 1971.

Parliamentary Debates (Hansard). House of Representatives. Official Report. vol. 95, no. 3, 9th Sept., 1971, col. 744. *See* no. 188.

25. ——. Statement on the State of Emergency. *Parliamentary Debates (Hansard). House of Representatives. Official Report.* vol. 94, no. 15, July 20, 1971, cols. 1806–1838, + Appendix II (List of weapons and implements found in the University), cols. 1941–1944 (English text, cols. 1823–1838). Reprinted as: "Prime Minister's statement on insurgency". *Ceylon Today.* vol. 20, nos. 7–8, July–August 1971, pp. 1–8.

The first comprehensive statement on the insurrection by the Prime Minister, following "a chronological pattern as far as is possible so that the whole subject can be seen in perspective by Honourable Members". Revealed that the total number in custody at the time was approximately 14,000, of whom approximately 4,200 surrendered on the Amnesty. "In my estimation, which is based on the information that is available to me, the total deaths do not exceed 1,200". This figure included Police and Service casualties. The particulars of police and service personnel killed or wounded were as follows: Police 35 (194); Army 15 (89); Navy 6 (16); Air Force 4 (13). The numbers in brackets are those injured. The total number of police stations attacked was 74. The Prime Minister also stated that she had no evidence of any foreign involvement in assisting and supporting this insurrection. The special reasons for the closing down of the North Korean Embassy in mid-April were reiterated. "In conclusion, I might say that this insurgent uprising has dealt a severe blow to this country, particularly in economic terms, at a time when we had to strain every nerve and sinew to ensure rapid economic growth."

26. ——. Address to the United Nations General Assembly, New York, October 12, 1971. Full text. *Ceylon Daily News.* October 14, 1971, p. 6.

27. ——. Statement by the Prime Minister: socio-economic proposals [presenting the Five Year Plan]. *Parliamentary Debates (Hansard). House of Representatives. Official Report.* vol. 95, no. 15, Nov. 9, 1971, cols. 2066–2093 (English text, cols. 2080–2093).

28. ——. Speech during the Second Reading of the Appropriation Bill 1971–72. *Parliamentary Debates (Hansard). House of Representatives. Official Report.* vol. 96, no. 10 (pt. II), Nov. 25, 1971, cols. 2208–2242.

29. ——. Prime Minister pays tribute to dead policemen. Speech at unveiling of memorial in Colombo on April 10, 1972. *Ceylon Daily News.* April 12, 1972, p. 6.

37 police officers of all ranks lost their lives in the insurrection.

30. ——. May Day message to the nation. *Ceylon Daily News.* vol. 57, no. 103, May 1, 1972, pp. 1 + 2.

31. ——. Country not back to normal. Emergency regrettable necessity.

Speech at United Front May Day rally in Colombo. *Ceylon Daily News.* vol. 57, no. 105, May 3, 1972, p. 3.

32. ——. Statement of Government policy. *National State Assembly Debates. Official Report.* vol. 1, no. 4, June 23, 1972, cols. 188–260 (English text, cols. 245–260).

References to the program of rehabilitation of denetus, and the large number (7,703) realesed after January 1972.

33. ——. Prime Minister decries doctrines of conflict. Text of address at SLFP All-Island Youth Conference, Kandy, Dec. 17, 1972. *Ceylon Daily News*, December 18, 1972, pp. 1 + 3, *see also* nos. 96, 101, 110, and 113.

34. ——. Speech by the Prime Minister during the debate on the Opposition Motion for the appointment of a "Select Committee to investigate an alleged conspiracy to destroy sovereignty of the people". *National State Assembly Debates. Official Report.* vol. 10, no. 5, 6th March 1974, cols. 972–996.

The documents referred to at col. 975 in the speech were tabled in the House and published as Appendices I–II, cols. 995–1012. They consist of letters exchanged between the Leader of the Opposition and the Prime Minister, in the aftermath of Mr. Jayawardene's statement in the National State Assembly on January 10th, 1974. *See also* nos. 133–136, & 192.

35. ——. Statement by the Prime Minister re. documents tabled by the Leader of the Opposition on 6.3.74. *National State Assembly Debates. Official Report.* vol. 10, no. 6, pt. 1, 21st March 1974, cols. 1090–1111. *See also* nos. 133–136, & 192.

36. ——. We follow only SWRD's path to Socialism. Text of Prime Minister's address at the 23rd annual sessions of the Sri Lanka Freedom Party, December 28, 1974. *Ceylon Observer Magazine Edition.* vol. 9, no. 21, Dec. 29, 1974, pp. 1 + 3 + 6 + 9.

In a wide-ranging survey of political history in the country since the formation of the SLFP in 1951, the Prime Minister made an extended reference to the insurrectionary threat in 1971 and the consequent disruption of national life.

37. ——. I will maintain independence, national security. P.M.'s reply to L.S.S.P. General Secretary's statement. Text of Prime Minister's statement. *Ceylon Observer Magazine Edition.* vol. 10, no. 2, Jan. 12, 1975. p. 1.

Mr. Bernard Soysa's statement, which was published in the newspapers of January 10th complained of the imposition of the sudden curfew directed against the Ceylon Federation of Labour trade union procession and meeting on November 16th, 1974 and the ban on paramilitary activities by political parties, both of the left and right. In her reply Mrs. Bandaranaike referred to national security being menaced by the very organisations which assisted the United Front in May 1970 and subsequently supported the JVP activities. The Ceylon

Federation of Labour in a statement in reply to the Prime Minister said that the Curfew of the 16th November was unnecessary and ill-advised, and an instance of the use of State power against the working class. The statement was published in the *Ceylon Daily News*, vol. 10, no. 17, Jan. 20, 1975, p. 1. This particular episode and exchange of views was a pointer to the growing rift between the L.S.S.P. and the right wing of the United Front leadership. It led to the dismissal of the three L.S.S.P. Ministers in the Cabinet in August 1975, and the party withdrew from the Government.

38. BHARATI, Agehananda. (*formerly* Leopold Fischer). Monastic and Lay Buddhism in the 1971 Sri Lanka Insurgency, in Bardwell L. Smith, ed., *Religion and Social Conflict in South Asia* (Leiden: E. J. Brill, 1976), pp. 102–112.

Originally read at a Panel on "Radical change in a non-radical society: the 1971 insurgency in Sri Lanka" on 1st April 1973, at the Annual Meeting of the Association for Asian Studies held in Chicago. The author, a Professor of Anthropology in Syracuse University, N.Y., was in Ceylon during the period of the insurgency, researching ideological change and the Buddhist clergy. He was tempted to extend his inquiries into the phenomenon of radical behaviour by Buddhists, and the polarisation of "political Buddhism" in the period April–June 1971. The several factors leading to leftist ideological inclinations among priests and novices are enumerated, and the significant correlation between Marxist inclinations and sympathy for the insurgents is evaluated. Factors contributing to a Marxist orientation among monks are further suggested on the basis of the writer's observations. The bulk of the rebels "were young villagers disenfranchised from political power, devoid of potential and theoretical access to the political and economic power structure", and there were no viable mediating power echelons between the society from which the insurgents came, and the administrative and political elites in the country. The monks involved in the insurrection emerged from the same milieu. An earlier contribution by Bharati, "Serendipity suddenly armed: the 1971 Sri Lanka insurgency", appeared in *Quest* (Bombay), No. 80, February 1973.

39. BHATTACHARYA, Debesh. Violence in Sri Lanka: a Ceylonese dream shattered by political upheaval. *Current affairs Bulletin* (University of Sydney, Dept. of Adult Education). vol. 49, no. 6, Nov. 1972, pp. 184–190, 3 tables.

A historical account of the development of the radical youth organisation, the JVP, in opposition to the establishment left of centre or middle-path governing groups since 1965, and the reasons for its armed adventure in April 1971, provoked in large measure by increasing government repression of the movement. The weaknesses in the organisation and ideology of the JVP are evaluated to explain its failure when exposed to the destructive forces of the government.

40. BLACKTON, Charles S. The Ceylon insurgency, 1971. *Australia's Neighbours* (Australian Institute of International Affairs, Victoria). 4th series, no. 76, July–August 1971, pp. 4–7.

The author, Professor of History, Colgate University, Hamilton, New York, was a Visiting Fellow at the University of Ceylon in the period of the insurrection. Much of the material in this early article was later refashioned for no. 41.

41. ——. Sri Lanka's Marxists. *Problems of Communism* (Washington). vol. 22, no. 1, Jan.–Feb. 1973, pp. 28–43. map.

An analysis of the challenge posed to the established socialist leadership by the JVP and its insurgent strategy. The dynamic radicalism of disillusioned youth since 1965 is contrasted with the foot-dragging middle path parliamentary road to socialism of the conventional Marxist parties in alliance since 1964 with the Sinhala-Buddhist SLFP. The dilemma of the left is discussed against the background of the rise of the JVP and its abortive revolt.

42. ——. The 1971 insurgency in Ceylon (Sri Lanka) 18 pp. (Cyclostyled text).

Paper read at a Panel on "Radical change in a non-radical society: the 1971 insurgency in Sri Lanka" on 1, April 1973 at the Annual Meeting of the Association for Asian Studies held in Chicago. Traces the causes for the 1971 uprising through the origin and development of the Janata Vimukti Peramuna, and its rapid involvement in the political process, in the period following the election to power of the United Front in May 1970. The events of April and May 1971 are described, and prominent features isolated. This paper remains unpublished. For earlier investigations of this dramatic happening by the same author, *see* nos. 40 and 41.

43. ——. The Marxists and Ultra-Marxists of Sri Lanka since Independence. *Ceylon Journal of Historical and Social Studies* (Peradeniya). new series. vol. 4, nos. 1 & 2, Jan.–Dec. 1974, pp. 126–133.

A brief analysis of the Fabian-style record of the established Marxist parties evolving within the British model of a parliamentary system until dissent with these practices led to the significant emergence of ultra-Marxist groups, especially among the young, which spearheaded the climactic insurgency of April 1971. The interaction of the new ultra-Left with the established Marxists after this traumatic experience, and the continuing dilemmas of Marxism in Sri Lanka are examined. The results of the failure of the JVP revolt are summed up thus: "The eruption of the Ultra-Left was nevertheless the watershed of modern Ceylonese history. The rebels of '71 would partly shape the future. Despite adolescent aspects, vagueness of precept and plans, and disregard for individual rights, the JVP stated clearer than any party manifesto the call for united action to build a self-reliant Sri Lanka on egalitarian lines. The deprived youth may intuitively have acted in the name of the future poor of Sri Lanka."

44. Brass, Paul R. Political parties of the radical left in South Asian politics. *Radical politics in South Asia*; ed. by Paul R. Brass and Marcus F. Franda. Cambridge, Mass., M.I.T. Press, 1973. Ch. 1, pp. 3–116, 12 tables, map.

The development, performance and current tribulations of Marxist parties and their disaffected new left outshoots in Ceylon are also discussed in this perceptive study, esp. on pp. 12, 32, 102, 103, 114 and 116. The impact of the insurrectionary radical movement of the JVP is also assessed.

45. Caspersz, S. J., *Father* Paul. Sri Lanka: a society in transition. *Impact. A monthly Asian magazine for human development.* (Manila). vol. 7, no. 10, Oct. 1972, pp. 339–341.

The worsening political, social and economic situation in the context of stagnation, inertia and stasis in which the April insurrection took place, and threw a flare over the grim prospects for the future.

46. ——. *Towards a sociological analysis of the youth struggle in Sri Lanka 1971. (A critique of educational effectiveness in a developing area)*. vi, 113 pp., 13 tables,

fold. map. (Advanced Certificate in Educational Sociology thesis. University of Oxford, 1973. Unpublished typescript).

The author, a Master of Arts of Oxford, and Rector of St. Aloysius College, Galle from 1963–1971, has presented in this brief dissertation a keenly argued hypothesis in two parts. Firstly, he maintains that the structures of education have been dysfunctional for the attainment of the goals of education, and secondly, that this dysfunctionalism is crucial in the analysis of the youth struggle in Sri Lanka in 1971. Attempts to establish that the explosiveness of the structures and the operation of education had by an inevitable logic to result in the upheaval of 1971. Father Caspersz makes significant use through citation of some of the transcripts of statements made to the authorities by suspects (including Wijeweera) now admissible before the Criminal Justice Commission in progress. A version of the now famous "Five Lectures," which provided the movement with its main ideological drive, is also made use of in his sociological analysis of what he terms a contemporary "situation of shattered hope". The author believes that the "Five Lectures" "seem to have been first excogitated by Wijeweera and the inner core in late 1967 or early 1968, then delivered, discussed with various groups of listeners, continually amended and brought up to date at the time of each successive class". They had instant success in winning over dedicated recruits to the movement. Wijeweera's order of the lectures is as follows: "The first lesson was the Economic Crisis, second Independence, third Indian Expansionism, fourth the Leftist Movement and fifth, The Path the Revolution in Ceylon should follow". Contents: Ch. 1, The hypothesis and its background, pp. 1–18; Ch. 2, The course of events, pp. 19–36; Ch. 3, Educational disfunctionalism, pp. 37–65; Ch. 4, Educational seeds of revolt, pp. 66–94; Ch. 5, The ideology of the struggle, pp. 95–106. Among the tables are five revealing religious and caste affiliations of suspected insurgents, and suspected insurgents classified by single year of age and sex, and age group and highest examination passed. The map shows the areas of the 1971 insurrection, and pp. 14–15 are left blank for illustrations when the thesis is eventually published. This notable contribution has remained unpublished.

47. Center for Radical Studies. Colombo. *Are we ready for a workers' and peasants' govt.*? [Centre for Radical Studies, 101/50 Kew Road (Susitha Industrial Printers, 1334, Kotte Road, Rajagiriya) 1973]. 112 pp., 11 tables (some fold).

The ideas in this document, produced at a point of extreme crisis for Ceylonese society, have been developed out of discussions with groups operating both within and outside the existing political parties. The document is unsigned, and no copyright is claimed. For purposes of the law, Mr. Gamini Gunawardene has taken full responsibility for the ideas expressed in the book. The document seeks to maintain that the deepening political and economic crises cannot be solved within the framework of the existing social and political structure. It offers a way forward through the establishment of a Workers and Peasants Government. It sets out the way in which such a government will function as the organ of a true democracy, and describes the social and economic organisation on which it will rest. The programme is offered for discussion and criticism so that the ideas on view may be developed and clarified. The abolition of the present Constitution is seen as a cardinal and first step in the implementation of the programme. The first radical document to emerge from the "underground left" after the revolt of 1971. A summary of this publication under the same title appeared in *Stranger in his land*, by R. W. Crossette-Thambiah. (Colombo, 1974). pt. III, pp. 162–184.

48. ——. *Let us discuss our problems.* [Colombo, Gamini Gunawardene, 1974]. 25 pp.

A sequel to the same organisation's *Are we ready for a workers' and peasants' govt.*?, published in 1973. Reflections and concrete proposals for political and economic transformation of society so that the economic crisis can be surmounted. The document provides a framework in which progressive organisations of the exploited classes can clarify and develop their ideas. Suggests that the Emergency be lifted, the Criminal Justice Commission Act of 1972 repealed, all April 1971 participants given an unconditional pardon, and the repressive apparatus of the State disbanded.

49. *Ceylon: beginning of a revolutionary struggle.* London, Ginipupura (Spark) Publication [1971]. 4 pp.

An analysis of April for the future of the revolutionary cause in Ceylon, and the belief that though the first phase of the struggle has not been successful, the movement is not isolated, and has, on the contrary, struck deeper roots among a people steadily alienated from the government.

50. *Ceylon: betrayal of a peoples' struggle.* London, A Ginipupura Publication [1972]. 4 pp.

Analysis of the continuing emergency situation in Ceylon, from a quarter in London sympathetic to the JVP.

51. Ceylon. Birth of a revolution and of counter-revolutionary terror. *Peace Press. An international information service.* (London, Conflict Education Library Trust), vol 7, nos. 5 & 6, June–July 1971. 22 pp.

This issue devoted entirely to Ceylon contains the English translations of the article in *Nouvel Observateur* by Rene Dumont, and *Le Monde* (4 parts) by Jacques Decornoy.

52. The Ceylon Committee. London. *Announcement of formation of the Ceylon Committee, giving aims as well as sponsors and members of the Committee.* London, Bertrand Russell Peace Foundation, 1971. 2 pp.

The Committee with an international group of sponsors and members was formed on 16th September 1971.

53. ——. *Statement of the Ceylon Committee.* London, Bertrand Russell Peace Foundation, 1971. 4 pp.

The Ceylon Committee was formed to arouse world opinion about the situation prevailing in Ceylon, to support all resistance to the suppression of political freedom in Ceylon, to assist in the setting up of an independent Commission of Inquiry into the April uprising and the atrocities by police/armed forces, to direct world attention to the trials of suspects to ensure fair trials and to provide legal assistance, and to assist in the rehabilitation of families affected by the events.

54. ——. *Ceylon: a new state of crisis.* A statement by the Ceylon Committee, April 7, 1972. London, 1972. 2 pp.

55. ——. *Bulletins.* No. 1 (October 1971) 13 pp.; No. 2 (Jan. 1972) 16 pp.; No. 3 (April 1972) 15 pp.; No. 4 (August 1972) 15 pp.; No. 5 (Dec. 1972) 15 pp.; No. 6 (June 1973) 15 pp.

Each issue contained, besides an editorial, reports of government activities in relation to the insurrection and the continuing Emergency, analyses of legislative and administrative measures of a "repressive" nature, and accounts of the Committee's work in pursuit of its objectives.

56. CEYLON. The Governor-General. Proclamations by the Governor-General. By His Excellency the Governor-General – A proclamation on 16.3.71 (7.00 p.m.), declaring that by reason of the existence of a state of public emergency in Ceylon, the provisions of Part II of the Public Security Ordinance (Chapter 40), as amended by Act no. 8 of 1959, shall come into operation throughout Ceylon on the sixteenth day of March 1971. *The Ceylon Government Gazette Extraordinary.* no. 14,949/6 of Tuesday, March 16, 1971, 1 p.

57. ——. The Public Security Ordinance (Chapter 40). Regulations made by the Governor-General under Section 5 of the Public Security Ordinance, upon the recommendation of the Prime Minister. These may be cited as the Emergency (Miscellaneous Provisions and Powers) Regulations, No. 1 of 1971. *The Ceylon Government Gazette Extraordinary.* No. 14,949/7 of Tuesday, March 16, 1971, 15 pp.

These two *Gazettes Extraordinary* marked the beginning of a series of orders and regulations made by the Governor-General, upon the recommendation of the Prime Minister, under the Public Security Ordinance (Chapter 40), and under various regulations of the Emergency (Miscellaneous Provisions and Powers) Regulations, Nos. 1 & 2 of 1971, beginning with the Emergency (Curfew) Order published in *Gazette Extraordinary* No. 14,952/4 of April 5, 1971. *Gazettes Extraordinary* No. 14,952/13 of April 6, 1971 contained the order "proscribing the organisation commonly known as Janatha Vimukti Peramuna"; and No. 14,954/15 of April 23, 1971 contained the order banning the publication of nine newspapers – *Kamkaru Puwath*; *Janatha Vimukti*; *Gini Pupura*; *Rathu Balaya*; *Rathu Lanka*; *Tharuna Satana*; *Virodaya*; *Rathu Kekula*; and *Tholilali Seydi*. Shortly after April 5th the Government put into operation a very strict censorship of all news pertaining to activities in the country arising from the emergency. All news items, articles and editorials, including foreign news despatches were subject to the censorship of the Competent Authority, and the regulations also empowered him to prevent or restrict publication in Ceylon, or any specified area of Ceylon, of matter which would or might be prejudicial to the interests of public security. The reports in the local newspapers during April and May 1971 added up to very little, therefore, and the information revealed was too scanty for considered judgement. There were no eye-witness accounts of any actual fighting between the armed services and police and the insurgents. The daily official communiques issued by the Director of Information were terse, detached and undramatic, and it was difficult to read between the lines of these official hand-outs. Only during the first week of May at the time of the first amnesty did local correspondents get their chance of joining the armed services in a few of their forays against the retreating guerillas in various parts of the country. These reports appeared in the first two weeks of May, with accompanying pictures, in the *Ceylon Daily News*, *Ceylon Observer*, *Sun*, *Times of Ceylon*, *Ceylon Observer Magazine Edition*, *Times Weekender* and *Weekend*.

58. CEYLON. House of Representatives. Debate on the Address of Thanks. *Parliamentary Debates (Hansard). House of Representatives. Official Report. Session 1971–72.* vol. 94, no. 1, March 28, 1971, cols 6–24; (94(2) April 4, 1971, cols. 36–160; 94(3) April 5, 1971, cols. 166–322; 94(4) April 6,

1971, cols. 333–336; 94(5) April 21, 1971, cols. 371–375; 94(6) May 4, 1971, cols. 488–588.

The Debate was substantially confined to four days, and both the Emergency situation and the events of April were discussed by speakers on both sides throughout the proceedings.

59. ——. Vote on Account 1971–72. Debate. *Parliamentary Debates (Hansard). House of Representatives. Official Report.* vol. 95, no. 1, Sept. 7, 1971, cols. 28–180; 95(2) Sept. 8, 1971, cols. 208–455; 95(3) Sept. 9, 1971, cols. 645–762.

The insurgency figured prominently in the discussions.

60. ——. Supplementary Supply 1971–72 – Expenses in connection with Emergency. *Parliamentary Debates (Hansard). House of Representatives. Official Report.* vol. 95, no. 5, Sept. 24, 1971, cols. 930–966 (Police); cols. 966–967 (Army); cols. 968–987 (Royal Ceylon Navy); cols. 988–999 (Royal Ceylon Air Force); cols. 1007–1009 (Dept. of Prisons).

The Supplementary Estimates figures were respectively: Police – Rs. 15,302,500/ =; Army – Rs. 64,897,247/ =; Royal Ceylon Navy – Rs. 1,837,690/ =; Royal Ceylon Air Force – Rs. 22,466,545/ =; Prisons (Insurgent & Rehabilitation Camps) – Rs. 5,145,516/ =.

61. ——. Capital Levy Bill. Debate on Second and Third Readings. *Parliamentary Debates (Hansard). House of Representatives. Official Report.* vol. 95, no. 15, Nov. 9, 1971, cols. 2021–2065, 2093–2172.

The insurgency figured in the speeches.

62. ——. Debate on the Second Reading of the Appropriation Bill 1971–72. *Parliamentary Debates (Hansard). House of Representatives. Official Report.* vol. 96, no. 2, Nov. 15, 1971 – vol. 96, no. 10 (pts. I & II), Nov. 25, 1971.

Nearly all the speakers, beginning with Mr. J. R. Jayawardene, Leader of the Opposition, and including the Prime Minister, made substantial reference to the insurrection and the continuing Emergency during the debate which lasted nine days.

63. ——. Appropriation Bill 1971–72. Considered in Committee. Third Reading. Head 2 – Prime Minister; Head 14 – Minister of Defence and External Affairs; Head 15 – Army; Head 16 – Royal Ceylon Navy; Head 17 – Royal Ceylon Air Force. *Parliamentary Debates (Hansard). House of Representatives .Official Report.* vol. 97, no. 1 (pt. I), Nov. 30, 1971, cols. 31–239.

Under these Heads, many speeches dealt with the insurrection and continuing emergency.

64. ——. Criminal Justice Commissions Bill. Second and Third Readings. Debate. *Parliamentary Debates (Hansard). House of Representatives. Official*

Report. vol. 99, no. 1, April 4, 1972, cols. 86–188; 99(2) April 5, 1972, cols. 217–555. (Third Reading, cols. 465–555.)

The Bill was read for the first time on 23rd March 1972, and read a second time on March 24th and ordered to be printed. The vote on the Second Reading was 110 in favour, 24 against, with 2 declining, and on the Third Reading taken in the early hours of April 6th morning, 111 in favour and eight against.

65. ——. Motion of no-confidence in Government. *Parliamentary Debates (Hansard). House of Representatives. Official Report*. vol. 99, no. 5, May 2, 1972, cols. 862–1000; 99(6) May 3, 1972, cols. 1013–1191.

The motion was defeated by 103 votes to 9, with 2 abstentions.

66. Ceylon. Senate. Debate on the Address of Thanks. *Parliamentary Debates (Hansard). Senate. Official Report*. vol. 32, no. 1, March 28, 1971 – vol. 32, no. 21, June 17, 1971.

The Emergency situation in the country and the events of April were repeatedly discussed in the speeches on both sides during the Debate, which occupied seventeen days.

67. ——. Constituent Assembly – Debate on Motion. *Parliamentary Debates (Hansard). Senate. Official Report*. vol. 33, no. 2, June 19, 1971, cols. 100–148; 33(3) June 24, 1971, cols. 170–211; 33(5) June 26, 1971, cols. 279–336; 33(6) July 2, 1971, cols. 354–404; 33(8) July 4, 1971, cols. 496–542; 33(11) July 18, 1971, cols. 710–759; 33(12) July 23, 1971, cols. 771–830; 33(17) Aug. 3, 1971, cols. 1145–1197 (unfinished).

Motion: "This House is of opinion that, in view of the situation, prevailing in the country at present, the sittings of the Constituent Assembly should be postponed until such time as the people are free to express their views freely and without any fear or restraint".

68. ——. Army Regulation [amending Soldiers' Enlistment Regulations, 1955]. *Parliamentary Debates (Hansard). Senate. Official Report*. vol. 33, no. 24, Sept. 8, 1971, cols. 1654–1660.

The Emergency was the theme of the discussion on this subject.

69. ——. Failure of the Government to give priority to the Ceylon (Constitution and Independence) Amendment Bill. Debate on Motion. (First [and last] day). *Parliamentary Debates (Hansard). Senate. Official Report*. vol. 33, no. 29, Sept. 23, 1971, cols. 1991–2063.

This was the last meeting of the Senate, before it was abolished at midnight on October 2, 1971.

70. Ceylon. Department of Information. *Äyī*? [Why?]. Colombo, Dept. of Govt. Printing, [1971], 26 pp., illus. (photos.).

Sinhala text. A booklet issued by the Government containing pictures of insurgent activity and its suppression, designed to pose the question as to why a progressive and benevolent administration should have become the target of such "terrorism".

71. CEYLON. Parliament. *Criminal Justice Commissions Act, No. 14 of 1972.* Date of assent, April 18, 1972. Colombo, Govt. Press, Ceylon, 1972. 15 pp.

The Act under which the main trial of the 41 principal suspects arrested in connection with the April 1971 insurrection was held from June 12th, 1972 to December 20, 1974, when the sentences were handed down.

72. CEYLON. Royal Commission of Inquiry on [the] University of Ceylon, Peradeniya. *Report of the Royal Commission appointed to inquire into the University of Ceylon, Peradeniya.* [Katubedde, Sri Lanka University Press, printers, 1974, i.e., 1975]. Ch. XXVIII. 'Introduction of fire-arms, hand-grenades and other explosives into the Campus prior to April 1971", pp. 213–249.

By a Warrant under the Seal of the Island of Ceylon dated February 8, 1972, the Governor-General, Mr. William Gopallawa, appointed Mr. Walter Wimalachandra (Chairman), and Messrs. B. L. W. Fernando and V. W. Kularatne (Members) to be a Commission of Inquiry under the Commissions of Inquiry Act (Ch. 393) for the purpose of inquiring into and reporting on various matters connected with the administration and functioning of the University of Ceylon in a period beginning on 1 January 1960 and ending on 31 December 1971. Item 2 of the Terms of Reference related to the circumstances under which firearms, hand-grenades and other explosives had been brought into the University Campus and stored there before April 1971, and whether any steps had been taken by the Authorities of the University in this connection, and, if so, the steps taken. Item 3 referred to remedial measures to be adopted in matters arising out of the investigation of Item 2. This chapter unfolds a sequence of events from 1960 linked to the increasing trends towards student indiscipline, incidents of disturbance, strikes, etc., which serve as a background to the events of March 1971 and the explosion at Marrs Hall on the 20th March 1971. The section entitled "Background to the events of March 1971" (pp. 226–244) describes in some detail the growth and activities of the Samajawadi Sangamaya, the student wing of the Janata Vimukti Peramuna, on the Peradeniya Campus from the middle sixties. Its organisation, methods of enlistment, the "five lectures", the attractions of its ideology, the dramatic radicalisation of its activities, and pen-pictures of its leading members are given in the course of the discussion. The cache of arms and explosives found on the campus after March 20, 1971 is listed in Appendix "V"; a list of those university students and employees detained as result of Police inquiries is annexed as Appendix "W"; and, the structure of JVP organisations for Kandy district is at Appendix "X", (p. 243). The Appendices to the Report have not been published so far. The Report was handed in on February 28, 1974, and published a year later, by the University, and not by the Government as a Sessional Paper in the usual form.

73. CEYLON SOLIDARITY CAMPAIGN. London. *Bulletin* No. 1, April 1972. 12 pp., illus.

Present crisis in Ceylon. pp. 1–11.

74. ——. *Bulletin* No. 2, May 1972. 11 pp., illus.

Illegality legalised, pp. 1–7. An analysis of the Criminal Justice Commissions Act of April 1972.

75. ——. *Bulletin* No. 3, July 1972. 11 pp., illus.

Constitution for repression – Republic of Sri Lanka, pp. 1–5. Comments on basic flaws in the new Constitution; Political trials begin, pp. 10–11.

76. ——. *Bulletin* No. 4, December 1972. 17 pp., illus.

An appeal for international solidarity, by Rohana Wijeweera, pp. 6–9; Ceylon Government gags the press, pp. 9–11; The political trials in Ceylon today, pp. 12–16.

77. ——. *Bulletin* No. 5, April 1973. 15 pp., illus.

Gagging of the press – the Press Council, pp. 7–10; Treatment of political detainees – a letter from prison, pp. 11–13; A brief essay on the history of Ceylon from a Marxist viewpoint, pp. 13–15.

78. ——. *Bulletin.* Special Issue May 1973. 20 pp., illus.

An analysis of three years of government by the U.L.F. in Sri Lanka, pp. 3–9; Messages of solidarity, p. 10; Report of C.S.C. activities in Britain, p. 11; Letter to the Prime Minister from the Committee of Concerned Asian Scholars (U.S.A.), p. 12; Tourism at the People's expense, pp. 13–14; Republic Day celebrations at the Sri Lanka High Commission, pp. 16–17.

79. ——. *Bulletin.* April 1974. 17 pp., illus.

Editorial. pp. 1–3; "War on Want" Report on Sri Lanka's tea industry, pp. 4–7, illus.; Anura, the alchemist perseveres: or, a lesson in mythmaking, pp. 13–15; War on Want – what can be done? pp. 16–17.

80. ——. *Bulletin.* September 1974. 15 pp., illus.

Editorial "End the repression", p. 1; Report on activities (of C.S.F.), pp. 2–3. Rohana Wijeweera's Defence Speech in J.V.P. Trial, pp. 5–12. (Reprinted from *New Left Review*, no. 84, March–April 1974.)

81. ——. *End repression in Ceylon: victory to the Ceylonese revolutionary struggle.* 1972, 2 pp. (Cyclostyled leaflet).

82. ——. *Island behind bars.* London, Ceylon Solidarity Campaign, [1972]. 24, iv pp., 3 illus., map.

A collection of documents giving background information and analysis of the events in Ceylon, and the ensuing government measures to contain them. The Ceylon Solidarity Campaign was formed in London on April 23, 1971 on the initiative of three revolutionary Ceylonese organisations led by the Ginipupura group. Ten British revolutionary organisations came together to pledge active and continuing support for the struggle being waged by the JVP. The *Bulletin* produced regularly aims to give up-to-date information on new developments, and news of activities of the Ceylon Solidarity Campaign in Britain and other countries. An International Day of Solidarity was observed on October 18, 1972, to coincide with the dawn to dusk hunger strike organised by the Human and Democratic Rights Organisation (HADRO) in Ceylon. A striking poster in colour was issued to mark the occasion. The Campaign has adopted certain basic aims and demands in the broad context of helping to unite and mobilise all revolutionary organisations, labour movements and others willing to support the continuing revolutionary struggle of the Ceylonese masses against all forms of oppression.

83. Ceylon today. Pts. I & II; From a Colombo Correspondent. *Frontier. A political weekly.* (Calcutta). Vol. 5, no. 3, April 29, 1972, pp. 6–10; vol. 5, no. 4, May 6, 1972, pp. 5–9.

An uninhibited and incisive evaluation of the dilemmas of the traditional Marxist parties in Ceylon arising from their collaboration, as subsidiary partners, with the urban and rural bourgeoisie, in an unseemly attempt to usher in reformist modes of socialism. Argues, in the light of the magnitude of the revolutionary youth movement, that the youth in the rural areas, though not constituting an actual proletariat, yet possess the characteristics of a revolutionary class in the Marxist sense, and that it is wrong to describe them as petit-bourgeoisie. The writer makes a close analysis of politics in Ceylon since 1956, and highlights, in particular, the futility of establishing socialism through the bourgeois state machine – a tactic to which the established Left has also succumbed. In the second part of the analysis, the strategy and organisation of the revolutionary youth in the late 'sixties are appraised in appreciative terms. "The extent of the revolutionary consciousness and the ingenuity and indication of the leadership could be gauged by the fact that in five years they managed to organise a network of dedicated full-time underground cadres whose total strength reached around 100,000. They managed to capture the main student bodies at the universities, set up a major cottage industry in the manufacture of hand-bombs, and give two weeks military training to over 20,000 right under the nose of the police. The traditional Marxist parties, after 25 years, cannot boast even of 10,000 members, among whom those who would do anything to risk their jobs, let alone their lives, are few". The course of the uprising is traced, and the strategy of repression and terror employed by the threatened bourgeois state to wipe out the radical and militant youth movement, which sought to replace it by force.

84. Chou En-Lai. *Prime Minister of the People's Republic of China.* Letter to Mrs. Bandaranaike dated 26 April 1971. *Ceylon Daily News.* vol. 56, no. 124, May 27, 1971, p. 1. Reprinted: *New Left Review.* (London). no. 69, Sept.–Oct. 1971, p. 91; *Ceylon: the JVP uprising of April 1971.* London, Solidarity London Pamphlet no. 42, 1972. Appendix V, p. 47.

The Chinese Government broke its surprising silence and revealed its official attitude to the insurrection in this message of assistance. It characterised the prevailing conditions as "the chaotic situation created by a handful of persons who style themselves "Guevarists" and into whose ranks foreign spies have sneaked", and went on to deplore ultra left and right opportunism, "acts of rebellion plotted by reactionaries at home and abroad", and attempts to sow discord between the two countries. A long term interest free loan of 150 million rupees was provided in convertible foreign exchange. The formal document was signed in Colombo a short while after the release of the letter, and other forms of material assistance, in the shape of armaments and gunboats, etc., were provided later. The reports of these gifts appeared in the local newspapers and official documents from time to time. It is worth remarking that this significant letter was not published in any Chinese newspaper or journal, in Chinese or English, and it became internationally available when it was officially released by the Government of Ceylon in Colombo exactly one month later. The Chinese Government has not questioned the authenticity of the letter, however. It is also interesting to observe that the Chinese press has not carried up to now any references to the state of emergency prevailing in Ceylon since March 1971, or to the facts of the insurrection in April. On May 22, 1971 *Renmin Ribao* published a map on the revolutionary situation in the world, including a symbol denoting mass struggle in India, but nothing at all for Ceylon. During the Prime Minister's visit to China from June 24th to July 5th 1972 as a state guest, there was no mention of the insurrection and this specific timely assistance in the speeches, reports and communiques reported in the Chinese and local press. Even the *Renmin Ribao* editorial of June 25th welcoming the distinguished guests did not contain a single reference to this notable loan.

85. Civil Rights Movement of Ceylon. *Minutes of the Inaugural Meeting of the Civil Rights Movement of Ceylon held on 18 November 1971.* Colombo, The Secretary, C.R.M., 1971, 3 pp.

The organisation was committed to the protection and promotion of the civil rights and liberties of the people of Ceylon at all times. These rights and liberties were to be regarded as a necessary accompaniment to radical social and economic change and the movement towards an egalitarian society. As its immediate task the CRM was to concern itself with the question of the restoration of certain rights and liberties that have recently been suspended. The first Chairman was Prof. E. R. Sarachchandra, with Mr. R. K. W. Goonesekera as Deputy Chairman, and Mr. R. Siriwardena as Secretary. Mr. Goonesekera became Chairman in 1972, on the resignation of Prof. Sarachchandra, who was later appointed Ambassador of Sri Lanka in Paris. Besides the one listed, a number of other CRM statements, relevant directly or indirectly to the insurgency, were issued.

86. ——. *Letter to the Hon. Sirimāvo R.D. Bandaranaike, Prime Minister,* [on the restoration of certain rights and liberties of the people suspended since the declaration of the State of Emergency in March 1971], dated 10th December 1971. Colombo, 1971, 11 pp.

Extracts reprinted in *Ceylon Committee Bulletin* (London), No. 3, 1972, pp. 2–9.

87. Criminal Justice Commission. Attorney General opens case against insurgents. Leads evidence of police to establish nature and extent of the rebellion. *Ceylon Daily News.* vol. 57, no. 139, June 13, 1972, pp. 1 + 3.

88. ——. Attorney General names forty-one suspects. Second day of sittings. Evidence of Army, Navy, and Air Force officers. *Ceylon Daily News.* vol. 57, no. 140, June 14, 1972, pp. 1 + 2 + 10.

The Commission of five judges of the Supreme Court appointed to try those involved in the abortive rebellion of April 1971, commenced its sittings on June 12, 1972. The principal trial of the 41 suspects was brought to a conclusion on December 20, 1974. The Attorney General framed charges against 41 suspects on four counts. Only 40 of them were charged, and only 36 were actually produced before the Commission. Four suspects were reported by the prosecution to be either dead or absconding. Four of the 36 suspects pleaded guilty to the charges of conspiracy to overthrow the lawfully elected government, and waging war against it. The 41st suspect, J. A. P. Jayakody, surrendered before the Commission at the concluding stages of the trial, and the prosecution withdrew the charges against him in the main trial. He was to be charged later in a separate case linked to incidents in the Kurunegala area. On July 3rd, 1973, Chief Justice H. N. G. Fernando, Chairman of the Commission, observed that the evidence led by the prosecution had established a prima facie case of a conspiracy to overthrow the Government either by an insurrection or by an attack on police stations during the April 1971 uprising. This was after the Attorney General had on the same day closed the case for the prosecution after the evidence of 32 witnesses had been led over a period of 148 days of hearing. The procedure regarding the presentation of the case for the suspects was outlined in a subsequent order of the Chairman the same day. (*Ceylon Daily News.* July 4, 1973, p. 1). The local newspapers carried each day fairly representative accounts of the proceedings, with perhaps, the best coverage in the *Sun,* until the Government sealed the presses and offices of the Independent Newspapers of Ceylon Ltd. (Sun Group) on 20th April 1974.

89. ——. Order of the Commission. *Ceylon Observer* (Late edition). vol. 195, no. 238, December 20, 1974, pp. 1 + 3; *Ceylon Daily News*. vol. 59, no. 303, December 21, 1974, pp. 1 + 5.

On December 20, 1974 the Commission made order setting out its determinations, and delivering its sentences on the 36 suspects. Though the judgment in the inquiry had been prepared, delays in translation and printing prevented its publication at the same time. The 13th suspect, Rohana Wijeweera, was sentenced to a term of rigorous imprisonment for life, the only such sentence to be awarded. Thirty-one others were found guilty, and received varying sentences ranging from twelve to two years' rigorous imprisonment. Four suspects, including Mahindapala Wijesekera, were acquitted. In the case of three suspects – Susil Sirivardhana, S. D. Bandaranaike, and T. D. Silva – the sentences of 2 years' rigorous imprisonment were suspended.

90. ——. Wijeweera: life term reduced to 20 yrs. R.I. *Ceylon Daily News*. vol. 60, no. 15, January 17, 1975, p. 1.

The Criminal Justice Commission made order on January 16th, 1975, vacating the sentence of life imprisonment imposed on the 13th suspect, Rohana Wijeweera, and substituting a sentence of 20 years' rigorous imprisonment instead. The reasons for this order were to be stated in the final judgment. In the opinion of lawyers the Commission had exceeded its powers in imposing a sentence of life imprisonment on Wijeweera on December 20th, 1974.

91. ——. *Criminal Justice Commission. Inquiry No. 1.* [Proceedings in court on June 12th and 13th, 1972. Official record.] Colombo, Secretary, Criminal Justice Commission, 1972. 8, 8, 5, 2, 3, 2, 2, 4, 2, 5, 4, 6, 4, 7, 2, 2, 2, 1, 1, 14 pp. (= 84 pp). Mimeographed text.

This Commission was established by Warrant dated 16th May 1972 and issued by the Governor-General under Section 2 of the Criminal Justice Commissions Act. The law under which the Commission was established introduced for the first time the concept of a Commission possessing punitive powers. This piece of controversial legislation was, no doubt, intended to serve a very special and extraordinary situation – a situation, in which, among other things, the practice and procedures of the prevailing laws of the land were inadequate to administer criminal justice. The first public sittings of the Commission were held on June 12th and 13th 1972, and were in the nature of a prelude or curtain raiser to the proceedings of the inquiry that ensued from August 10th, 1972 to December 20, 1974. On these two days the Attorney-General, Mr. Victor Tennekoon, placed before the Commission certain reports from persons in the Police and Armed Services, "competent to speak of what happened during this period", to provide the five Judges with the background necessary to understand the more particularised evidence relating to the offences connected with the insurrection of April 1971. The authors of the reports, themselves, were called to read out their reports before the Commission, and this record of the proceedings contains fifteen reports presented on the two days. The Inspector-General of Police, Mr. Stanley Senanayake was the first to be called, and he gave a general picture of the gradual growth of a movement which, on April 5, 1971, put into execution their theories of armed revolution. Reports from a few police officers were followed by similar reports of operations during the insurgency by Army, Navy and Air Force officers. Insurgent attacks on police stations, their success and failure, and the consequent clearing of captured territory by combined operations in which the Army, Navy, Air Force, and Police joined in the Anuradhapura, Polonnaruwa, Kegalle, Galenbindunuwewa, Elpitiya, Kosgoda, Matara and Deniyaya, and other areas are narrated. The final report of 14 pages was by the Commander, Sri Lanka Air Force, Air Commodore P. H. Mendis, on "Insurgency operations of 1971". This report is marked "SECRET", and was dated 8th June 1972. Most of the reports are undated, and, those that do, bear dates in the very early part of June, 1972, a few days before the Commission began its sittings. Press reports of the proceedings appeared in the daily papers (*see* nos. 87–90). For reprinted versions of Air Commodore P. H. Mendis report, *see* no. 155. For the official record of the court proceedings from August 10, 1972 to December 20, 1974, *see* no. 92.

92. ——. *Criminal Justice Commission. Inquiry No. 1.* [Proceedings in court, August 10th, 1972–December 20, 1974. Official record]. Colombo, Secretary, Criminal Justice Commission, 1972–1975. 11,775 pp. Mimeographed text.

The proceedings in court each day were taken down by English and Sinhala stenographers, and a taped recording was also made. The tape was matched with the steno-record. The official record was in English, as stated by the Commission, but the Sinhala proceedings were produced separately and referred to as necessity arose. The benefit of the doubt arising from any mistakes or omissions in the English record was afforded to any suspect raising the issue. The production of the official record varied from two weeks to two or three months, and the English and Sinhala records were given out simultaneously. The five judges, however, received their copies in a week or so.

93. Crossette-Thambiah, R. W. The insurgency and aftermath. *Stranger in his land.* Colombo, Gunaratne and Co., printers, 1974. pt. II, pp. 95–135. "The Insurgency", pp. 96–101; "The eight days under insurgent rule", pp. 101–132; "Postscript", pp. 132–135.

The thoughts and reflections of a retired Ceylonese doctor in his sixties on the tide of insurrection as it flowed through the village of Bulathkohupitiya in Kegalla district, where he was living and working as a medical missionary. The description of the village under insurgent administration for eight days when the police deserted their station is revealing as to the self-discipline and sense of responsibility of the youth in revolt.

94. Crump, Julian. The struggle for Ceylon. *The Spokesman.* (Nottingham). nos. 13–14, June–July 1971, pp. 61–65, 1 pl.

The author is a British academic working in development economics who had spent some time in Ceylon close to the outbreak in April 1971. Underscores the perplexing situation in Ceylon where the gap between rhetoric and ideology is so gapingly large, and where a coalition of three "socialist revolutionary" parties is so unwilling and incapable of taking radical action. Speculates on the future for a genuine socialist revolution in Ceylon, with the JVP acting as a catalyst and vanguard.

95. David, Kumar. The 1971 rebellion. *Gauge. Magazine of the Engineering Students' Union.* (University of Ceylon, Peradeniya). vol. 2, no. 5, 1972, pp. 67–72 + 78.

The political nature of the 1971 insurrection is examined from the point of view of revolutionary Marxist tenets. An analysis of the class character of the participants is a prelude to concluding that the JVP was a racialist, chauvinist, petit-bourgeois rural youth movement exhibiting the crudest fascist attitudes in their methods and organisation. Their failure has only put the clock of socialism back considerably in that the reactionary right-wing forces have been strengthened. The author is a Lecturer in the Engineering Faculty of the University of Ceylon, a member of the LSSP, and a regular commentator on current Sri Lanka affairs in the *Nation.*

96. DECORNOY, Jacques. Interview with Ceylonese Prime Minister. An outline of anti-subversive activities. *Le Monde. Weekly* (English edition). June 3–9, 1971, p. 3.

An interview of nine questions and answers six weeks after the fighting broke out, in which the Prime Minister made some frank admissions. She surmised that the JVP substantially supported her election campaign in the belief that her administration would be more liberal than the UNP, and this climate would help the movement to organise themselves better for revolt. She also conceded that there did not seem to be any fundamental difference between the reports of JVP plans and tactics in April 1970 (as available to the then government and reported in the press) and what actually happened a year later.

97. ——. Ceylan, naissance d'une révolution. Pts. 1–4. *Le Monde.* Juin 16, 1971, pp. 4–5; Juin 17, 1971, p. 5; Juin 18, 1971, p. 6; Juin 19, 1971, p. 5, map.

The titles of the four parts were: 1. Péril Jeune contre sahibs bruns [Youth uprising against brown sahibs]; 2. Les bombes de la décolonisation [The bombs of decolonisation]; 3. Dans la jungle des campagnes [In the jungle of the countryside]; 4. Notre agent à Colombo [Our agent in Colombo].

98. ——. Ceylon – a case of persistent political myopia. *Le Monde. Weekly.* (English edition). July 1–7, 1971, p. 4.

A fairly full summarised translation of the four-part article in French listed as no. 97.

99. ——. Ceylon: birth of a revolution. *Peace Press. An international information service.* (London). vol. 7, nos. 5–6, June–July 1971, pp. 8–22.

A different English translation of the entire four-part French article by the same title in *Le Monde* listed as no. 97.

100. DE SILVA, Mervyn. An Eden's calm shattered. *The Washington Post.* May 23, 1971, pp. B1 + B5, 3 illus.; Reprinted: *Ceylon Today.* vol. 20, nos. 3–4, March–April 1971, pp. 20–25; as "Background to the crisis". *Ceylon Observer Magazine Edition.* June 8, 1971, p. 6.

The Chief Editor of the Lake House group of newspapers delineates the successive stages of welfare politics which produced the conditions in which radical youth leaders found a captive audience, leading to the explosion of April.

101. ——. April and its aftermath. April crisis has instilled in us a new sense of urgency, says Prime Minister. *Ceylon Observer Magazine Edition.* vol. 6, no. 38, Oct. 10, 1971, p. 6.

Full text of an exclusive two and a half hour interview given by Mrs. Bandaranaike to the Chief Editor of the Lake House group of newspapers, in which the Prime Minister expressed her hopes and fears for the future, and evaluated frankly the situation facing the Government as a result of the trauma of April.

102. ——. Sri Lanka: the end of welfare politics. *South Asian Review. The Journal of the Royal Society for India, Pakistan and Ceylon.* (London). vol. 6, no. 2, January 1973, pp. 91–109. Reprinted (in 3 parts); *Ceylon Observer Magazine Edition.* June 3, 10, 17, 1973.

An unbuttoned analysis of the Ceylonese political experience since 1948, with special emphasis on the role of the old left, alone and in league with the ruling Sri Lanka Freedom Party of the national bourgeoisie, in contributing to the rapidly deteriorating conditions of the current crisis. Discusses the failure of the existing political system, based on British style parliamentary democracy and state welfare schemes, to produce the desired dramatic economic and social change, and more important to satisfy the rising aspirations of the youth forces spawned by that very system. The "silent revolution" of 1970 shattered by the remarkable April insurrection a year later is also dissected, and the inevitable appearance of the radical new left liberation front is outlined against this background.

103. DE SILVA, Rohan. The revolt of the DDT generation. The insurgence in Ceylon may be the first move in the storming of the barricades. *Insight.* (Hong Kong). vol. 1, no. 7, July 1971, pp. 33–35.

Indicates that, besides the generation gap, the revolt of the young in Ceylon underscores the acute sense of letdown among the educated young, disenchanted by economic policies which hold out no hope for the postwar generation. Elitist politics have been dominated by issues of race, class and caste at the expense of clear economic objectives. Postwar political power games are replayed in the discussion of how the ideology of despair which led youth into open rebellion was dismissed too easily as subversive and Communist. If the role of the young is not recognised, and an opportunity for constructive participation not created quickly, the April insurgence could lead to "a total destruction of the elitist elements and the privileged caste group that has ruled Ceylon as if it were their private fiefdom". The title of the article derives its meaning from the fact that, as the result of the excellent malaria control programs adopted in the late 'thirties, the pressure of young population was greatest in the North-Western and North Central provinces of the island, especially the Kegalle and Kurunegala districts.

104. DEUTSCHER, Tamara. Letter from Ceylon. *New Left Review* (London). no. 64, Nov.–Dec. 1970, pp. 38–48.

A review of the political scene, with an early estimate of the radical JVP movement, by the widow of Isaac Deutscher, who spent a month in Ceylon in August 1970.

105. ——. Civil war in Ceylon. *Ramparts Magazine* (Berkeley, California). vol. 10, no. 1, July 1971, pp. 26–29. Reprinted as "What next in Ceylon?". *Journal of Contemporary Asia* (Stockholm). vol. 1, no. 3, 1971, pp. 67–73.

An estimate of the political confusion after the suppression of the insurrection, and the pointers to greater external influence in the attempt to head off future shock.

106. DEVANANDA, Yohan. *Sevaka. Violent Lanka. The day for slaughter. An interpretation of the revolt of April 1971.* Ibbagamuwa (Sri Lanka), Devasaranaramaya, 1972. 20 pp.; 2nd ed. (Dec. 1972). [5], 20 pp.

This tour-de-force analysis written in the heat of events at the end of May 1971 was cyclostyled for private circulation as a pamphlet at the end of May 1972 by the author, earlier known as John Cooray, a communitarian socialist "drop-out" Anglican priest, pursuing ascetic goals of community living and collective farming in the Kurunegala district. A long free verse ballad occupies pp. 1–11, and a commentary on the April insurrection follows on pp. 12–20. The second edition, seven months later, had a three-page preface containing explanatory remarks in view of comments made on the first edition. The main intention in the interpretation put forward in "*Violent Lanka*" has been to focus attention on the injustice and violence – both open and hidden – that lies behind the authorities, laws and institutions of society. The understanding behind the interpretation came out of common consultation and dialogue in a particular grass-roots situation – the Ibbagamuva People's Committee for Land Reform that began in 1970. Explains that the JVP was "undoubtedly part of the deep movement of liberation" despite their questionable strategy and methods, and was permeated by a genuine revolutionary spirit. "They shook a whole nation and called it to corporate penitence and corporate search for a more just and more effective way of life". A Sinhalese translation of "*Violent Lanka*", in many ways an orginal and creative work in its own right, has also been produced for private circulation. The ballad alone was published as an eight-page supplement to *CMS Newsletter*, no. 375, Nov. 1973 by the Church Missionary Society in London. It is introduced in the accompanying *CMS Newsletter* by an article entitled "Pilgrim to the barricades" by John V. Taylor, drawing attention to the significance of the poem in the context of Devananda's life and work, especially in connection with the April 1971 upheaval.

107. [Devinuwara, Sumith]. *Janata Vimukti Peramunē desapalanamaya nyāyātmaka ha samvidhānamaya padanama pilibanda vigrahayak.* [An analysis of the political, ideological, and organisational basis of the Janata Vimukti Peramuna]. *Vimuktiyē Udāva* [The Dawn of Liberation]. vol. 1, no. 1, March 1973, pp. [6]–[15]. Footnotes are given on 4 separate pages at the end of this unpaginated mimeographed first issue of a journal in Sinhala.

A Marxist-Leninist critique of the theory and practice of the JVP, as a petty bourgeois political organisation, and its perversion of revolutionary socialist objectives in rejecting the leadership of the proletariat in its struggle to transform the economy. Upholds the dictatorship of the proletariat, the destruction of the capitalist state machinery, and the elimination of private ownership as the only true strategy.

108. Dumont, Rene. La "Commune" de Ceylan et le chomage, produits du "populisme". *Esprit.* nos. 7–8, July–Aug. 1971, pp. 126–132.

The social welfare and "populist" policies of Ceylon governments since Independence contributed to the creation of a large and dissatisfied segment of radical unemployed youth, which resorted to violence when the expected electoral promises of the United Front Government were not forthcoming. The noted French agronomist was an adviser to the Government on agricultural programs, and spent some time in the country during this period. These articles were written shortly after he left Ceylon.

109. ——. La révolte des jeunes rebelles sans espoir, au centenaire de la Commune de Paris. *Paysanneries aux abois: Ceylon, Tunisiè, Sénégal.* Paris,Éditions du Seuil, 1972. Ch. 3, pp. 73–92.

The revolt of the youth without hope on the centenary of the Paris Commune. This is one of the three chapters on Ceylon in a book on the peasantry at bay in Ceylon, Tunisia and Senegal. The two other chapters deal with political "populism" aggravated by unemployment, and agrarian reforms in the cause of mobilising for economic independence.

110. FALLACI, Oriana. Ceylon: una tragedia sconosciuta. Photographs by Gianfranco Moroldo. *L'Europeo. Settimanale Politico di Attualita* (Milan). vol. 27, no. 32, Aug. 12, 1971, pp. 36–47, 9 col. illus.

A question and answer interview with Mrs. Bandaranaike, the Prime Minister, is on pp. 43–47.

111. ——. Un'inchiesta che ci fa capire l'Asia d'oggi. I draghi di Ceylon. Photographs by Gianfranco Moroldo. *L'Europeo*. vol. 27, no. 33, Aug. 19, 1971, pp. 36–47, 7 col. illus., 3 monochrome.

The well-known Italian political journalist visited Ceylon in connection with these reports on the situation.

112. FERNANDO, Tissa. Elite politics in the new states: the case of post-Independence Sri Lanka. *Pacific Affairs*. vol. 46, no. 3, Fall 1973, pp. 361–383.

After an introductory discourse on the dynamics of elite political systems, the actual workings of an elite model in the case of post-Independence Ceylon is investigated. Eschewing a conventional analysis of the formal political structure which too often serves as a misleading facade, the author surveys the political scene by examining the composition of the numerically small social elite which has wielded power, and its relationship to the non-elite who have no access to areas of crucial decision-making. The significant distinction between the governing elite and the non-governing elite is elaborated in the Ceylonese context, and how the dichotomy between those who wield power and those who are content to be ruled has been kept going skilfully by the former group. The emergence of an unprecedented new popular element introduced by the J.V.P. may constitute a "rival political structure", and provide an altogether new perspective through which to approach the interpretation of contemporary politics. The survival of elite politics on the old model appears to be seriously threatened by the unconventional forces thrown up by the recent events in Ceylon.

113. GILES, Frank. What went wrong in Ceylon. Mrs. Sirimavo Bandaranaike gives an exclusive question and answer interview to Frank Giles, Deputy Editor of the *Sunday Times*. *The Sunday Times*. October 31, 1971, p. 9. Reprinted as: "Embodiment of non-alignment". *Ceylon Daily News*. November 5, 1971, p. 4.

"As far as we know, the insurgency was entirely an indigenous affair, prepared and carried out by a movement of young revolutionaries, that has been building up for four or five years... There was no question of any outside support or influence". Stressed that the crisis helped to strengthen Ceylon's image of neutrality and non-alignment.

114. GILLILAND, Elizabeth. Ceylon the bitter harvest. *The Nation* (New York). May 10, 1971, pp. 582–584.

A free-lance journalist, editor and poet in Ceylon during the revolt comments on the happening. "Effective economic planning and leadership that can evoke forces of constructive change are desperately needed in Ceylon as the nation tries to do in one generation what took the West three centuries – to move from feudalism into the modern world... But in the immediate context, the answering of force with force seems to be the government's only recourse for dealing with what one hopes will be a short-lived bitter spring".

115. *Ginipupura Ceylon Spark.* London, Ginipupura publications, 1971, 6 pp.

Organ of a Ceylonese revolutionary group in London openly sympathetic to the aims and methods of the JVP. Issued after the April outbreak.

116. GOUGH, Kathleen. The South Asian revolutionary potential. *Bulletin of Concerned American Scholars* (San Francisco). 4 (1) Winter 1972: 77–96. Reprinted in: *Imperialism and Revolution in South Asia*; ed. by Kathleen Gough and Hari P. Sharma. New York, Monthly Review Press, 1973. pp. 3–42.

Explores the central problems of estimating the revolutionary potential and resistance movements in India, Pakistan and Ceylon, and the root causes of the failure of economic and social welfare programs set in motion by their respective governments since independence twenty-five years ago, which has provoked insurrection. The Ceylon situation arising from the emergence of the Janatha Vimukthi Peramuna in the mid-sixties, and the preemptive measures taken by the Government to repress the movement are discussed to explain the eruption of the mass struggle of youths in April 1971 (pp. 82–84). Certain interesting new features characterising the revolutionary socialist groups in South Asia are brought out, in the context of "severe repression", and the need to undertake reassessment and regrouping. The author, Professor of Anthropology at the University of Toronto, and well-known for her work in the field of Eastern anthropology, wrote the first version of this paper for the annual meeting of the American Anthropological Association in New York in November 1971, and this is a later revised and expanded version, which was also published as "Imperialism and Revolutionary Potential in South Asia", in *Monthly Review* (New York), 23 (10), March 1972: 25–45.

117. GUNASEKERA, Prins. *M.P. for Habaraduwa.* Statement in the House of Representatives on crossing from the Government to the Opposition Benches. *Parliamentary Debates (Hansard). House of Representatives. Official Report.* vol. 95, no. 6, Oct. 5, 1971, cols. 1078–1092.

The statement was in Sinhala, and a summarised censored version in English was published in the *Ceylon Daily News* October 7, 1971, p. 3, under the caption "Prins crosses over to the Opposition".

118. ——. Speech on Appropriation Bill, 1973. *National State Assembly Debates. Official Report.* vol. 3, no. 6, Nov. 21, 1972, cols. 960–1023.

119. ——. Persons taken into custody or detained [between 16th March–5th April]. *National State Assembly Debates. Official Report.* vol. 5, no. 3, Feb. 8, 1973, col. 168.

Mr. Gunasekera asked a question from the Prime Minister, "(a) Will she table a list of the names of persons who were taken into custody or detention at each police station in the island during the period 16th March to 5th April 1971? (b) Will she state the address, age and status of each of these persons?". The "*Schedule tabled in reply to questions for oral answer No. 5 at col. 168 of the Official Report of 8th February 1973*" was published as an Appendix to vol. 5, no. 3 in June 1973, and consisted of 162 pages of names, addresses and occupations of persons taken into custody at each police division throughout Ceylon during the period mentioned. A total of 5,067 persons are listed under 18 police divisions, and the breakdown of the statistics is revealing, as indicating the number of suspects already under arrest and immobilised before the first shots were fired in the insurrection: Colombo – 1,117; Kalutara – 221; Galle – 300; Kegalle – 166; Kalaniya – 269; Badulla – 69; Gampaha – 348; Mount Lavinia – 274; Nugegoda – 251; Matara – 165; Chilaw – 229; Batticaloa – 245; Ratnapura – 264; Kurunegala – 17; Anuradhapura – 151; Jaffna – 263; Nuwara Eliya – 265; Kandy – 453.

A corrected statement (deleting the names of children who had only accompanied their parents to the police stations) was tabled and published as an Appendix to vol. 7, no. 1, August 7, 1973. 154 pp.

120. ——. The fight for civil liberties in Ceylon. A question and answer interview with an American visitor on January 17th, 1972. *Intercontinental Press*. vol. 10, no. 8, Feb. 28, 1972, pp. 203–205.

Mr. Gunasekera is the Secretary of the Human and Democratic Rights Organisation, formed on November 5th, 1971.

121. ——. Persons who died in incidents of April 1971. *National State Assembly Debates. Official Report*. vol. 6, no. 7, June 7, 1973, cols. 1240–1248.

Mr. Gunasekera asked the Prime Minister whether she would make public, as she said recently she would, the names of all those who died in the incidents of April 1971, their addresses, ages, occupations, places and dates of death, and the circumstances in which the deaths occurred and whether memorials would be erected for them in every district of Ceylon, and if not why? The discussion developed into a verbal flurry of thrust and counterthrust between Mr. Gunasekera and members of the Government, and the question was stood down in the confusion.

122. GUNAWARDENA, Victor. The Insurgency. Pts. 1–4. *The Times of Ceylon Sunday Illustrated*. Dec. 21, 1975; Dec. 28, 1975; Jan. 4, 1976; Jan. 11, 1976.

A four-part survey of the insurrection, its background, participants, and aftermath. The concern of the writer is to shed light on the uprising as a historical event, outline the social injustices that gave rise to it, analyse the social composition of the rebels and their future, and draw lessons from this remarkable occurrence in the annals of revolt in any country.

123. HALLIDAY, Fred. The Ceylonese insurrection. *New Left Review*. no. 69, Sept.–Oct. 1971, pp. 55–91, 5 tables, map.

A searching and sympathetic appraisal of the unusual political origins of the JVP which masterminded the unexpected revolutionary explosion of April 1971. The theory and tactics of this unique radical youth movement with a decided ultra-Marxist approach, which developed as a split on the left from the pro-Chinese Communist party, are discussed in the light of their own statements in their papers. This article became almost required reading for the sheltered English-only speaking, Westernised Ceylonese intelligentsia, shocked out of their conventional wits by the astonishing verve and unsuspected strength of an underground radical Sinhala youth movement. The nature of the present economic and social crisis, which saw the emergence of the JVP as a political force, is examined, and the course of the insurrection, its repression, and the "permanent emergency" situation following it appraised. The complete text of Chou En-Lai's letter to Mrs. Bandaranaike dated April 26, 1971 is given on p. 91. The French translation of this article, "L'insurrection cinghalaise", was published in *Le Temps modernes* (Paris), no. 305, Dec. 1971, pp. 775–806; no. 306, Jan. 1972, pp. 1001–1025. A digest of Halliday's article appears in the same issue of *New Left Review* under the heading "Themes" on pp. 1–2. A revised and extended version of this article with the same title was published in *Explosion in a sub-continent. India, Pakistan, Bangladesh and Ceylon*; ed. by Robin Blackburn. Penguin Books, 1975. pp. 151–220.

124. HENSMAN, C. Richard. Rural revolution in Ceylon. *Venture* (London). vol. 23, no. 6, June 1971, pp. 17–20.

Probes the reasons for guerilla uprising in April 1971, and how Ceylon's most left-wing government ever provoked the country's first mass revolt. A very sympathetic outline of the rise to power and rapid influence of the JVP, and the repressive measures adopted by the Government to preserve itself in power. Suggests that the insurrection has precipitated the most profound and far-reaching change in the island's history since the British captured the Kandyan provinces, and the lines are drawn for a prolonged struggle between the underprivileged and rebellious rural (and urban) poor and the well-armed forces of law and order. The author is a Ceylonese broadcaster and writer living in London, and author of "From Gandhi to Guevara", "Rich against Poor", etc. A letter to the editor by Hugh Gray refuting certain assertions in Hensman's analysis was published in *Venture*. vol. 23, no. 7, July 1971, p. 31.

125. HOUTART, François. The insurrection of 1971 as the expression of the non-recognition of the dominated group in the political field. *Religion and ideology in Sri Lanka*. Bangalore, Theological Publications, St. Peter's Seminary; Colombo, Hansa Publishers Ltd., 1974. Ch. 2, ii, 4, pp. 341–365, 7 tables.

A discussion of the principal orientations of the formal political power in the years during which the movement developed, since its foundation in 1964, until it erupted into insurrection in 1971, serves as a prelude to the analysis of the J.V.P., on pp. 344–358. The social composition of the movement and the main outlines of its ideology are evaluated. Various sources have been used: official documents, the records of the principal trial which began in June 1972, the text of the Five Lectures of the J.V.P.; declarations made to the police by some of the leaders, including Wijeweera, and some personal interviews. The orientation of the political system after the insurrection is discussed on pp. 358–365.

126. HYDE, Douglas. *Ceylon's programme for the rehabilitation of political detainees*. Colombo, Dept. of Govt. Printing, Sri Lanka, 1972 [i.e., 1973]. [4], 15 pp.

Mr. Hyde, a former British Communist Party member and *Daily Worker* editor, was invited by the Government of Sri Lanka to express his views on the Rehabilitation Programme since April 1971 of the insurgent youth detained in camps. His report dated May 1972 is an evaluation of a year's work up to April 1972. He toured seven of the camps where suspected insurgents were incarcerated, and applauds the general scheme of rehabilitation, and arrangements in these institutions. His report, however, does not conceal a depressing gap between theory and practice even in the select camps inspected. After the hell-holes of Indonesia and South Vietnam, Hyde was obviously impressed by the human-touch organisation in Ceylon, though he is concerned, nevertheless, to emphasise the poor features even here – overcrowding, poor food, lack of opportunities for exercise, primitive hygiene, and the isolation from parents and friends. The Minister of Parliamentary Affairs and Sports, who had ministerial responsibility for these camps, contributes a "Foreword", and the report is published by the Department of Rehabilitation, functioning under the aegis of the same Ministry. Major extracts from the report were earlier serialised in the *Ceylon Daily News* in three instalments on June 27, 28 and 29th, 1972 on p. 4 each day, under the title "Report on Lanka's rehabilitation camps."

127. JAYAWARDENE, C. H. S. *Value changes of the emerging youth in Ceylon. The insurgence of 1971*. 28 pp. (Typescript).

The author of this paper, written in 1972, was formerly Senior Lecturer in Forensic Medicine at the University of Ceylon, and is now Professor of Criminology at the University of Ottawa. *See also* no. 216.

128. JAYAWARDENE, Junius Richard. *M.P. for Colombo South. Leader of the Opposition.* "In the name of God, go!". Speech on "Youth and the development programme", at a Youth Seminar in Colombo on March 10, 1971. *Times Weekender.* March 11, 1971, p. 1. Reprinted as: "Youth in revolt". *Selected speeches 1944–1973.* Colombo, H. W. Cave, 1974, pp. 92–94.

An appeal to the Government to abandon office, if they were unable to face up to the swelling youth problems.

129. ——. Who is behind it all? Statement in the House of Representatives. *Parliamentary Debates (Hansard). House of Representatives. Official Report.* vol. 94, no. 10, May 22, 1971, cols. 932–936. Reprinted: *Ceylon Daily News.* vol. 56, no. 121, May 23, 1971, pp. 1 + 7.

130. ——. J.R. clarifies co-operation. A question and answer interview. *Ceylon Observer Magazine Edition*, vol. 7, no. 4, Jan. 23, 1972, pp. 1 + 11.

131. ——. Time for co-operation. Appeal to all political leaders for united effort on common program. *Ceylon Daily News.* Jan. 25, 1972, p. 1.

132. ——. *Tharuna Viplavaya. Youth in revolt.* Colombo, Varuna Publishers, 1972. [6], 130 pp.

A collection of eight talks on a topical subject (including speeches in Parliament).

133. ——. The question of the release of all those detained without trial under Emergency regulations including those detained in connection with the 1971 insurgent activities. *National State Assembly Debates. Official Report.* vol. 6, no. 9, June 21, 1973, cols. 1659–1671.

This question led to a discussion in the course of which the Minister of Justice, Mr. Felix Dias Bandaranaike, vouchsafed the following information. Some 18,000 persons were taken into custody in connection with the April 1971 insurrection, of whom about 13,500 had been released after full inquiry, and there were less than 4,500 persons still in custody. Of the number released only 50 were re-arrested, indicating the success of the Government's rehabilitation program. The present Criminal Justice Commission hearing the main case against the 41 suspects would not be prolonged, and after charge sheets had been issued to suspects in custody who have still not been prosecuted, the C.J.C. had the power to pass suspended sentences, and the Minister further expressed the belief that many suspects would confess and seek pardon. The Government had no intention of following a vindictive policy in this matter.

134. ——. Statement in the National State Assembly on 10th January 1974 in tabling another statement made by him as Leader of the Opposition on behalf of the Opposition Members to His Excellency the President of the Republic of Sri Lanka on 3rd January 1974 at the President's House. *National State Assembly Debates. Official Report.* vol. 10, no. 1, 10th January 1974, cols. 107–112; Appendix I & II, cols. 134–144.

The English statement made to the President on 3rd January appears as Appendix I, cols. 138–139. Both statements referred to "plans" carried out at Attanagalla during the Opposition Satyagraha on 9th December 1973, and "tentative plans" which were not carried out at the Anuradhapura Satyagraha on 8th January 1974 owing to the government ban. These "plans" were to assist a revolutionary group within and outside Parliament to come into power.

135. ——. Speech on proposing an Opposition motion to appoint a "Select Committee to investigate an alleged conspiracy to destroy sovereignty of the people". *National State Assembly Debates. Official Report.* vol. 10, no. 5, 6th March 1974, cols. 813–862 (Sinhala text of speech, cols. 863–890).

The Leader of the Opposition accused the Government of accommodating within its ranks the "Janavegaya" group, including members of the Prime Minister's family, who form an inner Cabinet, constituting the real government in which most Ministers are only figureheads. This issue was first raised by Mr. Jayawardene on 10th January 1974, subsequent to which he met the Prime Minister on 11th January, and on the Prime Minister's refusal to appoint a Select Committee to investigate the evidence, the Leader of the Opposition wrote a letter to her on 15th January. This motion is a sequel to these events. The close connections of some members of the "Janavegaya" group with the J.V.P. both in Ceylon and in London are detailed in the statement, and the current moves to deprive the Opposition of the right to form a government democratically. Various episodes in 1971 which attempt to link the members of this group with the April insurrection are mentioned, and the continuing relationships of these persons with some of those incarcerated in connection with the April uprising and later released. Mr. Kumar Rupasinghe and Mrs. Sunethra Rupasinghe, the son-in-law and daughter of the Prime Minister, are two of the key members of this group, which is alleged to be active in undermining the proper processes of the prevailing democratic system, either by establishing a military government, by rigging the general election, or by cancelling it. At the end of the debate in which the Prime Minister replied to the statement, the motion was rejected by 99 votes to 25. *See also* nos. 34, 35, and 192.

136. ——. Statement on "Question of Privilege: Documents tabled in the Assembly". *National State Assembly Debates. Official Report.* vol. 10, no. 6, pt. 1, 21st March 1974, cols. 1088–1089; 1113–1122.

On March 21st, 1974, the Prime Minister made a statement in the Assembly that the documents produced and tabled in the House by the Leader of the Opposition in support of the Opposition Motion on March 6th, 1974, had been found to be forgeries, and castigated him for irresponsibility and a reckless desire for political gain. Mr. Jayawardene, in a statement prior to this on the same day, as well as in the statement immediately following, described the investigation as highly irregular and lacking in respect of the due processes of judicial inquiry, and parliamentary privilege. It had also been conducted with scant regard for the elementary principles on which the request for a Select Committee of the Assembly had been based.

137. JEYASINGHAM, Shakuntala Jean. Janatha Vimukthi Peramuna. *South Asian Studies. Bi-annual Journal of South Asia Studies Centre,* (University of Rajasthan, Jaipur). vol. 9, nos. 1 & 2, Jan.–July 1974, pp. 1–16, 1 chart, 1 table.

A Junior Research Fellow of the South Asia Studies Centre discusses the origins, development and ill-fated activities of "the only truly radical, revolutionary party in Sri Lanka, i.e., Janatha Vimukthi Peramuna (J.V.P.)". The article is based mostly on Criminal Justice Commission sittings in Inquiry No. 1 as reported in the Ceylonese daily press, and personal interviews with leaders of left parties, one of whom commented that only the JVP "could call itself left, but it was destroyed before it ever blossomed leaving the entire left movement in shambles".

138. Jupp, James. *The JVP insurrection of 1971 and its impact on the Marxist and socialist movements in Ceylon.* 22 pp.

Paper presented at the Centre of South Asian Studies Conference on Social Change in Sri Lanka held on 20–21 March, 1974 at the School of Oriental and African Studies, London University. The author, who teaches political science at the University of York, describes the events surrounding the April 1971 insurrection, and the emergence and involvement of the J.V.P. in this tragic catastrophe. After a quick survey of the actual insurrectionary phase, and its impact, the writer analyses the character of the JVP, its relations with the Marxist movement, the tactics of rebellion, and the opposition from fellow Marxists. In a final section the possibility of the 1971 eruption being as fundamental a dividing line in the political experience of Ceylon as the social revolution of 1956 is discussed. In *The Annual Register of World Events in 1972* (London, Macmillan, 1972) the writer had earlier dealt briefly with these same events on pp. 282–285, in his round-up on Ceylon.

139. The JVP on the Peradeniya Campus; by "Akbar". *Nation.* vol. 5, no. 28, May 1, 1971, p. 10.

By tracing the meteoric rise of the movement on the largest campus of the University of Ceylon, the author hopes some light will be thrown on important aspects of its appeal, which the United Front parties failed to counter or even understand till too late. Analyses the nature of the social and psychological cul-de-sac in which the majority of the students entering the universities were trapped, thus enhancing the quick-fire seductiveness of the JVP programme.

140. Kearney, Robert N. *The 1971 Ceylonese uprising: an ecological interpretation of its origin and fate.* Paper prepared for the Research Conference on Communist Revolutions at St. Croix, Virgin Islands, January 24–28, 1973.

Unpublished as yet. *See also* no. 10.

141. ——. The 1971 insurrection. *The politics of Ceylon* (Sri Lanka). Ithaca, N.Y., London, Cornell University Press, 1973, pp. 201–208.

An estimate of the political and psychological consequences of the April 1971 uprising, considered in the light of the swift rise and ruthless suppression of the radical youth movement.

142. ——. The Marxist parties of Ceylon. *Radical politics in South Asia*; ed. by Paul R. Brass and Marcus F. Franda. Cambridge, Mass., M.I.T. Press, 1973. (Studies in Communism, Revisionism and Revolution – No. 19). Ch. 7, pp. 401–439, map, 3 tables.

An account of the shifting fortunes of the cluster of Marxist parties and groups since 1935, with special emphasis on the Trotskyite L.S.S.P., and analysing their changing roles in populist politics and popular front coalitions of the decade since 1963. In the last section, entitled "The insurrectionary challenge", pp. 435–439, the author offers an estimate of the agonising effects of the insurrection of radicalised Sinhala youth on the domesticated old left parties in Ceylon, and their increasing predicament over using repressive and anti-democratic measures against the new left.

143. ——. Educational expansion and volatility in Sri Lanka: the 1971 insurrection. *Asian Survey*. vol. 15, no. 9, Sept. 1975, pp. 727–744, 10 tables.

Concerns itself neither with ideological ferment and schisms on the Left, nor with the motives and expectations of the leaders of the revolt, but with some aspects of the socio-political environment which led to the transformation of a small band of disaffected young Marxists into a spirited and significant movement of armed rebellion against the state in April 1971. The rapid expansion of education in the two decades preceding the event, and its contribution to the ripening of conditions of large-scale radicalism, deprivation and disaffection, arising mainly from unemployment, are discussed. The paper isolates the marked elevation of political volatility as a clear product of educational expansion.

144. —— & Jiggins, Janice. The Ceylon Insurrection of 1971. *The Journal of Commonwealth and Comparative Politics*. vol. xiii, no. 1, March 1975, pp. 40–64, 3 tables.

A further exploration of this unique political convulsion, and the distinctive features which accompanied its eruption, by the well-known American researcher into contemporary Ceylonese politics, assisted by an English postgraduate student. The composition of the insurgent movement, the demographic and socio-economic environment which provided the stimulus for its growth, the political background in which the revolutionary new left came to the fore, and the final plunge into rebellion are discussed in sequence. There are ninety-one footnotes on pp. 61–64.

145. Knightley, Philip. Ceylon Minister: how 8,000 youths nearly seized power. *Sunday Times*. June 6, 1971, p. 7. Reprinted: *Sun* (Colombo). June 7, 1971.

An interview in London with Mr. Felix Dias Bandaranaike, Minister of Public Administration, Local Government and Home Affairs (and later Justice). Description of the uprising where about 10,000 activists fought with home-made weapons and shot-guns, and managed to occupy large areas of the country in nine districts, compelling Government forces to withdraw to the cities. They may well have succeeded in seizing power, if only for a short time, if not for the timely assistance given by a combination of countries – Britain, U.S., India, Pakistan, U.S.S.R., Egypt, Yugoslavia and China.

146. Kuriacose, Thomas C. Sri Lanka and its youth. *Impact. A monthly Asian magazine for human development* (Manila). vol. 7, no. 10, Oct. 1972, pp. 344–346, 2 illus.

An honest analysis by a Catholic priest of the massive youth trauma, and one of its manifestations – the April insurrection, where thousands revolted for a cause. The acute crisis in a young nation where over 60% of the population is under 24.

147. Kuruppu, Neil. Youth movements and politics in Sri Lanka. *Christian Worker. Bulletin of the Chistian Workers Fellowship* (Colombo). Dec. 1972, pp. 3–6.

An analysis of the growing radicalism of frustrated youth, and a realistic appraisal of the events of 1971.

148. LERSKI, George Jan. Ceylon. *Yearbook on International Communist Affairs 1972*. Stanford (California), Hoover Institution Press, Stanford University, 1972. pp. 464–476.

The country profile is mainly taken up with a fairly detailed survey of the origins, development and activities of the J.V.P. leading to the April 1971 outbreak (pp. 464–469). The author, a Professor of History at San Francisco State University, taught politics at the University of Ceylon, Peradeniya in the early 'sixties.

149. LUBBOCK, Eric. *Lord Avebury. A letter to the Prime Minister dated "Colombo, 24th September, 1971"; with a postscript dated "Bandaranaike Airport, 28th September, 1971, 10.35 a.m."*. 5 pp.

150. ——. *A letter to Mr. Nihal Jayawickrema, Permanent Secretary, Ministry of Justice, dated "High Elms Farm, Downe Orpington, Kent, 15 October 1971"*. 2 pp.

Lord Avebury visited Ceylon on an official fact-finding mission for Amnesty International, but was requested to leave the country by the authorities, after a controversy over prison visits.

151. ——. An island behind bars. A personal assessment. *The Guardian*. October 2, 1971, p. 10. Partially reproduced in *Ceylon Committee Bulletin*, No. 1, Oct., 1971, pp. 4–5.

A report on the situation as he saw it during a week's visit to Ceylon for Amnesty International. *See also* nos. 4–7.

152. LUDOWYK, E. F. C. Ceylon: a communication. *The Spokesman*. (Nottingham). nos. 15–16, Aug.–Sept. 1971, pp. 65–66.

Takes up and sharpens some of the points in Julian Crump's article in the previous issue. Points out that in the vacuum left by the internecine rivalries in the Communist camp, and the defection of the revolutionary LSSP to the exploiter class, "it would be true to say that if after 1965 there had been no JVP it would have been necessary to invent it". Hints at the possibility that in the murky situation of March 1971, the Government "decided to provoke armed action by the JVP as the best method of settling with them". The author also commented on the insurgency in his account of "Independent Ceylon". *The Far East and Australasia 1972*. London, Europa, 1972. pp. 171–176, (esp. pp. 175–176).

153. MADAPATHA, Chrisantha *pseud.* [i.e., Chrisantha Rodrigo]. Popular Frontism in Sri Lanka. *Militant International Review* (London). no. 9, June 1974, pp. 24–40, 7 illus., map. tables.

An earnest and searching analysis of the political developments which led to the formation of the Popular Front alliance of the S.L.F.P., the L.S.S.P. and C.P. in 1968, and their subsequent victory at the polls in May, 1970 under the Common Programme of a United Front, pledged to socialist objectives. The economic and political transformations occasioned by the dictates of British Imperialism before 1948, and the strategies of "Independent" governments thereafter are analysed as a starting point for investigating the record in office of the U.F. Government since 1970, in the light of its avowed promises of radical reform and change, and the disturbing features and reactionary trends existing in the present situation. The rise and impact of the Janatha Vimukti Peramuna on national politics are also determined in the context of the failure of the United Front to deliver the goods.

154. MENDIS, L. A. T. Ceylon: self-sufficiency versus colonialism. *Peace News* (London). no. 1823, June 11, 1971, p. 2.

A Ceylonese in London traces the background to the April uprising, through his own mood of personal anguish and bewilderment.

155. MENDIS, P. H. *Air Commodore. Royal Cy. A.F.* The Air Force in counter insurgency – 1971. *Ceylon Today.* vol. 20, nos. 5–6, May–June 1971, pp. 13–23, 12 illus. Reprinted: *Sri Lanka Air Force 21st Anniversary Souvenir.* Colombo, 1972, pp. 17–20.

Recounts the key role of the R.Cy.A.F. (as it was then known) in supporting the land forces in suppressing the revolt.

156. *Message to international revolutionary movements and forces of anti-imperialism from the Janatha Vimukthi Peramuna (People's Liberation Front) of Ceylon.* [London, Privately published, 1970]. 8 pp.

Cover title: "Message from the J.V.P." A basic statement on the political context in which the J.V.P. had its origin, and expected to function so that the reactionary trends of bourgeois parliamentary democracy could be reversed, and true socialism achieved.

157. MIGNON, Thierry. The trials of the revolutionary leaders of the April 1971 insurrection in Ceylon. Summary of report. *Ceylon Committee Bulletin.* no. 5, 1972, pp. 1–4.

The author, a French lawyer, observed the current Criminal Justice Commission trial of the 41 principal suspects in progress since June 1972, as a representative of the International Federation of Human Rights.

158. NANAYAKKARA, Vasudeva. *M.P. for Kiriella.* Debray, Che and revolution. *Ceylon Observer Magazine Edition.* January 19, 1971.

A repudiation of Brian Crozier's article on the political thinking of Regis Debray, published in the *Observer Magazine* of January 4th, 1971, where the suggestion was made that Debray had abandoned his conviction in the efficacy of revolutionary violence after Guevara's death and Allende's victory in Chile. "We in Ceylon with our own experience and that in India surely know that parliament today is not merely a platform for socialism but a point of take-off in that direction. To accept this is not to accept also the absence of any need for armed revolt". Mr. Nanayakkara, the President of the LSSP Youth League, was arrested in the very first week of the April uprising and released from custody a year later in May 1972. The only Member of Parliament to be so incarcerated, no reasons were given at the time for his detention without charge or trial, and subsequent release. On June 28th, 1973, in the course of his evidence before the Criminal Justice Commission (Insurgency), Inspector of Police P.B.G. Aluwihare stated that he was aware that Mr. Vasudeva Nanayakkara was arrested in connection with the attack on the Hanwella police station on the night of April 5th, 1971. He also revealed that Mr. Nanayakkara was a supporter of the Mathrubhumi Arakshaka Sangamaya (Society for the Protection of the Motherland), the JVP splinter group led by Dharmasekera arrested in 1973 in connection with the attack on the American Embassy on March 6, 1971. (*Ceylon Daily News.* June 29, 1973).

159. ——. LSSP youth leader on socialist dilemma. *Ceylon Daily News*. vol. 57, no. 138, June 12, 1972, p. 3.

The first public speech at the Ceylon Law College on June 9th, 1972, after his release from custody, examined the predicament of a socialist in the context of the emerging contradictions within the world revolutionary movement. The dilemma facing the socialist in Ceylon was that the realignment of forces within the ruling coalition had still not taken place. The question was whether to continue to seek a breakthrough towards the revolution through a broad left front or to go on the offensive against the capitalist class from outside the government.

160. North Korean diplomats leave – on Government orders. Text of official communique. *Times Weekender*. April 17, 1971.

The Government was careful to explain that though the Embassy had been asked to close down and its staff to leave, diplomatic relations were not being severed. The North Korean Ambassador was seen off at the airport by the Chinese Ambassador. Over-enthusiastic and indiscreet propaganda which had not been curbed, despite a Government caution, was the reason given for this summary expulsion of the representative of a country which the United Front Government used to symbolise its new foreign policy after May 1970. The specific reasons for this action were given by the Prime Minister in her broadcast to the nation on April 24, 1971, which helped to abate the flood of rumour. *See* no. 25. Diplomatic relations were resumed in March 1975, following the visit of the Prime Minister's son to North Korea.

161. OBEYESEKERE, Gananath. Some comments on the social backgrounds of April 1971 insurgency in Sri Lanka (Ceylon). *Journal of Asian Studies* 33 (3) May 1974, 367–384, 9 tables.

This article in two parts by the former Professor of Sociology in the University of Ceylon attempts to draw out the sociological implications of the youth insurrection in April 1971. The main intent in Pt. I is to present a substantial sample of the statistical information the author has obtained on suspected insurgents in order to get a more accurate picture of their social backgrounds. The data was obtained through interviews by carefully selected senior government officials, and subsequently computerized by the Department of Census and Statistics. The data from 10,192 suspected insurgents (44.1 arrested by the police, and 55.9 through voluntary surrender) incarcerated in rehabilitation camps are interpreted with certain cautions. Caste, occupational and educational backgrounds are isolated with a view to evaluating the major thrust of the argument that the insurgents were mainly Sinhala-Buddhist youth belonging to the major castes, who were inconvenienced by economic dissatisfactions and the lack of social mobility into the ruling elites. Pt. II, entitled "The barbarians at the gates", explores the implications of the insurrection as an attack on the indigenous elite as a class, and not only against the government in power. The insurgents were not peasants, the J.V.P. was not a rural movement, and the insurrection was not a peasant revolt. Popular notions that the insurgency was activated by lowcaste based frustrations of rural students, and unemployed youth mainly from the universities are dispelled. The fieldwork and interviewing were done in Sri Lanka, and the author personally directed the research on the insurgency itself. This paper, with the same title, was first presented at a Panel on "Radical change in a non-radical society: the 1971 insurgency in Sri Lanka" on 1, April 1973 at the Annual Meeting of the Association of Asian Studies held in Chicago, and later substantially revised for publication. The author has been Professor of Anthropology at the University of California, San Diego, since January 1972.

162. OBEYSEKARA, Jayasumana. *pseud.* Revolutionary movements in Ceylon. *Imperialism and revolution in South Asia*, ed. by Kathleen Gough and Hari

P. Sharma. New York, London, Monthly Review Press, 1973. Ch. 5, pp. 368–395.

Discusses the birth and emergence of the Janatha Vimukti Peramuna against the background of the conflicting socialist ideologies and haphazard practices of the established left in Ceylon since Independence. Indicts the Government on the brutal suppression of the movement when it was beginning to mobilise the disenchanted, and offer an alternative to the United Front. The author, a one-time ardent L.S.S.P. activist, has now left the party. This article was written in January 1972.

163. PERERA, Victor *pseud.* The April uprising of insurgent youth. (A view point). *Christian Worker. Bulletin of the Christian Workers Fellowship* (Colombo). May 1971, pp. 3–7.

Isolates for examination certain features of the insurgent movement which merit attention, and which, at the same time, contributed to its lack of a proper social content and sincere Marxist direction. The drawbacks in the thinking and organisation of the radical groups, as well as the outstanding deficiencies in the attitude of the Government to the movement for rapid change, are described with a view to sharpening the tasks of the progressives in this situation, and as a warning for the future.

164. PERINBANAYAGAM, R. S. Civil strife and doctrine of responsibility: a comment on the events of Ceylon. *Economic and Political Weekly* (Bombay). 6 (50) Dec. 1971: 2491–2492.

Analyses the inevitability of military and police repression sanctioned by a democratic government in the face of revolutionary violence against it. The author, a Ceylonese, teaches sociology in the City College of New York.

165. PHADNIS, Urmila. Insurgency in Ceylon: hard challenge and grim warning. *Economic and Political Weekly* (Bombay). vol. 6, no. 19, May 8, 1971, pp. 965–968.

An informed and acute appraisal of the April insurrection, its antecedents, and prospects for the future. Written a month after the eruption, depending largely on newspaper reports from Ceylon.

166. ——. Insurgency in Ceylonese politics: problems and prospects. *Institute for Defence Studies and Analyses Journal* (New Delhi). vol. 3, no. 4, April 1971, pp. 582–616.

The unique nature of the Ceylonese insurrection, and the political implications for the future of the crucial questions raised by it.

167. ——. The UF Government in Ceylon: challenges and responses. *The World Today* (London). vol. 27, no. 6, June 1971, pp. 267–276.

Analyses the present crisis in Ceylon, which appears to be a judgement on the present Government's performance in the context of its electoral pledges. The ability of the system to meet the government's socialist commitments and the political credentials of the Prime Minister are equally at stake.

168. ——. Crisis for the Old Left in Ceylon. *Venture* (London). vol. 23, no. 10, Nov. 1971, pp. 10–12.

Examines the challenge to the traditional "establishment left" by the new agitational movements of radical youth.

169. ——. At the cross-roads. *Tribune* (Colombo). vol. 17, no. 32, June 20, 1972, pp. 7–8.

A study of the government's predicament on the first anniversary of the April insurrection.

170. ——. Crisis of consensus. *Tribune* (Colombo). vol. 17, no. 43, Oct. 19, 1972, pp. 10–13.

An analysis of the present dilemma arising from the doubtful authority of the present Government.

171. ——. Sri Lanka today. *Current History: a world affairs monthly.* (Philadelphia). vol. 63, no. 375, Nov. 1972, pp. 210–213 + 230.

The new political formulations and domestic compulsions introduced by the United Front government, aggravated by the 1971 insurrection, coupled with recent international developments, are the critical variables contributing to the low posture in foreign policy.

172. PRASAD, Dhirendra Mohan. Che Guevarist insurgence: politics of violence in Sri Lanka. *Young Indian* (New Delhi). 3 (29–30) Special number on violence, 1973: 47–54.

Estimates the value of the J.V.P. revolt in the context of the declining economic and political situation, and its importance as a lever in promoting swift and radical change.

173. PUROHIT, Vinayak. Ceylon: emerald island turned bloody red. *Economic and Political Weekly* (Bombay). vol. 6, nos. 30–32, July 1971, pp. 1521, 1523–4.

Decries the Sino-Stalinist revisionism and social reformist leadership that provoked the insurrection of April 1971, and hails the desperate valour of the JVP against the combined might of repressive forces at home and from abroad. A criticism of the Prime Minister's speech in Parliament on July 20th, 1971.

174. Revolt in Ceylon '71. Introductory note to the "Calendar-chronicle". *Tribune. A journal of Ceylon and world affairs* (Colombo). vol. 17, nos. 1–3, June 30, 1971, pp. 2–3.

175. Revolt in Ceylon. Calendar-chronicle. Parts I–III. I – Writing on the wall (Jan. 31st, 1971–Mar. 15th, 1971); II – Declaration of Emergency (Mar. 16th, 1971–April 4th, 1971); III – The attack begins (April 5th–May 31st, 1971). vol. 17, nos. 1–3, June 30, 1971 – vol. 17, no. 21, Feb. 29, 1972.

A series of fourteen articles giving a blow-by-blow account of the build-up to the April insurrection, and the events of April–May 1971. The chronicle is based on factual reports, official communiques and government statements from English language newspapers (dailies and weeklies) published in Colombo, and extracts from Ceylon Broadcasting Corporation news reviews. Neither editorial and other comments, nor reports and articles in foreign newspapers and journals have been included in the compilation of this digest. It serves as a convenient summarised version of the information available to readers in Ceylon.

176. Revolutionary Marxist Party (Ceylon Section of the Fourth International). *The Political situation in Ceylon and the rebuilding of the left movement under revolutionary Marxist leadership. Political resolution of the Revolutionary Marxist Party (Ceylon Section of the Fourth International – December 1973* [Colombo, Mahabodhi Press, printers, 1974]. 34, [1] p.

The Lanka Sama Samaja Party (Revolutionary) changed its name to the Revolutionary Marxist Party on 29th December 1973. An evaluation of the prevailing political situation which takes into consideration the short-lived threat to the United Front Government from the radical youth movement – the J.V.P. Accuses the Government of deliberately suppressing and destroying the J.V.P. because it posed the most serious and main threat from the Left. The analysis of J.V.P. fortunes is on pp. 5–10, and the impact of the insurrection is also referred to in other parts of the discussion. The statement is signed by Bala Tampoe, Secretary of the Revolutionary Marxist Party.

177. Right wing "Communism": a senile disorder. *Ginipupura Ceylon Spark.* London, Ginipupura Publications, 1971, pp. 2–5.

Condemns the rigidly pedantic attitude of the "old left" social democrat leaders of Ceylon in viewing the untimely insurrection as an infantile brand of "left wing communism". Suggests the coming together of all true revolutionary groups as a first requisite for the future of radical politics in Ceylon. In an article in the *Bangkok World* of April 2, 1973, p. 15, entitled "The new woman to watch in Sri Lanka", G. K. Navaratne writes about the radical political leanings and affiliations of Miss Sunethra Bandaranaike, the elder daughter of the Prime Minister, and her husband Kumar Rupasinghe, both at one time active in left-wing student politics in England. Rupasinghe returned to Ceylon in 1972 and married Sunethra Bandaranaike later in the year. Navaratne writes, "they were active in the London Branch of the ultra-left People's Liberation Front of Sri Lanka. Rupasinghe edited the PLF journal Ginipupura (Spark) published from London". After his return he was one of the founders of the Jana Vēgaya Movement, a new-left group within the United Front umbrella, in 1973.

178. Robson, Ronald. Ceylon's stars. *The Listener* (London). vol. 85, no. 2197, May 6, 1971, pp. 574–575.

179. Ross, Michael. *The struggle for Trotskyism in Ceylon.* New York, Labor Publications, Inc., 1972. 69 pp. ("*Bulletin*" Pamphlet Series – 9).

The material in this pamphlet originally appeared in the *Bulletin*, weekly organ of the Workers League. The first section appeared in the Oct. 18th, 1971 issue (vol. 8, no. 7) and it ran consecutively until November 15th, 1971 (vol. 8, no. 11). A bitter attack on and exposure of LSSP policies and strategies which has led this Marxist party to abandon the true international socialist struggle in favour of the opportunist role of consorting with and within the forces of reformism and revisionism. The analysis, both historical and theoretical, leads inexorably to the author's view that the hands of the LSSP (part of the Fourth International for years) are also soiled with the blood of April 1971.

180. RUDRA, Ashok. Spartacus in Ceylon. *Frontier. A political weekly* (Calcutta). vol. 4, no. 7, May 29, 1971, pp. 6–8.

181. ——. On the threshhold. *Frontier.* vol. 4, nos. 24–25, Sept. 25, 1971, pp. 5–8.

A Marxist-Leninist view of the insurrection, comparing the Naxalite movement with the JVP. "Ceylon insurrection has not been killed. It cannot be killed".

182. SAMARAKKODY, Edmund. *Letter to the Prime Minister by the Revolutionary Sama Samaja Party dated 22nd April 1971.* Dehiwela (Ceylon), 1971, 2 pp.

183. ——. *Ceylon youth in armed uprising.* Mount Lavinia (Ceylon), 1971, 16 pp.

This cyclostyled folio pamphlet first issued in Ceylon on 15th May 1971 was later in the same year published in London with a separate "Addendum" of two pages. The Secretary of the R.S.S.P. (the one-time leading theoretician and activist of the L.S.S.P.) analyses the meaning of the insurrection for the political future of the island. Opines that the armed struggle poses the first real challenge to parliamentary processes and the established regime, and concedes that, despite the escalating radicalisation of youth in the 'sixties, both strategy and tactics have to undergo a serious evaluation, so that coming revolutionary struggles for the socialist causes will lead to greater success. The later two page addendum issued with the London reprint, contains an analysis of the lessons for radical politics in Ceylon.

184. ——. Interview with Samarakkody in September 1971. *Ceylon: the JVP uprising of April 1971.* London, Solidarity, 1972, pp. 3–16.

Sections of an extensive interview recorded in Colombo with a founder of the revolutionary movement in Ceylon. The questions and answers cover the attitudes and social basis of the JVP, its posture on foreign affairs, the significance of the People's Committees "elected" after May 1970, the continuing repression and censorship, the present attitudes of the LSSP (R), and the degree of LSSP degeneration.

185. ——. *Statement of the Revolutionary Sama Samaja Party on the expulsion order on Lord Avebury of Amnesty International.* 8th October, 1971. Dehiwela (Ceylon), 1971, 2 pp.

186. SANMUGATHASAN, Nagalingam. An analysis of the April events in Ceylon; by a Ceylonese Marxist-Leninist. *Frontier* (Calcutta). vol. 4, no. 35, Dec. 11, 1971, pp. 5–10. Reprinted in: *A Marxist looks at the history of Ceylon (1972).* Ch. 6, pp. 97–114; London, Mao Tse-tung Thought Institute, 1972. 12 pp., with an introductory note by A. Manchanda of the Mao Tse-tung Thought Institute.

A Maoist review of the situation written from prison which contains the hope that the foredoomed and foolhardy insurrection of April 1971, besides showing up the myth of Ceylon being a bastion of "bourgeois parliamentary democracy", reveals important pointers for the future. Believes that this pseudo-revolutionary movement was called into being to oppose the growing influence of Mao Tse-tung thought in Ceylon, and to discredit the revisionist theories of Trotskyites and Moscow Communists playing the parliamentary game. Condemns the strong individualism and distrust of the working class which was characteristic of the JVP. In ruling out mass participation, its theory was the very antithesis of the theory of people's war as expounded by Mao. The JVP perverted to its own quick use the systematic advocacy of a revolutionary path as the only means for social change, consistently done by the Marxist-Leninist Ceylon Communist Party since it split from the Ceylon Communist Party in 1964.

187. ——. *Letter to the Prime Minister dated 7th Feb. 1972.* Colombo, Ceylon Communist Party [Peking Wing], 123, Union Place, Colombo 2, 1972, 5 pp.

Mr. Sanmugathasan, General Secretary of the Peking Wing of the Ceylon Communist Party was detained in prison from 12th April 1971 to 31st January 1972, without charge or trial. The letter was written on his release from custody, and complained about the manner of his arrest and the treatment he received in prison. Emphasised his hostility to the JVP, and his exposure of their program. Shortly after his release from prison, Mr. Sanmugathasan left for Peking, and returned to Ceylon later in the year after visiting Europe too. While in England his two books, *A Marxist looks at the history of Ceylon* (118 pp.), and *A short history of the Left movement in Ceylon* [5], 83, [32] pp.), were privately published. These were apparently difficult to obtain in Ceylon on account of certain Customs restrictions, and have not been on sale in local bookshops. In London he also addressed a public meeting in June 1972 organised by the Ceylon Committee, and a summary of this speech was published in its *Bulletin* No. 4 (August 1972), pp. 8–10. *A Marxist looks at the history of Ceylon* was reprinted and published in Colombo in 1975. [6], 102 pp.

188. SENANAYAKE, Dudley Shelton. Letter to the Prime Minister dated 23 April 1971. *Parliamentary Debates (Hansard). House of Representatives. Official Report.* vol. 94, no. 6, May 4, 1971, cols. 501–522. Reprinted: *Ceylon Daily News.* vol. 55, no. 107, May 6, 1971, pp. 1 + 7. For reply by Prime Minister, *see* no. 24.

189. SOLIDARITY. London. *Ceylon: the JVP uprising of April 1971.* London, Solidarity, 1972. 50 pp., illus., map. (Solidarity pamphlet, No. 42).

An attempt to assess the insurrection, its genesis and consequences, critically, and "demythologise" the situation. Emphasises that despite the tremendous courage and total dedication, the strategy and tactics of the J.V.P. (and its political ideas on how to exercise power) were so hopelessly confused, that only defeat could occur. This contribution seeks to draw out the lessons of the senseless conflict. The main contents are: The Samarakody interview, pp. 3–16; Background to the uprising, pp. 17–32; Epilogue, pp. 32–34; Third worldism or socialism, pp. 35–40; Appendices, pp. 41–47; Footnotes, pp. 48–50. Keen insight, percipient realism and an unsparing incisiveness of writing contribute to a detached examination of this remarkable event.

190. SRI LANKA. NATIONAL STATE ASSEMBLY. Statement of Government Policy. Debate. *National State Assembly Debates. Official Report.* vol. 1, no. 5, July 4, 1972, cols. 340–456; 1 (6) July 5, 1972, cols. 493–668; 1 (7) July 6, 1972, cols. 714–873; 1 (8) July 7, 1972, cols. 896–1046.

191. ——. Appropriation Bill, 1973. Second Reading Debate. *National State Assembly Debates. Official Report.* vol. 3, no. 2, Nov. 14, 1972 – vol. 3, no. 10 (pt. II) Nov. 27, 1972.

During the two debates which lasted four and nine days respectively, matters arising from the insurrection, and its continuing consequences were referred to by most speakers on both sides.

192. ——. Debate on the Joint Opposition Motion to appoint a "Select Committee to investigate an alleged conspiracy to destroy sovereignty of the people". *National State Assembly Debates. Official Report.* vol. 10, no. 5, 6th March 1974, cols. 813–1031.

When the Assembly divided at the end of the debate, the motion was defeated, 25 voting for and 99 against. *See also* nos. 34, 35, 133, 134, 135, 136.

193. TYAGUNENKO, V. Paramount task before developing countries. *Soviet Review* (New Delhi). vol. 9, no. 1, Jan. 1972, pp. 24–37.

An analysis of radical left youth movements and the April 1971 revolt as a serious set-back to the forces of reformism under coalition sponsorship, pp. 33–34. *See also* no. 2.

194. VAN DER KROEFF, J. M. The Sri Lanka insurgency of April 1971: its development and meaning. *Asia Quarterly: a journal from Europe* (Brussels). No. 2, 1973: 111–129.

A detailed evaluation of the impact and continuing significance of the J.V.P. adventure in political radicalism and violence in Sri Lanka. Its educational implications and repercussions are given special attention. The author teaches at the University of Bridgeport, Conn., U.S.A., and has written frequently on contemporary Ceylonese politics.

195. WALSH, Michael. Ceylon, did the "guerillas" fall, or were they pushed? A Tribune inquiry. *Tribune: Labour's Independent Weekly* (London). vol. 35, no. 17, April 23, 1971, p. 16.

Surveys a palsied situation after the United Front took office in which the JVP and other radical left groupings would become increasingly antagonistic. Suggests, however, that it is probable the Government forced the JVP into armed insurrection and violent defiance for fear of its rapidly growing influence. The aggressive hostility and allegations against the movement for a whole year ahead of April, and later repressions close to the events, also support this idea of a preemptive strike.

196. [WARNAPALA, W. A. Wiswa]. Politicus *pseud.* The April revolt in Ceylon. *Asian Survey* (Berkeley, California). vol. 12, no. 3, March 1972, pp. 259–274.

The author, a lecturer in political science in the University of Ceylon, and presently, Counsellor in the Sri Lanka Embassy in Moscow, is concerned in this meaty contribution to point out that the variety of social, economic and political factors which stimulated a large section of Ceylon youth to "wage war against the Queen" were not of recent origin, but part and parcel of the political and economic experience of the island, in post-independence times particularly. These factors are probed with a view to identifying the nature and extent of the uprising, and its impact on the present political system and modes of functioning. The deepening dissatisfaction with the performance and postures of the traditional left is highlighted, especially in allowing its radical and revolutionary objectives to be blunted and adulterated by alliance with reformist forces. The meteoric emergence of the People's Liberation Front

(JVP) is largely blamed on the fissiparous and quarrelsome conventional Marxist parties in Ceylon, who had dominated the socialist scene for over thirty years. Stresses that the JVP is a political force not to be lightly dismissed despite its violence, lack of organisation and political depth, adventurism, and sad rejection of the Ceylon working class.

197. ——. Sri Lanka in 1972: tension and change. *Asian Survey*. vol. 13, no. 2, Feb. 1973, pp. 217–230.

A rapid survey of the political and economic situation in the year following the insurrection. The various attempts at repairing the fabric of national life, weakened by the violent crisis of 1971, through new economic programs, constitutional measures and legislative reforms are described. Despite certain forward-looking and aggressively realistic economic reforms being implemented, the ever-present climate of tension in most areas of national life and the view of the administration that a threat to the security of the State is very live interfere substantially with the process of change – an interference which is a luxury Sri Lanka can ill afford at this time.

198. ——. Sri Lanka in 1973: a test for both rulers and the ruled. *Asian Survey*. vol. 14, no. 2, Feb. 1974, pp. 148–156.

An unenthusiastic and depressing survey of the worsening economic and lack-lustre political situations in Ceylon, and the grim prospects for the future. A raw estimate lacking optimism, and at the same time neglecting to discuss the new forces emerging within the United Front – portending a significant departure from conventional parliamentary procedures.

199. ——. The Marxist parties of Sri Lanka and the 1971 insurrection. *Asian Survey*. vol. 15, no. 9, Sept. 1975, pp. 745–757.

Discusses in broad terms the dimensions of the crisis facing the Marxist parties immediately after the insurrection of April 1971, in the context of their attitudes, perspectives and strategies, both within and outside the United Front coalition. The traditional Marxist assessment of the revolutionary movement led by the JVP, and the impact on its thinking and responses thereafter are examined in two phases – the period before and the period after the revolt. The analyses of the respective crises confronting the Communist Party (Moscow), the LSSP, and the C.P. (Peking) are treated separately, as well as the repercussions in the trade union movement aligned to coalition partners in the present government. The crisis in both identity and legitimacy for Marxist parties is probed in some depth in the light of their commitment to stable and middle-road parliamentary goals.

200. WICKREMESINGHE, Cyril Lakshman. *Bishop of Kurunegala*. Pastoral address. Lessons from the civil war. *Ceylon Churchman*. vol. 67, nos. 10 & 11, October–November 1971, pp. 341–343.

201. ——. *Emergency regulations: for whose benefit*. Colombo, Civil Rights Movement of Ceylon, January 1972, 5 pp.

The English press in Ceylon did not publish this, but a shortened version in Sinhala translation was published in *Ättha*, a Sinhala left-wing daily, on 24th January 1972. It was available for limited circulation in mimeographed form.

202. ——. *Government by immunity or Government by participation. Some recent legislative changes*. Colombo, Civil Rights Movement of Ceylon, 1973, 6 pp.

This was also available for limited circulation in mimeographed form.

203. WIJETUNGA, W. M. K. "Insurgency 1971". *Sri Lanka in transition.* Colombo, Wesley Press, printers, 1974, pp. 93–97.

Perhaps the most daring, though still rather limited, discussion of the April insurrection to be published in Ceylon. Many of the comments are critical of government responses and performances vis-a-vis the youth movement. There are further observations on the insurrection on pp. 131–132. The author is a Lecturer in History at the Vidyodaya Campus, University of Sri Lanka (Ceylon), and served the Government as Chairman, State Printing Corporation for three years from 1970. He is presently President of the Vidyodaya Campus.

204. WIJEWEERA, Rohana [i.e., Patabandige Don Nandasiri Wijeweera]. *Janata Vimukti Peramuna. C.I.A. Kārayo*? [People's Liberation Front. C.I.A. agents?]. Speech made at a special assembly of the Sri Lanka Vidyōdaya University Socialist Society on 14th July 1970. Gangodawila, Sri Lanka Vidyōdaya University Socialist Society, 1970. [2], 56 pp., front. (port. of Wijeweera).

A keynote address made soon after his release from custody in July 1970, which was ordered by the new United Front Government. Wijeweera had been arrested by the UNP Government two weeks before the May 27th General Elections the same year. An exposition of the JVP political philosophy, and an appeal to radical youth to join the party and help usher in the true Marxist-Leninist revolution. Some misconceptions regarding the movement are repudiated.

205. ——. "*An appeal to the peoples of the world*". A four-page mimeographed English translation of the original Sinhalese text entitled: "Lōdanan veta ayāchanayaī" in three folio sheets written from prison in 1972. Reprinted: *Frontier. A Political weekly* (Calcutta). vol. 5, no. 2, Sept. 2, 1972, pp. 11–12; *Ceylon Solidarity Campaign Bulletin.* no. 4, Dec. 1972, pp. 6–9; *World Outlook: a weekly international supplement to The Militant* (New York). Nov. 3, 1972: 2; *Ginipupura Ceylon Spark.* April 1974. 4 pp. leaflet. London, 1974.

206. ——. Statement in writing to the Criminal Justice Commission. Abridged text. *Ceylon Daily News.* Sept. 30, 1972; and other papers. Reprinted: *Tribune.* vol. 17, no. 46, Nov. 10, 1972, pp. 20–23.

207. ——. Speech to the Criminal Justice Commission – 2 November 1973. *New Left Review* (London). No. 84, March–April 1974: 85–104. Reprinted: Ceylon Solidarity Campaign. *Bulletin.* Sept. 1974: 5–12; *Explosion in a sub-continent. India, Pakistan, Bangladesh and Ceylon,* ed. by Robin Blackburn. Penguin Books, 1975. pp. 221–251; concluding portion (abridged), *Frontier* (Calcutta). vol. 7, no. 35, Dec. 21, 1974, pp. 6–8.

The spirited, moving and sustained defence of his position vis-a-vis the April 1971 insurrection by the thirteenth suspect and acknowledged founder and leader of the Janata Vimukti Peramuna. The speech has been curtailed to present the leading themes and principal features of the statement made at the commencement of the examination of this suspect. His political education and path to Marxism, the question of violence in the transformation of capitalism to socialism, the tasks of the revolution in Ceylon, and the "origins of the April incidents" are some of the important matters discussed. Wijeweera was sentenced to rigorous imprisonment for life on December 20th, 1974, when the Criminal Justice Commission handed down its verdicts on the 36 suspects in the main case arising out of the April 1971 insurrection. He was the only suspect to receive this sentence, and the speech remains an example of personal assertion of principle in revolutionary commitment. On January 16th, 1975 the Commission made a fresh order substituting a term of 20 years' rigorous imprisonment in place of the previous sentence.

208. ——. *Statement produced at the C.J.C. Inquiry No. 1.* 32 pp. (Mimeographed text).

The statement of the 13th suspect was recorded at the Quarters of the Sub-inspectors of the Jaffna Police from 24–27 September 1971. Wijeweera refused to sign the statement. He was sentenced to rigorous imprisonment for life on 20th, Dec. 1974, and this sentence was reduced to 20 years' rigorous imprisonment on 16 Jan. 1975. *See also* no. 209.

209. ——. *Transcript of Rohana Wijeweera's tape-recorded statement.* (English translation). 366 pp. (Mimeographed text).

This was a production in the trial, and the tape was marked as S13. The Sinhala transcript was marked S13A, and the English translation S13B. The interrogation and recording of Wijeweera's statement took place in a building next to King's House in the Jaffna Fort. He was first interrogated on July 17 and 18th, 1971, by a team led by Mr. Ian Wikremanayake, assisted by Inspectors Zernie Wijesuriya, B. A. Jeyanathan, Suwaris, Upali Seneviratne, and Assistant Superintendent of Police S.B.W. de Silva. No recording took place on these two days. He was confronted with five suspects in the main case on the first of these days. The actual recording took place from 19th–25th July 1971, and the interviewing was done by the same team, excluding Jeyanathan, who developed appendicitis and left Jaffna on 19th July morning. The entire statement affords an unique insight into the makings of a revolutionary mind, and the origins and astonishing growth of the movement known as the Janata Vimukti Peramuna, of which Wijeweera was undoubtedly the mainspring. The exposition of the Ceylonese political scene, and its evaluation in Marxist-Leninist terms are also important ingredients in the statement.

210. Wilson, Alfred Jeyaratnam. Ceylon: a new Government takes office. *Asian Survey.* vol. 11, no. 2, Feb. 1971, pp. 177–184. Reprinted: Montreal, McGill University Centre for Developing-Area Studies (Reprint Series No. 19), 1972.

An analysis of the likely new political forms and their economic counterparts in consequence of a left-of-centre coalition government taking office in May 1970.

211. ——. Political changes in Ceylon. *Pacific Community. An Asian Quarterly Review* (Tokyo). vol. 2, no. 2, Jan. 1971, pp. 369–376.

The perspectives and menacing portents of the political situation dominated by the rising aspirations of the rural majority, and in particular the resurgent radical youth, looking to the United Front Government for fulfilling the promises held out by Mrs. Bandaranaike and her socialist partners in May 1970. The author was Professor of Political Science in the University of Ceylon, and resigned in 1972 to become Professor of Political Science in the University of New Brunswick, Canada.

212. ——. Recent political developments in Ceylon. Rising expectations still to be satisfied. *The Round Table. The Commonwealth Journal of International Affairs* (London). no. 241, January 1971, pp. 137–145.

An analysis of the first six months of United Front rule, and the difficulties ahead in the way of implementing economic and political change.

213. ——. Ceylon: the People's Liberation Front and the "revolution" that failed. *Pacific Community*. vol. 3, no. 2, January 1972, pp. 364–377. Reprinted: Montreal, McGill University Centre for Developing-Area Studies (Reprint series No. 23), 1972.

Outlines the predicament of Mrs. Bandaranaike's left-oriented administration in the wake of the JVP insurrection which has left a virtually insoluble economic problem on her hands. Discusses the highly conspiratorial character of the JVP movement, and the clandestine tactics employed to spread the revolutionary message. Speculates that even if the JVP had ousted the United Front Government, it is doubtful if they would have been allowed to consolidate the overthrow, and hints at a probable counter-coup by the armed forces with the assistance of conservative factions. But through failure it has created maximum embarrassment for Mrs. Bandaranaike, and hope for a future regrouping.

214. ——. Ceylon: a time of troubles. *Asian Survey*. vol. 12, no. 2, Feb. 1972, pp. 109–115.

A detailed report on the Government's new economic program, hastened by the impact of the insurrection and ensuing crisis.

215. ——. Political transformation in Ceylon: new policies take shape. *Round Table*. no. 246, April 1972, pp. 241–248.

The new political manoeuvres and economic changes arising primarily from the effects of the youth insurrection, which the Government survived through the use of extreme force.

216. Wriggins, William Howard and Jayawardene, C. H. S. Youth protest in Sri Lanka (Ceylon). *Population, politics and the future of Southern Asia*; ed. by W. H. Wriggins and James F. Guyot. New York, London, Columbia University Press, 1973; Ch. 10, pp. 318–350, map.

This analysis of the effort of a segment of Sri Lanka's youth to seize power by direct assault in April 1971 demonstrates the complexity of the relationship between demographic changes and a dramatic political event. The article examines Ceylon's rapid rate of population growth, the sharp increase in the actual number of young people in the population, and the mutually reinforcing educational and political processes that are changing traditional values and rapidly inflating the expectations of the young. These changes are contrasted with the stagnating economy and the worsening trade position. A very high rate of unemployment, especially among the educated, is a result. The authors stress that none of these demographic, social or economic conditions – alone or together – would have sparked off the political events reviewed if a dynamic political leadership in the J.V.P. had not mobilized a daring and desperate segment of youth to take unprecedented risks on behalf of an almost magical belief in the one-day revolution. The map gives the main areas of insurrectionary activity. The first author is Director of the Southern Asia Institute at Columbia University, and the second is Professor of Criminology at the University of Ottawa. *See also* no. 127.

217. Yalman, Nur. *The challenge of dialectical reason.* A paper presented at the Decennial Conference of the Association of Social Anthropologists, Oxford, 9–11 July, 1973. 43 pp. (Typescript).

A discussion of how theoretical developments in the paradigm of social anthropology affect the challenging problem of change in social systems. Some of these questions centering around the issue of alienation, and the dilemma of disaffection and affection towards a social order are examined in connection with two major social conflagrations in recent times – the student revolutions in Turkey and in Ceylon. The radical explosion in Ceylon in April 1971 is explored in terms of the author's dynamic theory of internally divided societies and disoriented cultures. "The People's Liberation Front in Ceylon", pp. 27–34. The social context, with its increasing educational dysfunctionalism, was largely responsible for the rise of the Janata Vimukti Peramuna – with its vision of a truly Marxist-Leninist society and a genuinely egalitarian Buddhist system. The author, a Professor at Harvard University, is well known for his researches into Ceylonese kinship and religious systems. This paper was to be included in a volume of ASA studies to be published in 1975 by the Malaby Press and J. M. Dent in England.

218. Youth unrest. *Christian Worker* (Colombo). April 1971, pp. 6–8.

An analysis of the "new left" movement among radical youth, who are posed with the question of "a job or revolution". Written on the eve of the insurrection. The office of the Christian Workers Fellowship in Colombo was sealed and their activities investigated briefly in April 1971, before they were permitted to continue.

"As for you: when it gets to the point
That man is the helper of men,
Think back on us
Forebearingly". – Bertolt Brecht

CONTRIBUTORS

Robert D. BAIRD is Professor of History of Religions at the University of Iowa, from which university he received his Ph.D. in 1964. He has done field work in India on two occasions: in 1966 as a Postdoctoral Fellow in Asian Religions of the Society for Religion in Higher Education, and in 1972 as a Faculty Fellow of the American Institute of Indian Studies. He is the author of *Category Formation and the History of Religions* (Mouton, 1971); co-author of *Indian and Far Eastern Religious Traditions* (Harper and Row, 1972); and editor of *Methodological Issues in Religious Study* (New Horizons, 1975). He is also the author of numerous journal articles including "Human Rights Priorities and Indian Religious Thought" (1969); "Mr. Justice Gajendragadkar and the Religion of the Indian Secular State" (1972); and "Religion and the Secular: Categories for Religious Conflict and Religious Change in Independent India" (1976).

Fred W. CLOTHEY is Assistant Professor in History of Religion at the University of Pittsburgh. He received his M.A. (1965) and Ph.D. (1968) in History of Religions from the University of Chicago and taught at Boston University until moving to Pittsburgh in 1975. He was in India in 1966–67 as a Fellow of the American Institute of Indian Studies and in 1971–72 as a co-ordinator of the GLCA Year in India program. He is the author of *The Many Faces of Murukaṉ: The History and Meaning of a South India God* (Mouton, 1976) and the director of three films on the festival experience in South India. He is currently completing a volume on Śaiva ritual and a volume of translations of Aruṇakiri, popular Tamil mystic, and editing the forthcoming volume: *Śiva: Myth, Rite and Attitude.*

H. A. I. GOONETILEKE joined the University of Sri Lanka (Ceylon), Peradeniya as an Assistant Librarian in 1953 and has been its Librarian since 1971. A Bachelor of Arts of the University of London, he holds postgraduate degrees in Library Studies from the Universities of London and Madras and obtained the Fellowship of the Library Association of Great Britain and Ireland by thesis in 1966. At University College, London he won the Cowley Prize. He has been a participant at various international and regional conferences in cataloguing and documentation, and has contributed many articles to professional and learned journals, as well as monographs. He is best known for *A Bibliography of Ceylon*, a continuing and major exercise in the exploration of the literature on his country, three volumes of which have been published so far by Inter Documentation Campany, Zug, Switzerland. In 1973–74 he was a Senior Specialist Fellow of the JDR 3rd Fund (New York). He is currently pursuing the theme of the changing image of Sri Lanka through foreign eyes and two volumes of travel essays on European and American visitors in the 19th and 20th centuries are in the press.

Gerald James LARSON is Professor of Religious Studies at the University of California, Santa Barbara. He teaches in the area of South Asian religion and philosophy. He also teaches courses in classical Sanskrit and Pali. He holds the Ph.D. in the history of religions from Columbia University in New York City (1967). He has been on the faculty at UC Santa Barbara since 1970. He is the author of *Classical Sāṃkhya* (Delhi: Banarsidass, 1969) and editor and contributor to *Myth in Indo-European Antiquity* (Berkeley: UC Press, 1974). He has also written numerous articles and reviews on South Asian religion and thought. For the 1976–77 academic year, Professor Larson was a senior fellow of the American Institute of Indian Studies and the Indo-U.S. Subcommission on Education and Culture at Banaras Hindu University, Varanasi, India. At Banaras Hindu he was also an honorary visiting professor in the area of Indian philosophy.

Sheila MCDONOUGH is Professor of Religion at the Sir George Williams Campus of Concordia University, Montreal, where she has been since 1963. She taught for three years at the Kinnaird College for Women, Lahore, Pakistan, and for one year at the Selly Oak Colleges, Birmingham, England. She received her doctorate from the Institute of Islamic Studies, McGill. Her publications include *The Authority of the Past* (AAR Monograph, 1970) and *Jinnah, Maker of Modern Pakistan* (Boston: D. C. Heath, 1970).

Franklin A. PRESLER is an Instructor in Political Science at Kalamazoo College. He received his B.A. from Oberlin College in 1965 with a major in religion. He is presently completing his doctoral dissertation in political science from the University of Chicago, where he also taught as a Lecturer in 1974–76. His article is based on research conducted in Madras and Tamil Nadu in 1973–74, under a grant from the Social Science Research Council.

Bardwell L. SMITH is the John W. Nason Professor of Asian Studies at Carleton College, Northfield, Minnesota. He also served as Dean of the College, 1967–72. He has received his B.A., B.D., M.A., and Ph.D. from Yale University and was a member of the Yale University Council, 1969–74. During 1972–73 he did research at the School of Oriental and African Studies, University of London, on a grant from the American Council of Learned Societies. He has edited a number of books, among them: *The Two Wheels of Dhamma: Essays on the Theravada Tradition in India and Ceylon* (American Academy of Religion, 1972); *Tradition and Change in Theravada Buddhism: Essays on Ceylon and Thailand in the 19th and 20th Centuries* (Leiden: E. J. Brill, 1973); *Unsui: A Diary of Zen Monastic Life* (Honolulu: University Press of Hawaii, 1973); *Hinduism: New Essays in the History of Religions* (Leiden: E. J. Brill, 1976); *Religion and Social Confiict in South Asia* (Leiden: E. J. Brill, 1976); and *Essays on T'ang Society: The Interplay of Social, Political and Economic Forces* (Leiden: E. J. Brill, 1976), co-edited with John Curtis Perry.

George W. SPPENCER is Associate Professor of History at Northern Illinois University, DeKalb, Illinois, where he has taught since 1967. There he teaches the histories of India and Japan, as well as various topics in comparative world history, including banditry, millennarianism, and utopian communities. His wife, Elaine, teaches German history and related subjects in the same department. He received his B.A. in History from the University of Maryland, College Park (1961) and his M.A. (1963) and Ph.D. (1967) degrees from the University of California, Berkeley. His articles have appeared in the *Journal of the Economic and Social History of the Orient*, the *Indian Economic and Social History Review*, *Numen*, *Asian Profile*, and the *Journal of Asian Studies*. His most recent article is "The Politics of Plunder: The Cholas in Eleventh Century Ceylon" (1976). The bulk of his research deals with topics in the history of South India from the sixth through the fourteenth centuries. He is especially interested in political, economic, and religious themes and their interaction, and he has a long-standing interest in the history of plundering activities by both states and local communities.

Joanne Punzo WAGHORNE is Assistant Professor of Religion Studies a tthe University of Massachusetts at Boston. She holds an M.A. and Ph.D. from the Divinity School, University of Chicago in the History of Religions. The research for her dissertation, "Images of Dharma: The Epic World of C. Rajagopalachari" was completed in India under the Department of Politics and Public Administration, University of Madras. An earlier article on C. Rajagopalachari, "Rajaji – The Kathakar", appeared in the *Journal of the University of Madras* (January, 1975). Her present research focuses on a general overview of systems of priesthood in India which have influenced the political structure. She is also interested in comparative studies in epic and heroic literature.

Eleanor ZELLIOT is Associate Professor of History at Carleton College, Northfield, Minnesota. Her Ph.D. thesis at the University of Pennsylvania was on "Dr. Ambedkar and the Mahar Movement" and she has since published a number of articles on that still dynamic movement, including its latest phases, the conversion to Buddhism and the literary movement known as *Dalit Sahitya*. On her recent sabbatical in India, she pursued the study of Eknath, a 16th century saint-poet whose work offers a different field for the investigation of the meaning of religion and literature to the course of history.

DATE DUE